From Athens to Zagreb

A First-Hand History of Hearts in Europe

From Athens to Zagreb

A First-Hand History of Hearts in Europe

Mike Buckle

Luath Press Limited
EDINBURGH
www.luath.co.uk

First published 2012

ISBN: 978 1 908373 41 0

The paper used in this book is sourced from renewable forestry
and is FSC credited material.

The author's right to be identified as author of this book under the Copyright,
Designs and Patents Act 1988 has been asserted.

Printed in the UK by MPG Books Ltd., Cornwall

Typeset in 11 point Sabon

Contents

This book is dedicated to the memory of Tom Heaney Jnr,
a great Jambo and a great friend.

Acknowledgements

I would like to express my thanks to everyone who has helped in providing material for this book. Former players, Alex Young, Robin Stenhouse, Billy Higgins, Donald Ford, Roy Kay, Eammon Bannon, Craig Levein, Scott Crabbe, Gary Locke, Jeremy Goss, Robbie Neilson and Christophe Berra have all been very helpful in relating 'inside stories' of their European adventures.

Also, well known Hearts men, Willie Bauld Jnr, Bob Aitchison, Scott Wilson, David McLetchie, Leslie Deans, Callum Anderson, Gary Cowan, Drew Goldie and John Fairbairn, the composer of the second most famous Hearts song, have been equally generous in sharing their memories of special games.

Other individuals who deserve mention are Davy Allan and Callum Marshall for use of so many photographs, David Speed for providing historical information, Duncan Mills for his excellent work on the cover design, Mel Knight at Mirrorpix, Christine Russ and Joe Ferrari. It would be remiss not to mention Gavin MacDougall, Kirsten Graham and Jennie Renton at Luath Press, so thank you all.

Finally, I would like to express my special appreciation to one of the finest actors Scotland has ever produced, Ken Stott, for agreeing to write the Foreword to the book.

Foreword by Ken Stott

We are a Hearts family: me, my father, and his father before him. We are also a Heriot's family; I was educated there, as was my father, who went on to become a teacher and assistant headmaster there.

And so it was for us, a source of immense pride that the great Alan Gordon was also a Herioter. In fact, by the time he was 17 years old, he was going to school during the week, excelling in maths and economics, and turning up at Tynecastle on a Saturday to play for the Hearts.

Not long before he passed away, I had the pleasure of meeting Alan and he filled me in on some of the details of the story, which had already assumed the status of legend in our house.

It was 1961, Hearts were doing very well, another great European night loomed – Inter Milan at San Siro – and Tommy Walker included Alan in the squad. It was a Wednesday night game so he'd need to get time off school. Now, Alan imagined that the then headmaster would be sharing the general excitement (Hibbies excluded) that was felt by the whole school when he went to formally ask his permission for time off to play.

But he was in for a shock. Not only was permission not granted, he was told that if he decided to go, he needn't bother coming back to school! As you can imagine, for us kids the answer to that was pretty much a no-brainer, but for Alan it was an entirely different matter. A gifted footballer and a gifted pupil, he was simply heartbroken.

He raced home and appealed to his father to intervene. Although very sympathetic, his father told him that there was nothing to be done and that he must think about his life and career when football was finished.

Alan was horrified; things were going from bad to worse. He decided to go straight to the top. He got through to Mr. Walker on the telephone and was astonished to hear that not only did he agree with his father, he also agreed with the headmaster. He told him that he'd be sorely missed, but it was the right thing to do.

When match day came around, Alan sat mournfully in class and my father, who happened to be his English teacher, said, 'We all feel very sorry for you [Hibbies excluded, again] but take heart in knowing that yours is a shining example to others of the importance of education.'

Well, when Alan told me this, I laughed uproariously and replied, 'And what did you make of that statement?'

He said, 'Of course I wanted to kill him – and then I thought, maybe he's right, maybe they're all right. And I know that... now !

Hearts lost 4-0 that night and I sometimes wonder, had Alan played, might the score have been very different.

Alan did eventually make his European debut a couple of years later in the second replay against Lausanne, but not before he was once again prevented from playing in a European tie, this time due to a clash of dates with exams. However, after his previous experience this was an easier decision for him to accept.

When what was undoubtedly a shining career with Heart of Midlothian was over, Alan went on to shine, maybe not so brightly but certainly more constantly as a Chartered Accountant for many more years to come.

I have enjoyed watching many games against European opposition at Tynecastle and look forward to seeing the grand old club in many more in years to come. I am sure that like me, when you read Mike's book, many forgotten memories of magical evenings of the past will come flooding back.

Ken Stott

CHAPTER I

1958–59 European Champion Clubs Cup

HAVING SWEPT ALL BEFORE THEM the previous season, after winning the league title in record-breaking style, it was no real surprise that expectations were high that Hearts' domestic success could be repeated into Europe.

When the draw was made in Paris on 2 July, Hearts were paired with the Belgian champions Standard Liège. A staff reporter in the *Scotsman* boldly forecast, 'It seems a safe prediction that the Edinburgh club will not have to face a deficit for the second leg.' A reasonable assumption, as the Belgians were all part-timers who really were a band of the proverbial 'butchers, bakers and candlestick makers'. Their season did not even start until the Sunday following the first leg.

It was therefore a relatively confident squad of players that headed out of Turnhouse on Tuesday 2 September for the game in Liège the following day. Also on board the specially chartered BEA Viscount for the two-hour flight were 13 intrepid supporters. One of them, 17-year-old Bobby Aitchison from Musselburgh, was reported by the *Edinburgh Evening News* as having had to 'ask permission from his mother' to travel.

As the team stepped off the plane at the Liège-Bierset airport around mid-morning, they were instantly hit by the heat-wave that had been sweeping the Continent for the previous few days, and when they went to train in the Sclessin stadium, they found the weather had taken its toll on the pitch. The surface was brick-hard.

This may have influenced Tommy Walker's decision to change the right-hand side of the forward line, with both Andy Bowman and Jimmy Wardhaugh being brought into the side that had beaten Raith Rovers at the weekend. Jimmy Murray and Johnny Hamilton were the unfortunate two to make way.

However, the strangest decision he made was to start Dave Mackay at inside right, a move that baffled many. Walker's thinking was that Dave had the perfect qualities to nullify the effect of Standard's best player, Jean Mathonet.

STADE DE SCLESSIN – WEDNESDAY 3 SEPTEMBER 1958
ROYAL STANDARD DE LIÈGE 5 (JADOT 17 & 89; PITERS 35; BONGA-BONGA 73; HOUF 78)
V
HEARTS 1 (CRAWFORD 14)
REFEREE: P SCHWINTE (FRANCE)

For the first 20 minutes Hearts took the game to Standard and it seemed that Walker's tinkering with the set-up would pay dividends. They survived a scare when after 11 minutes Liège came close to opening the scoring with a terrific shot from Marcel Paeschen that rattled the crossbar. This spurred Hearts on, and three minutes later Ian Crawford became the first Hearts player to score in a European competition after Jimmy Wardhaugh and Willie Bauld had prized open the home defence. There was a hint that the ball had gone out of play – the linesman flagged for a throw but the French referee, M Schwinte, chose to ignore his colleague and the goal stood.

Hearts' celebrations were short-lived. Liège hit back immediately through Jean Jadot, who grabbed the equaliser, ably assisted by Denis Houf and Bonga-Bonga. From that point on, the part-timers slowly began to take control of the game and Hearts fell behind on 35 minutes when André Piters gathered the ball on the right and let fly from fully 30 yards. It certainly was a setback but Hearts had a chance to get into the game again in the remaining ten minutes when left back Henri Thellin had to go off for treatment to a head cut after a clash with Dave Mackay. Try as they might, though, Hearts could not make the most of their numerical advantage and went in behind at the interval.

For the second half Liège were back to full strength – Thellin played on with three stitches in the wound. Hearts began to struggle and were thankful to Gordon Marshall, who brought off a string of good saves to keep them in the game. But with 17 minutes remaining, he was left helpless as the home team increased their lead with a fine individual effort from Bonga-Bonga, a goal their play richly deserved. Denis Houf crashed in a fourth five minutes later and it was a dispirited Hearts side that played out the time remaining. It was not a great surprise when Jadot completed the rout with his second goal of the game in the last minute.

ROYAL STANDARD DE LIÈGE: NICOLAY(T) HAPPART THELLIN BOLSÉE MARNETTE MATHONET PITERS JADOT BONGA-BONGA HOUF PAESCHEN
HEARTS: MARSHALL KIRK THOMSON CUMMING GLIDDEN BOWMAN BLACKWOOD MACKAY BAULD WARDHAUGH CRAWFORD

After the game the Hearts manager was magnanimous in defeat: 'Standard were much the better team and I admired the way every player worked on and off the ball. As for Hearts, I can only say that we were very disappointing and assure you that we can be better.' Following their worse defeat in any competition for 18 months, this was surely something of an understatement.

Hearts returned to Edinburgh the following morning to prepare for the second leg, still hopeful of overturning the four-goal deficit. Their confidence was boosted by a customary win over Hibs at Easter Road, this time by 4-0. By contrast, Liège lost their opening game of their season by 1-0 at home against Waterschei Thor.

TYNECASTLE PARK EDINBURGH – WEDNESDAY 10 SEPTEMBER 1958
HEARTS: 2 (BAULD 55 & 63)
V
ROYAL STANDARD DE LIÈGE: 1 (GIVARD 57)
REFEREE: L FAUQUEMBERGUE (FRANCE)

For the game at Tynecastle, Standard's Hungarian manager Géza Kalocsai looked to protect his four-goal advantage by fielding a more defensive-minded side. Jean Mathonet was dropped for Leopold Anoul, Joseph Givard replaced the troublesome Jean Janot and Jean Nicolay took over in goal from his brother Toussaint.

Despite the second half of the game being broadcast live by STV (for which Hearts received the princely sum of £525), a healthy crowd of 39,000 turned out to see the first ever European Cup tie at Tynecastle. Liège decided to carry out their pre-match exercises behind the main stand, giving some of the early arrivals their first glimpse of the opposition even before they went through the turnstiles.

The visitors also caused a stir at kick off when they took the field in an all white outfit that lacked a shirt number. This made it difficult to recognise any of the Standard team, apart from the distinctive Paul Bonga-Bonga, the Belgian Congo-born centre forward.

As could be expected it was Hearts that took the game to the visitors, but there was no way through the resolute Belgian defence despite all their best efforts. Crawford, Hamilton, Murray and Blackwood were all thwarted by a combination of desperate defending and poor finishing and the sides went in at the interval square.

With Hearts attacking the Gorgie Road end, the game resumed the way the first 45 minutes had finished with Liège (now with numbers on the back of their shirts) content to soak up the pressure, sometimes using rather robust challenges to thwart the Maroons. The breakthrough eventually came on 55 minutes when a Bobby Blackwood corner was nodded on by Dave Mackay to Willie Bauld, who swept the ball into the net.

This should have been the signal for the goal chase to begin but immediately 'Les Rouches' came out of their defensive shell. In their first real attack of the game, two minutes after Hearts had gone in front, Josef Givard fired in the equaliser with a spectacular strike from 20 yards.

Unlike the game in Liège, Hearts' heads did not go down and no one worked harder to restore the lead than Willie Bauld. He received some rough treatment from the visitors but they could not stop him heading home a free kick from Bobby Kirk after 63 minutes.

Hearts continued to seek the goals they needed but their efforts lacked the required finesse. Jimmy Murray was unlucky when his shot came back off the bar, Dave Mackay was first to the rebound but couldn't get enough on his effort. It looked as though the ball had crossed the line before being scrambled away to safety. Monsieur Fauquembergue, thought otherwise, and waved play on. The French whistler annoyed the home support again when he denied Hearts a penalty when Johnny Hamilton was the victim of yet another fierce tackle from Gilbert Marnette, well inside the box. It was all too much for one fan who threw a bottle on to the park and the game was stopped. The delay allowed Liège to reorganise and they saw out the remaining minutes of the match in a resolute manner, becoming the first Belgian side to qualify for the second round since the inception of the competition.

HEARTS: MARSHALL KIRK THOMSON MACKAY GLIDDEN CUMMING BLACKWOOD MURRAY BAULD CRAWFORD HAMILTON (J)
ROYAL STANDARD DE LIÈGE: NICOLAY (J) HAPPART THELLIN BOLSÉE MARNETTE ANOUL PITERS HOUF BONGA-BONGA GIVARD PAESCHEN

Not for the first time, a Scottish team had been ousted from the competition by a European opposition with superior tactical awareness – and often, a more physical approach to the game. Standard Liège had certainly left their mark at Tynecastle in more ways than one, something that Willie Bauld Jnr can testify to:

> I was only five years old at the time of the games, so I don't really remember either of them. My dad never used to talk much about any game really, but the Liège game was different.
>
> As a souvenir, all the players were given an ashtray with the Standard crest. Perhaps it would be considered a strange choice of gift these days but back then it was quite acceptable to Dad, as it is no great secret that he enjoyed a cigarette or two.
>
> It always remained on display in the house but if any visitor went to use it my father would quip, 'Not that one, I'm still paying for that with the bruises on my legs.'
>
> I know that when he walked off the park at the end of the game

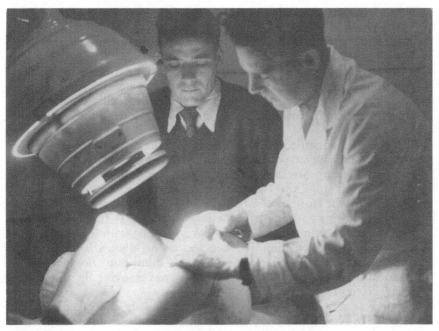

Willie Bauld receives attention after suffering from some rough treatment at the hands of Standard Liège (courtesy of Tom Wright)

both his socks had been torn in wild tackles by the Belgian players. But it was not in his nature to complain and I am sure he was happy that he got the better of them on the night with his two goals, even although Hearts didn't qualify for the next round.

Although Willie Bauld Jnr was not at either of the games, the afore-mentioned Bob Aitchison still has great memories of Hearts' first venture into Europe. Over 50 years later, he recalls the thrill of following his team to Belgium:

My parents, Jock and Grace, were avid Hearts supporters, so much so that my mother was the Secretary of the Musselburgh Hearts Supporters club. Their great friend at the time was John Fairgrieve, the football writer for the *Daily Mail*.

A few days before the first game he asked them if they were interested in travelling to Belgium for the European Cup tie as he knew there were still a few seats left on the official flight for paying supporters. Unfortunately they were both working, but they were delighted for me to go, with John agreeing to look after me.

Needless to say, I was thrilled to bits – aged 17 and going abroad on my first flight, and with my heroes!

Although I had recently been on a school trip to Germany, I needed a full passport to allow me to travel to the game. So I rushed through to the Glasgow Passport Office on the day before the flight, where a very helpful staff member wished me a pleasant trip and that hopefully it would be worth it.

Everything happened so quickly and soon I was sitting on the plane with all the players, officials, press and about a dozen other supporters. The flight was very smooth. We arrived at a Belgian Air Force base and then were taken by coach about 60 miles to our hotel in the centre of Liège.

After we had settled in, we all went with the players to their early evening training session at the Standard Liège ground. On returning to the hotel, I had my first taste of 'continental style' steak. It was virtually uncooked but somehow I didn't care, I was just so excited to be in Europe with the Hearts.

The following morning I got a message to say that Tommy Walker would like to see me in his room. I was tingling with a mixture of excitement and trepidation as I knocked on his door. I had a slight feeling of standing outside the headmaster's study, but I needn't have worried. He asked me nicely about how I was enjoying the trip and what subjects I was going to study at university.

He was very keen to buy a present for his wife and asked me to help him as I had a knowledge of French. The whole squad then drifted along the centre of Liège and Freddie Glidden asked me to help him buy a doll for his daughter. I was amazed that none of my heroes could speak French and struggled to work out the value of the Belgian Francs. In later life I had Freddie's grandson as one of my pupils at Craigroyston High School and was absolutely astounded to find out that the great man's relative was a Hibby!

At the game we were put in the enclosure below the grandstand. We made a lot of noise when Hearts opened the scoring but became more and more subdued as the home team rattled in five.

It was a very quiet group (and I would think very hung-over for some) who made their way back to Edinburgh. However, there was still the second leg to look forward to and the players all seemed keen to do battle again.

On the Thursday evening, back in Musselburgh, I duly reported for training at Olive Bank for the juvenile side I played for, Musselburgh Union. As I arrived one of the committee shouted to me, 'Yer team got thrashed in Belgium last night.' After three wonderful days, my sharp reply was, 'Yes I know... I was there!'

CHAPTER 2

1960–61 European Champion Clubs Cup

AFTER COMPLETING A MAGNIFICENT league and League Cup double the previous season, Hearts returned for a second bite of the European Cup cherry in 1960. However, when the draw was made in Paris on 7 July they could hardly have been handed stiffer opposition: Sir Stanley Rouse pulled out the name of Portuguese champions Benfica, with the first leg to be played at Tynecastle.

Having to fit in a deciding League Cup game against Clyde after finishing level in the group stage on points and goals for and against, the European tie was fixed later than normal, for Thursday 29 September.

It's fair to say that Hearts had experienced a mediocre start to the season, eventually losing out to Clyde in the League Cup play-off game. In the league, a straightforward thrashing of Hibs was followed by two draws against lowly Dunfermline and Airdrie. Despite this, hopes were high when Bella Guttmann brought his men to town.

The Hungarian manager was thorough in his preparations for the tie, arriving in Edinburgh the Monday before the game. Benfica's journey had taken 11 hours, their flight from Lisbon having gone via Paris and London. The players were put on a strict regime of rest followed by more rest.

Meanwhile Tommy Walker had taken the Gorgie side away to their retreat in Peebles where they enjoyed a couple of rounds of golf and daily training in Peebles Rovers' ground, Whitestone Park. These activities were supervised by Johnny Harvey as Walker headed back to Edinburgh to host the Portuguese giants.

From their base in the Carlton Hotel, the visiting party had entertainment laid on which included a shopping trip along Princes Street, a bus tour of Edinburgh and surrounding area and a dinner at Tynecastle. There the Hearts directors gifted a tartan rug for their opposite numbers and stylish tartan ties for the players. The following day, big George Thomson was to be even more generous to the visitors.

TYNECASTLE PARK EDINBURGH – THURSDAY 29 SEPTEMBER 1960
HEARTS: 1 (YOUNG 81)
V
SPORT LISBOA E BENFICA: 2 (ÁGUAS 37; AUGUSTO 73)
REFEREE: M LEQUESNE (FRANCE)

For the game, Alex Young was selected to play at outside right, his fourth position of the season and Gordon Smith at outside left as Hearts lined up an attacking formation. As happened in their previous forays, it was the home side that started the brighter.

As early as the third minute, Alex Young was sent through on goal by Willie Bauld but Costa Pereira was quick to narrow the angle and Alex shot into the side net. Alex continued to lead the Benfica a merry dance and more chances fell to Gordon Smith and Jimmy Murray but the game remained level.

However, against the run of play, it was the visitors who took the lead on 37 minutes. It started with a simple punt up the park from Pereira which was flicked on by Mario Coluna. It looked like a simple task for George Thomson to clear and he tried to head it back to Gordon Marshall, but all he ended up doing was to present Águas with easiest of chances to make it 1-0.

In the second period Hearts continued to search for the equaliser. John Cumming, Jimmy Murray and – trying to atone for his earlier error – George Thomson, all went close, but with 17 minutes to go Benfica doubled their advantage after another slip from Thomson – this time he failed to cut out a through ball to Santana, who whipped the ball into the middle for José Augusto to beat Gordon Marshall from a few yards.

Hearts did manage to throw themselves a lifeline with nine minutes left when Alex Young was rewarded for his hard work throughout. After Andy Bowman found Willie Bauld with a pass, Willie's run drew the Portuguese defence and he picked out Alex, who wasted no time in slamming the ball into the net. It was the least their play in the second half deserved and it certainly set up the tie for the game in Lisbon in six days' time.

HEARTS: MARSHALL KIRK THOMSON CUMMING MILNE BOWMAN YOUNG MURRAY BAULD
WARDHAUGH SMITH
SPORT LISBOA E BENFICA: PEREIRA JOAO CRUZ SARAIVA GERMANO NETO AUGUSTO SANTANA
ÁGUAS COLUNA CAVÉM

The following Saturday Hearts played newly promoted Dundee United at Tynecastle in what should have been a comfortable moral boosting league victory. However, they stuttered to a 1-1 draw against the lowly opposition, hardly the best preparation for the tie in Lisbon.

Hearts take a break from training at Peebles prior to the European Cup tie against Benfica in September 1960. Left to right, back row: George Thomson, Willie Bauld, Billy Higgins, Jim Cruickshank, Gordon Smith, Andy Bowman, Bobby Blackwood, Jimmy Murray, Gordon Marshall, Alex Young, Donald McLeod. Front row: Davie Holt, Bobby Kirk, John Cumming, Tommy Henderson, Jimmy Milne, Johnny Harvey

Once again Hearts chartered a BEA plane (at a cost of £1,266 13s)for the the away leg. Setting out from Tynecastle at 6AM, they flew to Lisbon via London; after a delayed arrival in Portugal, nine hours later the squad were met by Benfica officials who put their official team bus at Hearts' disposal. It was a world apart from anything available in Scotland, the vehicle being the final word in luxury, even having a treatment area for any player suffering from the strains of the arduous journey (it was not needed, though, as the team were transported to the Mundial Hotel on the outskirts of Lisbon).

They headed out that evening to the Estádio da Luz for a light training session. The game was to have a 9.45PM kick off, so Johnny Harvey wanted to get the players used to the conditions they would face the following day. At the stadium they again found facilities light years away from back home. Built only six years earlier, the 65,000-capacity ground was as spectacular as could be found anywhere in Europe.

On the day before the game the Hearts team perhaps felt more at home – the weather took a turn for the worse and it rained all day, confining their training sessions to the gym, with both Jimmy Milne and Willie Bauld receiving treatment for niggling injuries.

By kick off Jimmy Milne was considered to have recovered sufficiently from his groin strain but Willie had not been able to shake off the injury that had kept him out against Dundee United. This meant that Alex Young continued in the centre and Gordon Smith was brought back into the side at outside right.

ESTÁDIO DA LUZ – WEDNESDAY 5 OCTOBER 1960
SPORT LISBOA E BENFICA: 3 (ÁGUAS 8 & 60; AUGUSTO 49)
V
HEARTS: 0
REFEREE: J BARBEREN (FRANCE)

The teams were met with a spectacular fireworks display and music from several bands laid on to celebrate the inauguration of the third tier of the East Side stand. However, the ground was only half full to watch the visitors quickly getting into their stride with Bobby Blackwood being the first to test Alberto Pereira in the hunt to bring the sides level, but the international keeper held well.

Hearts were on top but were caught by a sucker punch in the eighth minute and Benfica doubled their overall lead after George Thomson was harshly adjudged to have impeded José Augusto. The free kick was headed into the net by José Águas in what was Benfica's first attack.

It was a blow to Hearts' aspirations but they continued to dominate. Benfica defended well, despite some dubious tackles that went unpunished by the French referee. Some of his decisions were baffling to say the least, none more so than when Jimmy Murray received a stern lecture after Augusto scythed down Bobby Blackwood.

Monsieur Barberan's most disgraceful decision was reserved for moments before half-time when Germano tripped Alex Young as he was homing in on goal. Not for the first time the ref saw nothing wrong, and Hearts went in at the break two goals down on aggregate.

Although, midway through the first half, John Cumming had picked up a shoulder injury that restricted his movement, the skipper played on through the pain barrier. Neither he nor the referee could be blamed four minutes into the second period when the defence was carved open by Caven, allowing Augusto to put the tie beyond Hearts.

The visitors fought on and Ian Crawford almost grabbed what would only have been a consolation goal. The home side piled on the agony with 30 minutes left when Águas pounced on a loose pass back from George Thomson and flicked the ball past a helpless Gordon Marshall.

Even after Benfica was reduced to ten men when Saraiva left the field, injured Hearts could not find a way through as the game ended in what looked to be a convincing win for the Portuguese champions.

SPORT LISBOA E BENFICA: PEREIRA ÂNGELO CRUZ SARAIVA GERMANO NETO AUGUSTO SANTANA ÁGUAS COLUNA CAVÉM
HEARTS: MARSHALL KIRK THOMSON CUMMING MILNE BOWMAN SMITH MURRAY YOUNG BLACKWOOD CRAWFORD

Despite the 4-1 aggregate scoreline, Benfica's performance had not impressed the experts of the Edinburgh press. One wrote: 'Benfica are no world beaters. They do not begin to compare with the greats of other Continental sides.' Perhaps a little harsh on the Portuguese, given that almost eight months later they ended Real Madrid's dominance in the tournament, defeating Barcelona 3-2 in the final. It could have been Jam Tarts in the final, though, as Hearts legend Alex Young recalls:

> To be honest, we were very naive back then. We were a good team and could beat anyone in Scotland, but like other Scottish teams before us we were outmanoeuvred when it came to playing European opposition. I had never heard of Benfica before the games, let alone having seen a team line up with four at the back – we always played with just three – and the Portuguese were good at exploiting their numerical advantage.
>
> Mind you, in the second leg we missed a couple of sitters in the opening spell and I have to admit I was one of the sinners. Had either or both of them gone in then I'm sure we would have won the game.
>
> As it turned out, those two games were the only times I played for Hearts in Europe. Curiously, when I was at Everton I did play against the likes of Inter Milan, Vålerengen and Real Zaragoza – all teams associated with Hearts in later years. We even played Dunfermline and Kilmarnock in the Inter-Cities Fairs Cup. But I will always wonder what might have been, had we taken our chances in Lisbon.

CHAPTER 3

1961–62 International Inter-Cities Industrial Fairs Cup

AFTER A RELATIVELY POOR SEASON, Hearts entered the Inter-Cities Fairs Cup for the first time. It was the first season that the organisers had relaxed the 'one city, one team' rule, so after an International Meeting at Porthcawl under the chairmanship of Sir Stanley Rous and attended by Hearts' Wilson Strachan, both Hearts and Hibs were chosen as Scotland's representatives. The Easter Road men were no strangers to the competition, having reached the semi-final the previous season when they were beaten after three games by Roma. History shows that they put out holders Barcelona in an earlier round, but what is not generally known is that the Spaniards were also competing in the European Cup where they were eventually beaten in the final by Hearts' conquerors Benfica – the side that they put out against our city rivals being a shadow of the side that played in the major European competition.

In the first round Hearts were drawn in Group D, which included Inter Milan, Valencia, Nottingham Forrest, Cologne and Lausanne, but were eventually paired with Union Saint-Gilloise from Belgium.

The first leg was to be played in Brussels on Wednesday 27 September. For the relatively short journey they left Tynecastle at 8.15AM on Tuesday morning. However, travel delays in both Edinburgh and London meant that they did not arrive in Belgium until 4.15PM, hampering their build up to the game. After checking into the Hotel Amigo near the Grand Place in the heart of Brussels, the party headed to the Stade Joseph Marien in the Dudenparc to watch a game between Valenciennes of France and Belgian side Alast. The idea was to give the team a feel for the stadium they would be playing in, but although the ground had a 30,000 capacity there were very few spectators present.

The following day Tommy Walker decided to change the side that had been beaten 2-0 by Dundee the previous Saturday and brought in Norrie Davidson and John Docherty.

PARC DE DUDEN – WEDNESDAY 27 SEPTEMBER 1961
ROYALE UNION SAINT-GILLOISE: 1 (VAN VAERENBERGH 18)
V
HEARTS: 3 (DAVIDSON 30 & 79; BLACKWOOD 23)
REFEREE: P ROOMER (HOLLAND)

A heavy downpour an hour before kick off played its part in restricting the crowd to only 4,000, although the fact that Les Unionistes, still without a league victory, were sitting second bottom of the league may have been more significant. They gave their fans a lift, though, when they went ahead after only 18 minutes when Camille van Vaerenbergh was allowed to fire in a low shot that eluded Gordon Marshall. However, it didn't take long for Hearts to respond.

After a further five minutes of play, André Vanderstappen had to be at his best in the Gilloise goal when he pulled off a great save to deny Norrie Davidson at the expense of a corner. Johnny Hamilton took it short to Bobby Blackwood who managed to squeeze it in from an acute angle.

It was another corner from 'Hammy' that led to Hearts taking the lead after half an hour. This time Vanderstappen could not reach his kick and Norrie Davidson had the easiest of chances to head into the net.

From then on in, Hearts controlled the game but without adding to their lead, much to the frustration of the 40 or so National Servicemen who had made a five-hour journey from Cologne to watch the game.

The Belgians nearly threw themselves a lifeline in the 73rd minute when a free kick from Jean Claes took a deflection, sending Gordon Marshall the wrong way. Luckily Willie Polland was on hand to clear the ball off the line. This seemed to act as a wake-up call to the visitors and 11 minutes from time, a perfect pass from Billy Higgins allowed Norrie Davidson to get his second and Hearts' third goal of the night.

ROYALE UNION SAINT-GILLOISE: VANDERSTAPPEN DE VOGELAERE BRUYLANTS SCHRAEPER CLAES HAECK KIALUNDA VAN VAERENBERGH MARTENS VAN WILDER JANSSENS
HEARTS: MARSHALL KIRK HOLT CUMMING POLLAND HIGGINS ROSS HAMILTON (J) DAVIDSON DOCHERTY BLACKWOOD

For the return leg Gilloise manager Henri Dekens was forced to make several changes in his line-up due to his part-time players being unable to get time off work. Their star player Paul Vandenberg was also unavailable as he was required for the International team in a World Cup qualifier.

For their part Hearts also made a couple of changes, with two-goal hero Norrie Davidson dropping out through injury. Into the side came Willie Bauld, Willie Wallace and Robin Stenhouse who had made a scoring debut against Airdrie four days earlier. Billy Higgins had suffered from concussion during the same game but had recovered in time to take his place in defence.

TYNECASTLE PARK – WEDNESDAY 4 OCTOBER 1961
HEARTS: 2 (CLAES O.G. 71; STENHOUSE 87)
V
ROYALE UNION SAINT-GILLOISE: 0
REFEREE: A POULSEN (DENMARK)

With a two-goal cushion, it was assumed by the 18,000 fans who turned up for the game that Hearts were a safe bet to qualify for the second round. This confidence obviously spread to the team and they looked fairly complacent with their early efforts. Despite this, the Belgians could not take advantage, which all added up to a rather lacklustre first half.

There was little for the crowd to get excited about but what little there was came in the shape of Robin Stenhouse. Twice he combined well with Willie Bauld but twice Union keeper André Vanderstappen was his equal.

Things did improve slightly in the second half, with Stenhouse again appearing to pose the main threat. With the game remaining goalless, the crowd became restless and the sound of slow handclapping reverberated around Tynecastle.

Even when the first goal did come, with 19 minutes to go, it did little to appease the disgruntled fans. A speculative shot from Willie Wallace looked to be going well wide until it took a deflection off centre half Jean Claes, sending it past the helpless Vanderstappen and putting the tie beyond doubt.

With just three minutes left, Hearts finally gave the fans something to shout about with a wonderful goal. Johnny Hamilton wove a piece of magic on the right wing then crossed the perfect ball for Robin Stenhouse to place a powerful header past the bewildered Union Saint-Gilloise keeper.

History had been made. Hearts qualified for the second round of a European competition for the first time.

HEARTS: MARSHALL KIRK HOLT CUMMING POLLAND HIGGINS HAMILTON (J) STENHOUSE BAULD
WALLACE DOCHERTY
ROYALE UNION SAINT-GILLOISE: VANDERSTAPPEN BRUYLANTS SCHRAEPER HAECK CLAES CLOSE
VAN CAUWELAERT VAN VAERENBERGH MARTENS KIALUNDA JANSSENS

When the second round draw was made in Rome a week later, Hearts were paired against Inter Milan, who had progressed at the expense of FC Köln after winning 5-3 in a play-off game.

The Italians breezed into Edinburgh by train from London on Sunday 5 November, the day before the game, and immediately found fault with

Robin Stenhouse celebrates scoring against Union Saint-Gilloise at Tynecastle in October 1961 (courtesy of Robin Stenhouse)

their accommodation. Hearts had booked them into the Roxburghe Hotel but manager Helenio Herrera deemed that it was not of a suitable standard for his stars. After a few frantic phone calls, Inter decamped along Princes Street to the North British where the standard was considered of a more satisfactory nature.

The following day the side made a visit to Tynecastle but did not bother to hold a training session and only stayed for ten minutes. When asked about the lack of practise, manager Herrera simply replied, 'Training? But why? We play tonight.'

Billy Higgins had been suffering from flu and had missed the win over St Johnstone two days earlier, but he recovered in time to be restored to the team that would face the Italian league leaders.

TYNECASTLE PARK – MONDAY 6 NOVEMBER 1961
HEARTS: 0
V
INTERNAZIONALE MILANO: 1 (HUMBERTO 32)
REFEREE: K HOWLEY (ENGLAND)

Only around 17,500 turned out to watch what was to be a masterful demonstration of the 'new' 4-2-4 system by an Inter side that was minus at least five of their regular players. Other than during the first ten minutes, the Italians controlled every department of the game and eased their way to a well deserved victory.

Although they could turn defence into attack in an instant, the visitors had been confined to long-range shots at goal. Gordon Marshall had to be at his very best to keep out a shot by Humberto, then again when full back Armando Picchi tried his luck from 35 yards. With 32 minutes on the clock, it took a defensive error to break the deadlock. Willie Polland, looking to cut out a pass by Mario Mereghetti, allowed the ball to run through to Lorenzo Bettini. The inside right wasted no time in squaring the ball to the unmarked Jorge Humberto, who had little difficulty beating Gordon Marshall from eight yards.

Inter continued to dominate, playing fast-flowing football; plus, they demonstrated that they had a steely side to their game when firstly Giacinto Facchetti and then Enea Masiero had to be warned by the referee for rough treatment of Danny Ferguson and Billy Higgins respectively.

Hearts did get the ball in the net just before the end of the half when a free kick from Johnny Hamilton floated beyond Ottavio Bugatti. Unfortunately as it was heading into the net, Willie Bauld, who had gone up to nod it in, only managed to let the ball hit his arm and the 'goal' was rightfully ruled out.

After ten minutes of the second half, it was the visitors' turn to have a

Willie Bauld's disallowed goal against Inter Milan, Tynecastle, November 1961

goal chalked off. When he found the net for a second time, Humberto's goal was deemed offside. The Milan side continued to dominate and seemed content to hold on to their one-goal advantage. They were nearly made to pay, though, when Danny Ferguson had a great chance to grab what would have been an undeserved equaliser five minutes from time. Slack, defending for once, allowed Danny a clear sight of goal only six yards out, but his shot was hurried and sailed high into the terracing.

Hearts had been handed a footballing lesson with the 1-0 scoreline certainly not reflecting the difference between the sides.

HEARTS: MARSHALL KIRK HOLT CUMMING POLLAND HIGGINS FERGUSON ELLIOT BAULD
WALLACE HAMILTON (J)
INTERNAZIONALE MILANO: BUGATTI PICCHI FACCHETTI MASIERO GUARNERI BALLERI BICICILI
BETTINI HUMBERTO MEREGHETTI MORBELLO

After the game Hearts were roundly criticised for their performance and the use of the 4-2-4 system, but Inter manager Herrera had some advice for his Hearts counterpart: 'Stick to the 4-2-4 system, it will pay off in the end. But you must learn to move the ball quickly from defence to attack and teach your forwards to beat their opponent over the first two yards. Do that, and goals should come.'

The gulf in class between the sides was readily conceded by Hearts director Nicol Kilgour. 'The gap between foreign and home football was shown up vividly,' he said, going on to bemoan the fact that there had been so few through the turnstiles to watch the game. 'We expected a much better crowd for Inter. They are one of the best teams to visit Scotland for a long time.' This view was echoed by Wilson Terris, chairman of the Scottish League: 'I wish I knew the reason for the poor turnout. Inter were a splendid team. The difference between the Scots and Italians was once again the man off the ball. The man in possession had three or four colleagues unmarked, waiting on the pass,' he remarked.

Two weeks later Hearts headed for Milan without Danny Ferguson, who had been called up by the Army to play in a Forces cup tie in Aldershot. His place was taken by John Docherty who seemed to be something of a cup expert, having only featured in League Cup sides, plus the two previous Fairs Cup games.

On arrival at Lynette Airport on Monday 20 November, they were informed that the game on Wednesday would have a 2.00PM kick off, not 7.30PM as had been expected. This revelation threw Johnny Harvey's training plans into disarray as he had wanted to get the team accustomed to the stadium under lights. Instead of the impressive San Siro, the squad performed their routines in the nearby Redaelli stadium on the Tuesday morning. The afternoon and early evening were given over to a sightseeing trip to Lake Como and Lugano.

The players were delighted when their hosts presented them with gold watches embellished with the Inter club crest, a slightly different class of gift than the tartan travelling rug given to the Italians in Edinburgh. Hearts also received an engraved trophy, and reciprocated with a musical cigarette box with the Hearts crest engraved on the lid.

Only three hours before kick off, Coach Herrera announced that he was making *nine* changes to the side that had been announced by Signore Comombo, the club secretary, the day before. This meant that Inter were starting with eight reserve-team players, although this was not to prove to be any real advantage to Hearts and only served to underline the gulf in class between the two sides.

NUOVO STADIO CALCISTICO SAN SIRO – WEDNESDAY 22 NOVEMBER 1961
INTERNAZIONALE MILANO: 4 (HITCHENS 11 & 68; MORBELLO 31; HUMBERTO 46)
V
HEARTS: 0
REFEREE: V CABALLERO (SPAIN)

Before a mere 12,000 spectators, Hearts started quite brightly – as in the first game – with Billy Higgins, Willie Wallace and Bobby Blackwood all causing problems. But it wasn't long before the home side got into their stride, with Franco Zaglio and English international Gerry Hitchens both testing Gordon Marshall.

Indeed, it was the Englishman who opened the scoring after 11 minutes when some slack defending in the Hearts ranks allowed him the time and space to beat Gordon Marshall with ease. Twenty minutes later and it really was all over as a contest when Morbello made it 3-0 on aggregate after being set up by that man Hitchens.

Hearts did have an opportunity to get back into the game when they were awarded a penalty three minutes before half-time. Remo Bicchierai was adjudged to have controlled a cross from Willie Wallace with his hand during a rare Hearts attack. Normal penalty-taker John Cumming had been injured in the build-up and needed lengthy treatment before the kick could be taken. He decided he could not be relied upon to take it, so Johnny Hamilton stepped up to the mark. His effort could not have been worse – he sent the ball high over the bar, leaving the Inter keeper untroubled.

After having missed this golden chance, Hearts fell further behind moments into the second half. Hitchens was again the provider, with a

The Hearts players and officials pictured in the San Siro Stadium Milan November 1961
Left to right, back row: Tommy Walker, John Cumming, Willie Polland, Bill Higgins, W Eadie
(Director), Jim Cruickshank, John Docherty, Gordon Marshall, W Strachan (Director), Roy
Barry, Robin Stenhouse, Johnny Harvey. Front row: Willie Wallace, Bobby Ross, Johnny
Hamilton, Bobby Kirk, Maurice Elliot, Davie Holt, Bobby Blackwood
(courtesy of Robin Stenhouse)

cross that allowed Humberto to head home. Things just weren't going
Hearts' way and when John Docherty incurred a knee injury moments
later it meant the 26-year-old had to see out the remainder of the game
limping out on the left wing. Man-of-the-match Gerry Hitchens punished
the visitors again after 66 minutes when he rounded off the scoring with a
well-taken goal. There might have been further embarrassment as another
effort by Hitchens was ruled out when a free kick had to be retaken, then
Franco Zaglio missed from the spot after he had been brought down by
John Cumming with five minutes left. The last chance fell to Willie Wallace,
but in an act typical of the game he crashed his shot against the bar when
he was left unmarked for the first time in 180 minutes of football.

INTERNAZIONALE MILANO: BUGATTI GIOVANNA FACCHETTI MASIERO BICCHIERAI BALLERI
PETRONI HUMBERTO HITCHENS ZAGLIO MORBELLO
HEARTS: MARSHALL KIRK HOLT CUMMING POLLAND HIGGINS DOCHERTY BLACKWOOD WALLACE
ELLIOT HAMILTON (J)

It had proved 'third time lucky' as Hearts at last progressed from the first
round in a European competition. They were then unfortunate to be drawn

against one of the best teams in Europe, so their subsequent elimination was no disgrace.

The ties provide great memories for a player with perhaps the best career goals per game ratio, and certainly European goals-per-game ratio in the history of the club, Robin Stenhouse:

Really it was all a bit of a blur at the time. First and foremost I was a Hearts fan. If I hadn't been privileged enough to be wearing the famous maroon jersey I would have been standing on the terracing shouting them on. But there I was sitting next to my hero, Willie Bauld, in the dressing room, ready to go out and play in the Fairs Cup.

I had made my first-team debut a few days earlier against Airdrie at Tynecastle and before the game I was obviously very nervous. Back in those days, they used to print the expected starting 11 in the programme and then would announce any team changes before kick off. I well remember hearing my name being read out, only for it to be greeted by silence. Then the announcer said, 'Number nine... Bauld,' – and the noise was deafening. Willie had been out of the team for over a month and everyone was delighted to see him back... including me.

Willie was magnificent to me. I remember Tommy Walker trying to give me some advice only for Willie to pipe up with something to the effect of, 'Ach, leave him alone boss, I'll make sure he's OK.' It was all I needed to hear. With his help I could hardly go wrong and I managed to get my name on the score sheet along with Willie himself (two goals of course) and John Cumming. We ended up winning 4-1.

I was happy with my performance and was even more delighted to learn that I had retained my place for the game against the Belgians the following Wednesday. We held a two-goal lead from the first leg over there and we were favourites to go through, but in Europe you never knew what to expect. However, we managed to win the game, and again, along with Willie Wallace, I was one of the scorers.

I was really on a high, but football being football I was soon brought back down to earth. I retained my place in the side when we travelled to Stirling for a league game. But unfortunately, we suffered a shock 3-1 defeat to lowly Albion and it was little consolation to me that I was the one to get our goal.

There was an opportunity for revenge only five days later when we played them at Easter Road in the semi-final of the League Cup. This time Willie Bauld came back into the team with Bobby Blackwood dropping out, and with his help we squeezed through 2-1 after extra time.

Next up was a tough trip to Pittodrie and although I hadn't scored at Easter Road I was still in the starting line-up. Before the game Tommy Walker told us to play in a 4-2-4 formation, explaining it was in anticipation of playing Inter Milan in the next round of the Fairs Cup, as that was the way the Italians would line up. I had never heard of it before and because I was only part-time at Tynecastle, I hadn't had the opportunity to practice this with the full-time boys. I needn't have worried, though, as I remember Danny Ferguson being sensational that day, making the whole thing work pretty well. We won again, with Johnny Hamilton and myself getting the goals.

The following two games were against the Old Firm, first Celtic in the league and then Rangers in the League Cup final. What a disappointment it was to me to find out that I had been 'rested' for the Celtic game, but I comforted myself that it was in anticipation of the cup final, or so I thought. Although I travelled through to Hampden as part of the official 13, I missed out, with Maurice Elliot, who had scored against Celtic, keeping the number eight jersey. In fact, he was to do so in the next few games and I never featured in the first team again. I did get included in the squad that travelled to Milan, but my only European experience was to be the game against Union Saint-Gilloise.

Towards the end of the season, it was obvious to me that I had faded from the first-team picture and it was no surprise when Tommy Walker called me into his office to tell me that the club were letting me go. I can't say I wasn't disappointed and just a wee bit puzzled, as I thought I had done enough in the five games I had played to show a bit of potential. I remember Jimmy Wardhaugh, who was by then a journalist, writing in his column that he could not understand 'why Stenhouse's name has mysteriously been missing from the first-team line-up since October'.

I know players these days would have their agent banging down the manager's door demanding answers, but back then there was no one to look after the player. I didn't question the decision, it was just one of these things and I got on with it. At least I had had the opportunity to have played not only for Hearts but also in Europe – and even more importantly, I had played alongside the legend that is Willie Bauld.

CHAPTER 4

1963–64 International Inter-Cities Industrial Fairs Cup

AFTER AN ABSENCE of a year, Hearts returned to Inter-Cities Fairs Cup action in 1963 when they were invited to take part by Willie Allan, the SFA secretary. In the draw they were paired against FC Lausanne-Sport, with the first leg to be played in Switzerland.

Despite having failed to qualify from the group stages in defence of the League Cup, Hearts had started the season brightly. Two comfortable wins against Hibs and Scotland's other Fairs Cup participants, Partick Thistle, plus a draw against Dunfermline, saw them set off in good heart. Only a few hours into the journey the mood changed when adverse weather in the London area forced their plane to land in Manchester to refuel. After a lengthy delay they were finally given the all-clear to continue their journey to the capital, where there was no plane available for the onward flight. As it happened, Hearts' old rivals Benfica were also fog-bound at the airport and there was plenty of time to exchange pleasantries as the Tynecastle boys suffered a further three-hour delay. They eventually reached Geneva some 14 hours after leaving Scotland. Exhausted from the journey, on arrival in Lausanne it was a case of straight to bed for the team.

On Tuesday after a light training session the squad took a sightseeing trip to Lake Geneva, then more rest. In the evening the traditional formalities were held, with the club being presented with a suitably inscribed silver water jug and the players received the rather novel gift of battery-operated shavers. Now clean-shaven, everyone had recovered sufficiently by match day to allow Tommy Walker to field the same 11 who had scored four times against Partick the previous Saturday.

STADE OLYMPIQUE DE LA PONTAISE – WEDNESDAY 25 SEPTEMBER 1963
FC LAUSANNE-SPORT: 2 (HERTIG 58; GOTTARDI 77)
V
HEARTS: 2 (TRAYNOR 26; FERGUSON 50)
REFEREE: G ADAMI (ITALY)

Six thousand spectators had gathered for the 8.30PM kick off in the grandly named but compact stadium. The home side posed little threat as Hearts took command – the only surprise was that it took as long as 26 minutes before they went in front. Tommy Traynor floated in a ball from 30 yards out but it looked a simple take for goalkeeper Rene Kuenzi. The sight of in-rushing Norrie Davidson obviously distracted him, as he ended up pushing the ball into his own net.

Hearts increased their lead five minutes after the break when another shot from 30 yards out beat Kuenzi. This time it was Danny Ferguson who beat the keeper, who looked very slow in getting down to the well struck drive.

The goal seemed to shake the Swiss from their lethargy and suddenly Hearts were playing a different side altogether. The comeback started eight minutes later when a move started by right half Hunziker was finished off by Charly Hertig. He nearly repeated the trick moments later but this time he was foiled by a good save from Jim Cruickshank.

The home side had their tails up, Hearts began to struggle and after 77 minutes Lausanne drew level when the ball broke to Peter Engler and the striker slipped it beyond the Hearts defence for Vottore Gottardi to chase. Cruickie came out to narrow the angle, but the Lausanne man remained composed and stroked the ball past the Hearts goalkeeper.

In a frantic final 13 minutes Lausanne nearly pulled off the win with the Tynecastle men having to thank both Jim Cruickshank and the referee for keeping them level. First the Hearts goalie brought off a world-class save from a Richard Dürr drive, then, seconds from the end, another shot, this time from Robert Hosp, thumped against the underside of the cross-bar. The ball looked to have crossed the line when it came down, but the Italian referee thought otherwise and Hearts had escaped.

FC LAUSANNE-SPORT: KUENZI GROBÉTY TACCHELLA HUNZIKER ARMBRUSTER SCHNEITER GOTTARDI DÜRR HOSP ENGLER HERTIG
HEARTS: CRUICKSHANK POLLAND SHEVLANE BARRY CUMMING HIGGINS HAMILTON (J) FERGUSON DAVIDSON WALLACE TRAYNOR

Hearts were still unbeaten and handily placed at fifth in the league when the Swiss part-timers made the journey to the capital two weeks later. Arriving early on Tuesday evening with only 13 players, they headed directly to Redford Barracks for a light workout. This was followed by the official reception in the Roxburghe Hotel, where Hearts made their usual presentation of a musical cigarette box to the club and tartan travel rugs to the players.

Tommy Walker meets the Lausanne players and officials at Turnhouse airport before the
Fairs Cup tie in October 1963
© The Scotsman Publications Ltd. Licensor www.scran.ac.uk

Perhaps underwhelmed by their hosts' generosity the previous evening, on the day of the game manager Jean Luciano decided that a shopping trip along Princes Street and a visit to Edinburgh Castle was the best way to prepare for the match, rather than a training session at Tynecastle.

TYNECASTLE PARK – WEDNESDAY 9 OCTOBER 1963
HEARTS: 2 (CUMMING 19; J HAMILTON 90)
V
FC LAUSANNE-SPORT: 2 (GOTTARDI 62; HOSP 88)
REFEREE: K DAGNALL (ENGLAND)

A stiff breeze swirled round Tynecastle as Hearts, using the same players for the fifth game running, started the second-leg tie playing into the wind. For the opening exchanges the game was fairly even, with Billy Higgins and John Cumming easily containing any threat from the Swiss. Then on 19 minutes, Cumming turned defence into attack and scored the opener.

Breaking down another attack, John strode forward and cracked in a shot from 25 yards. Possibly due to the wind, the ball took a swerve in mid-flight which deceived René Kuenzi, who remained rooted to the spot.

There were further opportunities to increase the lead but Hearts could not take their chances and ended up going in at the interval only one ahead, although their play merited more.

They were made to pay for their profligacy when Vittore Gottardi pulled Lausanne level with 62 minutes played. A cross from Charles Hertig found Robert Hosp whose miskick broke to Gottardi. As the Hearts defence waited for the referee to blow for offside, he swept the ball past Jim Cruickshank.

It was now end-to-end stuff, with Tommy Walker's side just holding the upper hand and Ely Tacchella twice having to make goal-line clearances. But with time running out and another draw looking likely, it was Lausanne who broke the deadlock. Another lightning break saw the ever dangerous Hosp put the visitors ahead.

There hardly seemed time for Hearts to hit back but they swept up the park and forced a corner. Tommy Traynor swung it into the middle and wee Johnny Hamilton was there to head an unlikely equaliser.

The terracing erupted but the cheers turned to jeers seconds later when Ken Dagnall blew for full time.

HEARTS: CRUICKSHANK POLLAND SHEVLANE CUMMING BARRY HIGGINS HAMILTON (J)
FERGUSON DAVIDSON WALLACE TRAYNOR
FC LAUSANNE-SPORT: KUENZI GROBÉTY TACCHELLA HUNZIKER SCHNEITER POLENCENT
GOTTARDI DÜRR FRIGERIO HOSP HERTIG

Hearts had certainly ridden their luck, but that ran out the next day at Tynecastle when after a toss of a coin by chairman Wilson Strachan they lost the decision as to where the third game would be played. Agreement was reached that the second match in Lausanne would be played six days later, on Tuesday 15 October.

Between the games Hearts went down to a surprise 1-0 home defeat to lowly Queen of the South. Billy Higgins and Norrie Davidson carried the blame – Tommy Walker brought in John Cumming and 20-year-old Alan Gordon.

Lausanne had also suffered a defeat, at the hands of La Chaux-de-Fonds. Despite this manager Jean Luciano decided to make only one change, with Kurt Armbruster replacing Eric Polencent.

STADE OLYMPIQUE DE LA PONTAISE – TUESDAY 15 OCTOBER 1963
FC LAUSANNE-SPORT: 3 (FRIGERIO 15; DÜRR 20 PEN; SCHNEITER 102)
V
HEARTS: 2 (WALLACE 30; FERGUSON 65)
REFEREE: R KREITLEIN (GERMANY)

It was a dry but chilly night in the Stade Olympique and Hearts were slow to get warmed up, finding themselves two down within 20 minutes. The first goal came after 15 minutes when the danger man from the first two games, Charly Hertig, presented Roberto Frigerio with the easiest of chances from a few yards.

Five minutes later and it was 2-0. Davie Holt was harshly adjudged by Herr Krietlein to have fouled Kurt Armbruster in the box. Richard Dürr stepped up and gave Jim Cruickshank no chance with his fierce kick. In the first game in Switzerland it had been Lausanne who had to comeback from a 2-0 deficit. Now it was Hearts' turn.

Slowly they began to creep back into the game, taking hold of midfield, and that was that area the first goal stemmed from. After 30 minutes John Cumming made progress into the Lausanne half, before stroking the ball to Johnny Hamilton on the left. Hammy wasted no time in whipping in his cross and Willie Wallace did the rest.

There was only one team in it now, but time and again the attacks either came to nothing or were ended by some cynical body checking by the Swiss. To Hearts' frustration, the German referee took no action against the Swiss but continued to find fault with the visitors, with both Willie Hamilton and Danny Ferguson's names ending up in his book. Hearts were not to be denied, though, and Danny Ferguson levelled things in the 65th minute when he blasted the ball past Kuenzi.

The Maroons continued to be the dominant side for the remaining 25 minutes but could not find the winner, with the game ending in a 2-2 draw for the third time. Hearts got the 30 minutes' extra time under way and Willie Wallace thought he had put them ahead in the first minute when he bundled the ball home. His celebrations were short-lived – the referee chose to rule it out for offside.

Ten minutes later disaster struck when, in a rare foray upfield, Lausanne won a corner. Vottore Gottardi's kick was poorly defended, allowing Heinz Schneiter time and space to beat Jim Cruickshank from six yards for what was to be the final goal in the marathon tie.

FC LAUSANNE-SPORT: KUENZI GROBÉTY TACCHELLA SCHNEITER HUNZIKER DÜRR GOTTARDI ARMBRUSTER FRIGERIO HOSP HERTIG
HEARTS: CRUICKSHANK SHEVLANE HOLT FERGUSON BARRY CUMMING TRAYNOR HAMILTON (W) WALLACE GORDON HAMILTON (J)

Despite being the better team by far over the three games, Hearts' failure to take their chances saw them fall at the first hurdle in a European competition once again. Playing in Europe was hardly a lucrative venture for the club as the accounts showed. The cost of the BEA flights alone were £810 14s 6d and these had to be offset against the receipts for the home gate, a mere £1,518 2s 6d (from a crowd of 11,715).

Hearts players arrive back in Edinburgh after getting eliminated from the Fairs Cup by Swiss side Lausanne. Left to right: Norrie Davidson, Roy Barry, Danny Ferguson, Bobby Broome, Tommy Traynor, Chris Shevlane. © The Scotsman Publications Ltd. Licensor www.scran.ac.uk

Serious thought would have to be given to accepting any future invitation into the Inter-Cities Fairs Cup. However, despite the lack of success in Europe, Hearts and Scotland stalwart Billy Higgins considers the experience to have been invaluable to the club:

> I was fortunate enough to be at Hearts when they first qualified for the European Cup and was at the home and away legs against both Standard Liège and Benfica before making my debut against Union Saint-Gilloise in the Fairs Cup in 1961.
>
> In truth, when we played Standard, we were just not ready for it – 'it' being the change in playing style, preparation, tactics and all that goes with playing outwith your normal environment. Our side was basically the same one that had romped home in Scotland the previous season and were full of confidence. That was reinforced when we scored first but after that we were not in the game. The return match again showed that, tactically, a 2-1 victory changed very little.
>
> In 1960 we faced a little-known club from Portugal called Benfica. Again, in reality we didn't seriously worry the team that went on lift the

trophy, giving some wonderful performances on the way. Maybe now this was the time to realise the values in team structure instead of the traditional Scottish way of having naturally gifted players. Certainly the players had it in mind!

The following season we tried to work to a new 4-2-4 formation and certainly attracted a lot of criticism from all quarters in the process. Success was erratic but then how quickly could you adapt? Notably, though, in the 61–62 season it worked against Rangers in the final of the League Cup where we drew 1-1 – but in truth, we should have won easily.

In Europe the 'new' system worked well against Union Saint-Gilloise but we were perhaps unfortunate to then draw Inter Milan. They were more used to playing 4-2-4 and, as might have been expected, we received another tactical lesson, especially away from home, where we lost 4-0 in a near empty stadium – we were obviously considered no threat to the local heroes – a further lesson that there is more to it than just running onto the pitch and depending on natural abilities.

With the team clearly uncomfortable with 4-2-4, the following years saw us experiment with a 4-3-3 formation which, in the early days, totally baffled some opposition in the Scottish league. While I don't claim that it significantly improved the performances in Europe, we did in fact play better in the fixture against Lausanne and again the following season against Zaragoza. On both occasions we deserved a better outcome.

Maybe the need to appreciate other techniques had gradually made sense. Did this also have a material impact on the incredible '64/'65 season? Who can say!

If there is positive comment from the ventures into Europe, it is that Hearts in the early '60s were most definitely in the vanguard with tactical team structures in the Scottish league. No such coaching was feasible in those days, and the fact that the team took it on themselves to try and break the mould in the face of much criticism speaks volumes for the players and staff. Times had definitely changed.

CHAPTER 5

1965–66 International Inter-Cities Industrial Fairs Cups

AFTER LOSING THE LEAGUE TITLE in the cruellest manner possible the previous season, Hearts found themselves participating in the Inter-Cities Fairs Cup when it could have so easily have been the European Cup. The rules for entry had changed by this time and it was now strictly on merit, so the club found themselves joining city rival Hibs and Dunfermline as Scotland's representatives.

Having received a 'bye' in the first round, by the time Hearts entered the competition the Scottish contingent was down to two, Hibs having fallen at the first hurdle against Valencia.

When the draw was made for round two on 8 October, Hearts were paired against Norwegian part-timers Vålerengen, no strangers to Hearts as the two sides had met in June on Hearts' tour of Norway, when goals from Don Kerrigan, Donald Ford, Roald Jensen and Willie Polland had led Hearts to a comfortable 4-1 victory, and so another easy victory for the Gorgie side was expected.

The first leg at Tynecastle has a historic significance – Hearts became the first Scottish side to be allowed by the SFA to list a substitute goalkeeper, with John Calder being named as Jim Cruickshank's replacement, should he be injured. As things turned out, it was Vålerengen's keeper who was to make a name for himself in the first leg.

TYNECASTLE PARK – MONDAY 18 OCTOBER 1965
HEARTS: 1 (WALLACE 43)
V
VÅLERENGEN IDRETTSFORENING: 0
REFEREE: W O'NEIL (IRELAND)

From the first whistle it was obvious that the Norwegian side had come to defend, and with the majority of their players being at least six feet in height, they looked ably built to carry out the job. Debutant Don Kerrigan, unfazed by their height advantage, brought out the best in Helge Sorlie in the visitors' goal. His save on 21 minutes was the pick of the bunch as he dived low to his right to turn a goal-bound shot onto the post. When Hearts did get the better of the keeper, he was capably assisted by his defenders as Mathisen cleared off the line from Willie Wallace after some great work by Donald Ford.

The 10,000 crowd watched as wave upon wave of Hearts attacks were thwarted until two minutes before the break when Donald Ford swung in a corner and the normally reliable Sorlie made his first mistake when he fumbled the ball to allow Willie Wallace to prod home.

The second half continued in the same manner as the first, with Hearts unable to pierce Vålerengren's rearguard. Kerrigan, Traynor and Polland all went close but time and again that man Sorlie prevented the home side from increasing their advantage.

As the game neared to a close tempers ran high and a frustrated Willie Wallace found his name going into the book for dissent after a free kick had been awarded against Hearts. At the final whistle Hearts had won but not by the margin they had wanted, which made the return leg the following week much trickier than anticipated.

Hearts players in the departure lounge at Turnhouse airport prior to flying to Norway for the Fairs Cup tie against Vålerengen in October 1965. Left to right, back row: Frank Sharp, Chris Shevlane, Willie Polland, Jim Cruickshank, Roy Barry, Derek Rutherford. Front row: John Cumming, Tommy Traynor, Johnny Hamilton, Danny Ferguson, Don Kerrigan, Alan Anderson © The Scotsman Publications Ltd. Licensor www.scran.ac.uk

HEARTS: CRUICKSHANK FERGUSON HOLT POLLAND ANDERSON CUMMING FORD TRAYNOR
WALLACE KERRIGAN HAMILTON (J) UNUSED SUB: CALDER
VÅLERENGEN IDRETTSFORENING: SORLIE EGGEN MATHISEN LARSON (T) PREASTEROD JACOBSEN
KNUDSEN LARSON (E) MARCOSSEN BORRENSEN SOREMAN

As had become customary, Hearts encountered travel problems en route to the second leg. This time, rather than flying, the squad took an overnight train to London in the hope of avoiding any delay due to weather conditions. The capital was, however, encountering one of its famous 'pea-soupers' and the team was again stranded at the airport. After a wait of several hours, they were eventually able to board the flight to Oslo, finally arriving at their destination 17 hours after leaving Edinburgh.

For the game, Tommy Walker selected the 11 that had pummelled the Scandinavians in the first leg. The same men had had found their shooting boots in the league game against Motherwell the previous Saturday, scoring five in the process.

BISLETT STADION – WEDNESDAY 27 OCTOBER 1965
VÅLERENGEN IDRETTSFORENING: 1 (KNUDSEN 72)
V
HEARTS: 3 (KERRIGAN 9 & 89; TRAYNOR 22)
REFEREE: H SCHALACH (HOLLAND)

Hearts, playing in an all white strip borrowed from their opponents, were quick out of the blocks and Sorlie, the hero of the first leg, was soon called into action. The Valerengen keeper was tested by both Kerrigan and Traynor as the visitors looked for the early goal that would surely settle the tie. The breakthrough came in the ninth minute, when a cross-cum-shot from Tommy Traynor rebounded off the bar to Don Kerrigan, who raced in to nod it home. Jim Cruickshank needed to be alert as the Norwegians tried to find a way back into the game and did well to get to a cross from Einar Larsen but his punch only went as far as Egil Olsen. But Cruickie was quick to react and managed to gather Olsen's shot easily.

After 22 minutes the tie really was over when Don Kerrigan and Tommy Traynor combined again. This time Don repaid the compliment when he slipped in the right winger, who beat Sorlie from six yards.

Hearts were now on cruise control, with Don Kerrigan running the show. They did get a fright 18 minutes from time whe, in a rare attack, Per Knudsen made it 2-1.

The goal enlivened the 18,000 crowd, but their encouragement did not stop Hearts tightening their grip on the game. Their endeavour was rewarded a minute from time when man-of-the-match Don Kerrigan got his second and Hearts' third, with the most spectacular strike of the night.

HEARTS: CRUICKSHANK FERGUSON HOLT POLLAND ANDERSON CUMMING FORD TRAYNOR
WALLACE KERRIGAN HAMILTON (J) UNUSED SUB: MURPHY
VÅLERENGEN IDRETTSFORENING: SORLIE EGGEN MATHISEN LARSEN (T) PREASTEROD JACOBSEN
KNUDSEN LARSEN (E) OLSEN BORRENSEN SOREMAN

After the match, a satisfied Tommy Walker said, 'Tonight's victory was a team effort. We will take anyone on in the third round.'

That 'anyone' turned out to be Real Zaragoza, who had won the trophy two seasons earlier, no easy task for round three. Like Hearts, they had started the season in reasonable form and lay fourth in their league by the time they arrived in Edinburgh on Monday evening. However, the squad was without goalkeeper and captain Enrique Yarza, who had sustained an ankle injury in the 3-1 win over Las Palmas the previous day. Also missing was influential inside left Juan Villa.

There was still a scattering of international players who set about upsetting the Tynecastle ground staff at their Tuesday training session. Firstly, the Spaniards turned up at 4.30PM instead of the agreed 7.30PM but after some negotiation it was agreed that they could carry out their exercises on the perimeter of the pitch. The weather over the previous few days had left the park very soft and Mattie Chalmers and his boys wanted it to be in prime condition for the game.

Zaragoza, however, were anxious to test out their young replacement keeper Aldea, who had very little experience as a senior player. To do this, they proceeded to hold an intensive 'shooting-in' practise, much to the annoyance of the groundsmen.

Hearts themselves had been denied the opportunity to play on the pitch due to its condition, but the men from Spain choose not to follow any such ruling. After the session, Zaragoza's French coach, Louis Hon, confident that his side would be too good for the Scots in the return leg in Spain, confessed that he would be happy to come away from Tynecastle with a draw.

TYNECASTLE PARK – WEDNESDAY 12 JANUARY 1966
HEARTS: 3 (ANDERSON 50; WALLACE 59; KERRIGAN 80)
V
REAL ZARAGOZA SAD: 3 (LAPETRA 10 & 87; ENDERIZ 30)
REFEREE: A JENSEN (DENMARK)

A crowd of 17,000 turned out (with gate receipts of £3,061 5s) on a bitterly cold night to watch what turned out to be the proverbial game of two halves. In the first 45, Zaragoza established a comfortable advantage but Hearts stormed back in the second period, only to be denied right at the death to give coach Hon the draw he desired.

The Spaniards went ahead after ten minutes when Marcelino broke through the Hearts defence. With the Brazilian Canário unmarked in the middle, he held on to the ball a little too long, allowing Alan Anderson the chance to put in a tackle. Unfortunately, the ball broke to Carlos Lapetra, whose shot from 20 yards beat Jim Cruickshank via the left-hand post.

A few minutes later and it could have been two, but Mr Jensen, the Danish referee, came to Hearts' rescue. Davie Holt tried to send a header back to his keeper but Canário nipped in and rounded Cruickie before slamming the ball into an empty net. His joy was short-lived when the ref disallowed the goal for offside. As the ball had been played to him by a Hearts man, it was a baffling but welcome decision.

Obviously riled by the perceived injustice, Canário extracted his revenge in the 30th minute. He did all the hard work, beating a couple of men before cutting inside from the left and laying on a chance that Uruguayan Eduardo Enderiz accepted with ease.

Hearts didn't have an answer to Canário, who had been part of the star-studded Real Madrid side that defeated Eintracht Frankfurt in the memorable European Cup final at Hampden almost six years earlier. He was unfortunate not to get the goal his play deserved when just before half-time he saw his shot thud back of the post with Jim Cruickshank

Real Zaragoza line up for a team photo outside Tynecastle prior to the Fairs Cup clash in January 1966

45

well beaten. Although the home side were down they were definitely not out and Alan Anderson played a true captain's part when he got them back in the game five minutes after the restart. Perhaps it was no surprise that the goal came when the menacing Canário was off the park receiving treatment, but big Alan's goal gave the boost the Tynecastle men needed.

The frailties of the stand-in keeper, Aldea, began to be exposed as Hearts pressed for the equaliser and it was a gift from him that saw the sides draw level. A cross from Johnny Hamilton found the head of Willie Wallace, but his effort looked to be easily covered by the Spanish goalie. That was until he tried to be a little too spectacular with the save and only succeeded in falling backwards into the net, clutching the ball.

Minutes later Aldea went down, claiming to have a shoulder injury and – probably more to save him any more embarrassment – was replaced by the tracksuit-wearing Vincente Cardoso. If Aldea was poor, Cardoso was worse. Hearts used this to their advantage, deservedly going ahead with ten minutes left.

Tommy Traynor did the lead-up work and Don Kerrigan did the damage with a shot on the turn that beat the slow-reacting Zaragoza keeper. It was the signal for the Tynecastle faithful to erupt and, unfortunately, for the visitors to begin their own mini-fightback.

Just as Hearts captain Alan Anderson had led the way with a goal, so did the Zaragoza captain, Carlos Lapetra, with a fine individual effort to make the scoreline 3-3 with only three minutes left.

HEARTS: CRUICKSHANK FERGUSON HOLT CUMMING ANDERSON MILLER HAMILTON(J) HIGGINS WALLACE KERRIGAN TRAYNOR
REAL ZARAGOZA SAD: ALDEA (CARDOSO) IRUSQUIETA REIJA ISASI SANTAMARIA VIOLETA CÁNARIO SANTOS MARCELINO ENDERIZ LAPETRA

The disappointment of losing the late equaliser was tempered by the fact that there was no doubt that the crowd had witnessed a fabulous game. If Hearts could produce the same standard of football in the second leg, then perhaps they might be able to dent the optimism of Louis Hon.

Despite the fact that any Scottish side had yet to win a European tie in Spain and that Zaragoza had only lost once at home, Hearts arrived in Zaragoza early on Monday evening in good spirit. For once they had no travel difficulties, despite their chartered BEA flight having to make two refuelling stops, in London and Bordeaux. The club had tried to offset the cost of the trip (£2,100) by allowing a small number of supporters to travel with the official party at £30 a head, but few had taken advantage of the offer.

The league game at Dundee two days earlier had been called off at the last minute due to a frozen pitch, so the team had trained at Tynecastle on the Sunday. Because of the break there were no injury worries, but Davie Holt was suffering from a bout of tonsillitis so did not travel, his place in the side being taken by Chris Shevlane.

If Zaragoza had upset the Tynecastle club with their training arrangements in Edinburgh, they did so again in Spain. When they arrived, Johnny Harvey was informed that the 11.30AM session he had arranged in the Romerada the following day had now been switched to 9AM to allow the home team to use the stadium at the later time.

Undeterred by this cynical gamesmanship, Hearts continued their preparations and were happy to line up with only the one change to the side that had finished so strongly at Tynecastle two weeks earlier. Zaragoza also made a change, with Rodri becoming the third goalkeeper to face the Scots.

ESTÁDIO LA ROMERADA – WEDNESDAY 26 JANUARY 1966
REAL ZARAGOZA SAD: 2 (SANTOS 5; ENDERIZ 22)
V
HEARTS: 2 (ANDERSON 26; WALLACE 77)
REFEREE: M KITABICAN (FRANCE)

Remarkably, there were similarities to this game and the thriller played out at Tynecastle when Hearts found themselves two down, only to storm back to finish level. Perhaps this was an even greater achievement, as they did so playing the majority of the game with only ten men.

The home side took just five minutes to take the lead, much to the delight of the 30,000 crowd. Jim Cruickshank just failed to reach a free kick from right back Reija and Santos was able to head the ball towards goal. It was uncertain if the ball had fully crossed the line before it was cleared but the referee awarded the goal. A contentious decision, and not the last the whistler gave in favour of the home side.

Despite being assisted by the referee, there was no doubt that the Spaniards were the better side and this was emphasised after 22 minutes when another free kick caused havoc in the Hearts box. It had been awarded after Tommy Traynor was penalised for an innocuous foul on Lapetra. Enderiz took the kick and Marcelino rose above everyone to place a powerful header behind Jim Cruickshank.

Once again there was a similarity to the first leg when Alan Anderson grabbed the goal that threw Hearts a lifeline. Having never scored all season, he followed up his first goal at Tynecastle with a second in Zaragoza. Four minutes after they had gone two down, he reduced the deficit with a great header when Tommy Traynor crossed from the right.

The goal was a signal for the home side to start to put in some unsavoury tackles. John Cumming received a bad knock after Marcelino had gone in high and late, a tackle that went unpunished. Worse was to follow when five minutes before the interval Danny Ferguson was injured in a tackle with Canário. The full back's injury was so severe he had to be carried from the field, leaving Hearts to play out the remaining 50 minutes with ten men.

Although the Spaniards' illegal tactics continued to go unpunished, George Miller, Johnny Hamilton and Chris Shevlane all managed to find their way into the referee's book.

In the second half Tommy Traynor was given the task of marking the dangerous Lapetra leaving *only* three men forward! Although on the back foot for most of the time, Hearts stunned the home team in 77 minutes with a great goal: Johnny Hamilton cleverly headed the ball through for Willie Wallace to run onto and crash a marvellous shot past the bemused Rodri.

In the remaining time it was all Zaragoza as Hearts defended stoutly. It looked like they might have been robbed of their finest result in Europe so far, when with eight minutes left, Marcelino had the ball in the net only for it to be ruled out for offside. It was about the only decision the referee got right all night, but as the angry Spaniards surrounded him there seemed a chance he could change his mind, although he stood by his decision.

At the death, Jim Cruickshank ensured a third meeting of the sides when he pulled off a magnificent save from Reija before the crossbar came to his rescue when a blockbuster from Santos had left him beaten.

REAL ZARAGOZA SAD: RODRI IRUSQUIETA REIJA ISASI SANTAMARIA VIOLETA CÁNARIO SANTOS
MARCELINO ENDERIZ LAPETRA
HEARTS: CRUICKSHANK FERGUSON SHEVLANE CUMMING ANDERSON MILLER HAMILTON (J)
HIGGINS WALLACE KERRIGAN TRAYNOR

After what had been a magnificent display from Hearts they fully merited a third bite at the cherry to overturn a very good Spanish side. Unfortunately, their luck ran out five minutes after the final whistle when Alan Anderson called 'heads' and the coin came down 'tails' in the coin toss to decide home advantage for the play-off.

The date for the deciding game was set for Wednesday 2 March. In the intervening five weeks the sides had contrasting fortunes. Hearts continued an unbeaten run that now stretched back to 13 November, while Zaragoza were in crisis.

They had not managed to solve their goalkeeping problem, with Yarza remaining on the injured list. Results had gone against them and Louis Hon was replaced by the legendary Czechoslovakian and man of many clubs, Ferdinand Daucik. Having steered both Barcelona and Athletico Bilbao to la Liga titles, he was seen as the man to change Zaragoza's fortunes.

However, in the three games prior to the Fairs Cup fixture, Los Banquillos had three consecutive 0-0 draws. There may have been an excuse for the first two, as they had been against Real Madrid and Barcelona, but the latest was against bottom club Majorca. Yarza had made his comeback in the match but he had to be replaced early in the second half and was already ruled out of the side.

Hearts, on the other hand, had no new injury concerns as they gathered in the Clarendon Hotel on Sunday 27 February after having defeated Aberdeen 1-0 the previous day. Following dinner and an overnight stay, the squad departed for Turnhouse and flight BFCH 255 to Bordeaux at 10.00AM. After a short stopover in France they continued on to Zaragoza finally arriving at their town-centre base, the Hotel Goya, at around 6.00PM.

Tuesday was split between a light training session and a sightseeing trip in Zaragoza as the players relaxed before the two sides met for the right to meet Dunfermline Athletic in the quarter-final.

ESTÁDIO LA ROMERADA – WEDNESDAY 2 MARCH 1966
REAL ZARAGOZA SAD: 1 (MARCELINO 80)
V
HEARTS: 0
REFEREE: B DI MARCHI (ITALY)

The performance of the French referee had been a talking-point of the last game between the two teams but incredibly Hearts pulled an even worse specimen out of the refereeing hat for this one. It is fair to say that Italian whistler Bruno di Marchi had as much influence in the outcome of the game as Marcelino who scored the goal that eventually split the sides.

From the off, Hearts set out their stall to defend and try to catch Zaragoza on the break with that responsibility given to Johnny Hamilton, Willie Wallace and Tommy Traynor. The referee began to play his part early on when Santamaria went unpunished for bringing down Willie Wallace by grabbing him round the waist with both hands. By contrast, Davie Holt was constantly pulled up for perfectly fair tackles allowing the Spaniards to pile the pressure on the resolute Tynecastle defence.

It looked as if the tactics had worked to perfection five minutes before the interval when Hearts thought they grabbed the opening goal they planned for. In a quick counter-at-tack Alan Anderson left his defen-sive duties to join in a foray into the Spanish half. A pinpoint cross from Johnny Hamilton picked him out beautifully and his header flew past Rodri. Unbelievably, the referee's whistle did not signal the goal but a mystery infringement.

The second half followed the same pattern as the first, with Hearts defending manfully and the Italian referee continuing to make puzzling decisions, usually favouring the home side.

Alan Anderson and Jim Cruickshank examne the trophy presented to the club by Real Zaragoza after the 2-2 draw in Spain January 1966
© The Scotsman Publications Ltd.
Licensor www.scran.ac.uk

Willie Wallace was downed in the box, a penalty anywhere else but not in La Romerada. The Italian whistler waved play on. Don Kerrigan almost got his name on the scoresheet when his volley was cleared off the line by left back Juan Zubiaurre, but still the stalemate could not be broken.

Sadly, a winning goal did come ten minutes from time and it went to the home side. Violeta was allowed to put a cross into the middle and Marcelino made a perfect run to meet it with his head to flash it past Jim Cruickshank.

Now it was Zaragoza's turn to defend in depth as Tommy Walker's men piled forward in search of the goal that would take the game into extra time They managed the task competently and it was left to the referee to dish out the final irony when he booked Violeta in the final minute for a rather innocuous foul on Johnny Hamilton.

REAL ZARAGOZA SAD: RODRI IRUSQUIETA ZUBIAURRE PEPIN SANTAMARIA VIOLETA CÁNARIO SANTOS MARCELINO VILLA LAPETRA
HEARTS: CRUICKSHANK POLLAND HOLT HIGGINS ANDERSON MILLER HAMILTON (J) CUMMING WALLACE KERRIGAN TRAYNOR

Hearts were out but not without putting up a magnificent fight and of course the help of an Italian official. Tommy Walker summed it up the following day when he said, 'He gave Anderson no protection at all and there were two obvious penalties.' Hearts considered making an official complaint but probably knew what the outcome would be and decided against the action. As Zaragoza then went all the way to the final (only to fail at the last hurdle against Barcelona after extra time), going out in such controversial circumstances is a classic case of 'so near yet so far'.

Despite a great career at Hearts that has been properly recognised with his induction into the Hall of Fame, the games against Vålerengen turned out to be the only two European ties that Donald Ford played in. The away leg came a couple of days after his 21st birthday and he can still remember the time vividly:

> As one of the 'younger' brigade at Tynecastle in 1965, my disappoint-ment at not being in the European Cup (the final day loss to Kilmar-nock took a *long* time to wear off) was not perhaps as deep as it must have been for the more seasoned members of the team. After all, we were still in a competition in Europe, even if the Fair Cities Cup was, in those days, a poor second. The potential excitement of foreign travel was still much anticipated – more so when we were drawn against a Norwegian team just a few months after (for me, at least) a highly suc-cessful end-of-season tour of that very same country.
>
> The 1-0 lead gained at Tynecastle in the first leg ought to have been wider, but breaking down a big defence intent on doing nothing more than rearguard fortification is never easy. As it turned out, the wider spaces we consequently enjoyed in Oslo made the second leg a whole lot less fraught than it might have been and a comfortable win – in spite of the nightmare journey to get there – was no less than we deserved.
>
> It was the next round, however, which grabbed the imagination. Real Zaragoza had both an exciting ring in the very name as well as a nucleus of class players. Sadly, the first leg was at Tynecastle.
>
> Don't let *any* comments by a manager or player about being happy to be at home first fool you. Ninety-nine per cent of the time, it is *hugely* in your psychological favour to be coming home – irrespective of the result on foreign soil – knowing exactly what has to be done. It is a two-way mental advantage. Almost certainly, the opposition will be as short of confidence and courage as the home side is bursting with both (who, for instance, can forget Hearts 4, Burnley 1 in the Texaco Cup second leg, or later, Hearts 5, Leipzig 1, as classic examples?
>
> With the like of Santamaria, Canário and Marcelino in their ranks, the presence of class had to be taken as read. To pull back from a two-goal deficit in the home leg and be within a fraction of then winning spoke volumes for the fight – and finishing qualities – in the Hearts' side. The Spanish equaliser, with just a few minutes left, was a real sickener.
>
> Despite not playing in the first leg, I was included in the party for the away game and the trip to Zaragoza was hugely entertaining and a great match, as I remember.
>
> Though not being involved again, I still remember sitting in the

stand and being riveted by a great game. It was threatened, however, by an appalling refereeing display which smacked, from start to finish, of favouritism. The suspicions aired by everyone with Tynecastle connections were compounded after it was all over. The courage of the team was immense, especially after Danny Ferguson had to be taken off after a horrific tackle by Marcelino. Coping with that, as well as awful refereeing decisions, many teams would have thrown in the towel.

However, a terrific, typical, Willie Wallace strike, some brilliant defending and another great goalkeeping display by Cruickie all saw me out of my seat as we earned a tremendous and well deserved draw.

After the whistle I made my way down to the dressing room where I found out that the drama wasn't finished – and neither was the biased refereeing. Tossing a coin in his room to decide the venue for the decider, the ref asked Alan Anderson to call. He shouted 'heads', the coin ran under the table, the ref swiftly got down to rescue it and, surprise, surprise, announced that it was 'tails'. Believe that, if you will!

In any event, for the return trip and third match we would have actually welcomed that French ref, as his replacement refereed even worse. We lost narrowly, having a great goal mysteriously disallowed, two penalty claims ignored and the most blatant show of 'homer' refereeing that anyone in our team had ever seen.

There was huge suspicion, though proof was difficult, obviously, that the Italian referee had been 'rewarded in advance' by unknown favours received from the Spanish club. How, otherwise, could such blatantly biased decision-making on the field be satisfactorily explained?

At any rate, we lost 1-0 to a goal from arch enemy and destroyer number one, Marcelino. It was sad that such a fine player showed all the worst features of field behaviour that could be imagined, went totally unpunished for them, then scored the winning goal. No wonder the whole Hearts party felt sick to the stomach… for a *long* time afterwards.

CHAPTER 6

1976–77 UEFA Cup Winners Cup

AFTER WATCHING THEIR favourites exit Europe at the hands of Zaragoza, Hearts supporters then had to live on a diet of Texaco and Anglo-Scottish cup appearances, as participation in Europe eluded them. Although the new competitions brought a welcome change during the normal season, visitors such as Oldham Athletic and Queen of the South just did not have the same allure as the likes of Benfica and Inter Milan.

A decade and three managers later, thanks to a Scottish Cup final appearance the previous season, fans were able to dust off their passports and head back into Europe. Despite a 3-1 defeat to Rangers, the Maroons qualified for the European Cup Winners Cup due to the fact that the Ibrox men had also won the league and were representing Scotland in the European Cup.

The first round draw saw Hearts paired with GDR cup winners Locomotive Leipzig in what would be the club's first trip 'behind the iron curtain'. Little was known about the East Germans, but their side did include the likes of Wilfred Gröbner and Wolfram Löwe, both of whom had been part of the GDR side that had defeated Poland in the football final at the summer Olympics in Montreal a couple of months earlier. Also included in the team were established internationals such as Henning Frenzel and Joachim Fritsche; in total the side contained players that had made over 110 international appearances.

Hearts were obviously a mystery to the Germans as well – their coach, Horst Scherbaum, decided to take in their game against Partick Thistle on the Saturday prior to their meeting in Leipzig. It is unlikely he saw anything to his advantage as the teams played out a rather dull 0-0 draw, with only the visitors' Alan Hansen showing anything like a European pedigree.

However, Leipzig themselves were showing none of the form that had won them the GDR cup the previous season and they could only struggle to a 1-1 draw against lowly Wismot the following day.

Hearts left for East Germany on the Tuesday morning and as per usual their journey to their European tie was not without incident. The scheduled BA flights between Edinburgh, London and Berlin went without a hitch but after arrival at Templehoff airport problems began.

The bus taking them across town got stuck in rush-hour traffic delaying the team's arrival at 'Checkpoint Charlie' – perhaps more of an inconvenience than a crisis. However, after entering East Germany they faced a three-hour journey to Leipzig and it was during this time that Dave Clunie reported feeling unwell. He was made as comfortable as was possible on a mid-'70s East German bus and then confined to his room immediately on arrival at the team hotel.

Another doubtful starter was Ralph Callachan, who was suffering from an ankle knock he had received against Thistle. However, after a light training session on the morning of the game, he was passed fit, along with Dave Clunie who had recovered sufficiently overnight to make the starting line-up. John Haggart also took the decision to restore Jim Cruickshank to the side, making him the sole survivor from the last Hearts team to play in Europe.

ZENTRALSTADION – WEDNESDAY 15 SEPTEMBER 1976
1. FC LOCOMOTIVE LEIPZIG 2 (SEKORA 2; FRITSCHE 17)
V
HEARTS: 0
REFEREE: N ZLATANOS (GREECE)

The game had a 4.30PM kick off and the 25,000 inside the 120,000 capacity Zentral Stadion did not have to wait long for the first goal as Hearts went behind with only two minutes played. After Lokomotive forced a corner the ball was cleared but it fell to right back Günter Sekora 25 yards out. His first-time volley fizzed past Jim Cruickshank to put the home side one up.

It was a whirlwind start that left John Haggart's men reeling. Although wingers Kenny Aird and Bobby Prentice both threatened to make a breakthrough, it was Leipzig who held the upper hand. Their dominance was reinforced 15 minutes later when another defender, Joachim Fritsche, added a second. John Gallacher was penalised for a foul on Dieter Kühn, who rolled the free kick into the path of Fritsche whose shot saw Jim Cruickshank beaten from 25 yards once again.

Despite the setback Hearts continued to look for the goal that would bring them back into the game. A chance fell to Drew Busby but the few Hearts fans in the vast stadium could only watch in horror as he ballooned the ball over the bar from the edge of the six yard box. It was a rare opportunity. The East Germans continued to dominate as John Gallacher headed off the line and Jim Cruickshank produced a series of fine saves to keep Hearts in the game.

In the second half both Willie Gibson and Cammy Fraser were introduced as the visitors shuffled the pack in search of a vital away goal. However, it was the hosts that got the golden opportunity to put the tie beyond doubt. With nine minutes to go, Wilfried Gröbner went down in the box as if he had been shot by a Stasi sniper as the bewildered John Gallacher looked on. The Greek referee, Nikos Zlatanos, had no doubt that it was big John and not some furtive member of the secret police that was to blame and pointed to the spot.

Up stepped the scorer of the second goal, Joachim Fritsche, who blasted the ball to Jim Cruickshank's right-hand side. Although he dived the right way, the ball was just out of the keeper's reach, but it was also just a little too wide and thumped back off the post to safety.

1. FC LOKOMOTIVE LEIPZIG: FRIESE SEKORA HAMMER GRÖBNER FRITSCHE ALTMANN (LISIEWICZ) MOLDT FRENZEL ROTH LÖWE KÜHN. SUBS UNUSED: NIKLASCH GEISLER BORNSCHEIN SCHUBERT
HEARTS: CRUICKSHANK BROWN KAY CALLACHAN (FRASER) GALLACHER CLUNIE AIRD SHAW (GIBSON) BUSBY PARK PRENTICE. SUBS UNUSED: WILSON JEFFERIES BURRELL

Hearts had been let off the hook but still faced a two-goal deficit in the second leg. Despite this, manager Haggart remained optimistic and was quoted after the game as saying, 'Hearts are capable of qualifying for the next round.' His opposite number, Herr Scherbaum, was also confident of progressing for round two. 'My team deserved the victory because we made a lot of chances,' he said. 'I want one goal in Edinburgh and then Hearts cannot win.' Time would tell which of the managers would be correct in two weeks' time, in what was to be one of the most memorable games ever witnessed at Tynecastle.

The team had an early start the following morning, setting off at 5AM for the three-hour bus journey back to the West, followed by the flights to London and Edinburgh. The journey took 11 hours in total, a tiring experience and probably not the best preparation for a league game two days later. However, it was a journey that Lokomotive would have to undertake for the return leg, which could turn out to Hearts' advantage.

It might have been the travel that had had an adverse effect on Lokomotive's performance on their six previous visits to the UK, as they had yet to depart with a victory. In Scotland both Hibs and Kilmarnock had beaten Leipzig, so the omens were good for a Hearts victory, but could they do it by the required number of goals?

Early on the morning of the game, Mohammad Ali had retained his world heavyweight crown against Ken Norton in Yankee Stadium, New York. He gained a bitterly disputed points decision after being unable to come up with a knockout punch. Later in the evening the Gorgie side definitely came up with a knockout blow in what still remains as one of the most amazing performances in a European tie by a Hearts side.

TYNECASTLE PARK – WEDNESDAY 29 SEPTEMBER 1976
HEARTS: 5 (KAY 13; GIBSON 28 & 84; BROWN 74; BUSBY 75)
V
1. FC LOKOMOTIVE LEIPZIG: 1 (FRITSCHE 41)
REFEREE: J DUBACH (SWITZERLAND)

Despite being two goals behind, the team's confidence was high and a healthy 18,000 paid £2.50 for a stand seat and 70p for a place on the terracing (or nothing if they had a season ticket) and turned out on relatively fine evening to see if the Maroons could overturn the deficit.

There had been a remarkable change in the weather: Edinburgh had suffered a deluge that lasted from mid-morning, relenting approximately an hour before kick off. The downpour had left the surface saturated but this did not stop Hearts going about their business from the off.

Drew Busby almost gave the home side the perfect start after Willie Gibson cleverly played the ball into the middle of the goal. The ball was met on the turn by Drew but his right-foot shot crashed against the post with Werner Friese rooted to his line.

The breakthrough did come, and as had happened in the first leg it was a defender that got the opener. With 13 minutes played Bobby Prentice picked out the onrushing Roy Kay who hit the ball sweetly with his right foot. Friese did well to get a hand to it, but the shot was unstoppable as it found its way into the net. Hearts were off and running.

It was a non-stop barrage and Bobby Prentice, Kenny Aird and Drew Busby all came close using a shoot-on-sight policy. But it was Drew's strike partner, Willie Gibson, who grabbed goal number two 15 minutes later. From a Jimmy Brown throw-in, Kenny Aird tried his luck from just inside the box, but when it looked as if the German goalkeeper would get to the ball first, Willie stuck out a boot and flicked it home. Tynecastle went wild as Hearts pulled the game level. Such was their ascendancy, it was surely just a matter of time before a third goal arrived, and in the 41st minute it did – unfortunately, to the visitors.

Although Lokomotive had been contained to a few raids, the dangerous pair of Dieter Kühn and Wilfried Gröbner had shown what they could do.

Drew Busby scores to make it 4-1 against Lokomotive Leipzig
© The Scotsman Publications Ltd. Licensor www.scran.ac.uk

Jim Cruickshank was relieved to see a header from Kühn drift past his post and then Jim Brown was in the right place to clear a Gröbner shot off the line. But it was the scorer of one of the goals in Leipzig, Joachim Fritsche who dashed Hearts' hopes when he tucked away a pass from Rainer Lisiewicz.

Lokomotive were now back in the driving seat and Hearts responded by replacing John Gallacher with Jim Jefferies at half-time. Kenny Aird made way for Graham Shaw ten minutes later as they tried to peg back the East Germans once again.

Werner Friese made a spectacular, point-blank save from Willie Gibson on the hour mark and then foiled 'Shuggie' Shaw on no fewer than four occasions. But he could do nothing 15 minutes from time when Hearts captain Jim Brown scored one of the most memorable goals ever witnessed at Tynecastle. Graham Shaw received the ball just inside the Germans' half before beating a couple of players and then passing to the captain, who was waiting on the right-hand side. Seeing the opportunity, Jim clipped the ball into the corner of the net – and don't expect him to admit it was intended as a cross!

The celebrations on the terracing hardly had time to die down before

The crowd spill onto the pitch at the end of Hearts' famous 5-3 aggregate victory over
Lokomotive Leipzig 1976
© The Scotsman Publications Ltd. Licensor www.scran.ac.uk

Drew Busby headed home after Friese made a mess of a corner from Bobby
Prentice. Tynecastle went wild again as Hearts went in front for the first
time in the tie.

As 'We want five, we want five' rang out around the terracing, the
celebrations began in earnest with six minute left when Willie Gibson
sealed a famous victory with his second goal after he could do little else
but put his head on a cross from Drew Busby to make it 5-1 on the night.

It was mayhem after the Swiss referee, Jean Dubach, blew the final
whistle, with the Hearts players being mobbed as youngsters (and some
not so young) ran onto the pitch. Although it was all good-natured, the
invasion did not amuse the UEFA match observer, SFA secretary Willie Allan,
and Hearts were eventually handed a fine of £250. It had been a remarkable
game but the win was no more than Hearts' performance deserved.

HEARTS: CRUICKSHANK BROWN KAY CALLACHAN GALLACHER (JEFFERIES) CLUNIE AIRD (SHAW)
BUSBY GIBSON PARK PRENTICE. SUBS UNUSED: WILSON FRASER BURRELL
I. FC LOKOMOTIVE LEIPZIG: FRIESE SEKORA HAMMER GRÖBNER FRITSCHE ROTH MOLDT
FRENZEL (BORNSCHEIN) LISIEWICZ LÖWE KÜHN. SUBS UNUSED: NICLASCH TRESKE SCHUBERT

Having spectacularly disposed of the East German cup winners, the next day Hearts were drawn against the West German cup winners, Hamburg. Where the East Germans had been something of a mystery, Hamburg were a different matter. Their European pedigree was well known – they had reached the final of the Cup Winners Cup in 1968, ending as runners-up to AC Milan.

Now, though, they were in a period of transition due in the main to an internal conflict between the coach, Kuno Klotzer and the club's general manager, Dr Peter Krohn. An economist by profession, Dr Krohn had been brought in three years earlier with a remit to sort the club's finances. Deep in debt in 1973, within two years this had been cleared and last season the German club had made a considerable profit.

However, he now thought that he could work his magic on the park and wanted to change the tactics, turning a defensive set-up into a more attacking formation. In their nine Bundesliga games so far, they had scored 12 times, but the usually watertight defence had leaked 11 goals and had just lost five to Bayern Munich in the German Cup. So, despite the presence of six internationalists, hopes were high that Hearts could pull off another famous victory.

The day before the game Hearts had a light workout at Tynecastle, then flew to Germany. They arrived at the Crest Hotel in Hamburg around 6.30PM and applied for the normal courtesy of being allowed to train in the stadium, but this was politely refused on the grounds that there was no one available to operate the floodlights.

On the day of the game the Edinburgh squad were subjected to more 'gamesmanship' when a further request to hold a training session in the Volkspark Stadion was refused due to Hamburg having scheduled their training session for the same time. Hearts duly had their workout on a public park behind their hotel on the outskirts of the city. Remarkably part of the warm-up included a game against a team of German journalists gathered to report on the Edinburgh men. It ended 1-1, but there were questions asked about the numbers the newspaper men deployed during the bounce game!

After the session, it was decided that Brian Wilson would be preferred to the more experienced Jim Cruickshank. Brian had made his league debut against Motherwell the previous Saturday but had got off to a nightmare start. After only 45 seconds he let the ball slip from his grasp to allow ex Hibbie Jimmy O'Rourke to put the Steelmen in front. Hearts had battled back to force a 1-1 draw, with Brian playing his part, but it was a risk throwing him in against the German giants.

VOLKSPARK STADION – WEDNESDAY 20 OCTOBER 1976
HAMBURGER SV: 4 (BJØRNMOSE 2; EIGL 34; REIMANN 59; GALLACHER OG 69)
V
HEARTS 2 (BUSBY 15; PARK 89)
REFEREE: V JARKOV (USSR)

By 7.30PM the missing lighting operative had been found but only 25,000 spectators – Hamburg's lowest attendance of the season – were in the vast stadium for the kick off. They did not have to wait long to see their favourites get on the goal trail. As in the first game in the previous round, Hearts got off to the worst possible start by losing a goal after only two minutes.

Klaus Winkler ran onto a measured pass through the middle of the Hearts defence from Willi Reimann. His fierce shot thumped back off Brian Wilson's right-hand post, but the ball rebounded straight to Danish international Ole Bjørnmose who found the net from 15 yards.

Despite the setback Hearts then matched the Germans in every department and grabbed a deserved equaliser after 15 minutes. Typically, it was Drew Busby that got his head on a cross from John Gallacher to beat Rudi Kargus in the Hamburg goal.

The home side restored their lead 20 minutes later when a Kurt Eigl strike squirmed out of Brian Wilson's grasp. Despite a last-gasp attempt to clear the ball by Roy Kay, the referee ruled that it had crossed the line before the full back had booted it away.

In the second half Hamburg began to tighten their grip on the game but John Gallacher made a timely intervention when Arno Steffenhagen looked likely to score and Brian Wilson atoned for his earlier error when he made a magnificent save at the feet of Manny Kaltz after the full back found himself one-on-one with the keeper.

Just before the hour mark Hearts spurned a great chance to level the game for a second time. Cammy Fraser, who had come on for Kenny Aird, sent Donald Park through unopposed but he rushed his shot and blazed the ball past the post. From the resultant goal kick, the ball was played up the park to Willi Reimann who lashed an unstoppable shot past Brain Wilson from an almost impossible angle.

Ten minutes later and Hearts looked down and out when 'Der Rothosen' scored a fourth after John Gallacher deflected a header from Manny Kaltz past his own goalkeeper. With seconds remaining they managed to throw themselves a lifeline when Donald Park made up for his earlier miss, blasting the ball into the net following a knock-down by Drew Busby.

HAMBURGER SV: KARGUS KALTZ RIPP WINKLER HIDIEN (SPINCKE) ZACZYK BJØRNMOSE EIGL

SPERLICH REIMANN STEFFENHAGEN. SUBS UNUSED: BLANKENBURG MAGATH ETTMAYER BERTL
HEARTS: WILSON BROWN KAY JEFFERIES GALLACHER CLUNIE AIRD (FRASER) PARK SHAW BUSBY
PRENTICE (GIBSON). SUBS UNUSED: CRUICKSHANK BANNON BURRELL

It was a vital second away goal, and after the events of the first round it gave manager Haggart hope. He was quoted as saying, 'I have the greatest respect for Hamburg after seeing them tonight, but Leipzig too impressed me in East Germany, and look what happened to them.' Unfortunately for John, there was to be no repeat performance of the previous round's heroics.

When Hamburg arrived in Edinburgh for the second leg they had once again just been hammered by rivals Bayern Munich, this time by a 6-2 scoreline in a Bundesliga game. Morale was low in the German camp. However, rumours were sweeping the city that the German team were being offered a massive £1,250 per man to qualify for the quarter-finals of the competition. It was obviously the incentive they needed to up their game, as they systematically destroyed Hearts from the beginning in a game that will probably only be remembered for the first-team debut of young Eamonn Bannon.

TYNECASTLE PARK – WEDNESDAY 3 NOVEMBER 1976
HEARTS: 1 (GIBSON 60)
V
HAMBURGER SV: 4 (EIGL 13 & 62; MAGATH 30 & 80)
REFEREE: R WURTZ (FRANCE)

The biggest crowd of the season paid gate receipts of £17,763 80p to attend Tynecastle to see if Hearts could once again claw back a two-goal margin against the German opposition. They were given a ray of hope as early as the first minute when John Haggart's men forced a corner with their first attack. Bobby Prentice played it short to Roy Kay whose cross found Willie Gibson. Unfortunately, Willie's header did not find the target and drifted narrowly past the post with Rudi Kargus rooted to his line.

It was an encouraging start and Hearts continued to create chances. After five minutes Drew Busby made space for himself inside the 18 yard box before passing to Jim Brown. His left-foot shot looked like being as good a goal as his cracker against Leipzig – that was, until Kargus showed the form that had seen him recently replace the legendary Sepp Maier in the international side as he brought off a fantastic, one-handed save.

As the home support was beginning to think their team were gaining the upper hand, Hamburg dashed their hopes with a slick breakaway goal. With 11 minutes gone the Germans broke out of defence with a series of

Willie Gibson scores Hearts' consolation goal in the 4-1 defeat at Tynecastle to Hamburg in the Cup Winners Cup, November 1976
© The Scotsman Publications Ltd. Licensor www.scran.ac.uk

passes that ended when Kurt Eigl hit a low shot towards Brian Wilson. Although it was a well enough struck, the keeper should have done better than to let it slip under his body and into the net.

The goal certainly dented Hearts' hopes yet still they pressed forward, with Graham Shaw and Willie Gibson having chances, but the pair were both denied by Kargus in the German goal. With Hearts chasing the game it left them exposed at the back, which Hamburg ruthlessly exploited after half an hour. In only their second attack of the game, danger man Eigl found his partner Felix Magath in acres of space to knock in goal number two.

In the second half John Haggart brought on Cammy Fraser in place of Jim Jefferies in an attempt to change the game. The swap immediately paid dividends when they went close through a shot from Drew Busby that had to be cleared of the line with Kargus helpless for once. On the hour mark the German keeper was finally beaten, giving the big crowd something to cheer about when Willie Gibson pounced after a header from Graham Shaw came back off the bar following a Bobby Prentice corner.

The crowd barely had time to contemplate another remarkable comeback when two minutes later Arno Steffenhagen broke free of his marker and ran in on goal. He somehow managed to collide with Brian

Wilson but he was first to react and tapped the ball to that man Eigl, who slammed it into an empty net.

The game was over as a contest and the terraces began to empty. Those who stayed on were able to witness the Germans adding salt to the wound ten minutes from time when Magath had the easiest of tasks to tuck away a shot from Willi Riemann that had rebounded off the post.

All that was left was for soon-to-be-Hearts-legend Eamonn Bannon to make his debut when he replaced Bobby Prentice in the last few minutes.

HEARTS: WILSON BROWN KAY JEFFERIES (FRASER) GALLACHER CLUNIE SHAW BUSBY GIBSON
PARK PRENTICE (BANNON). SUBS UNUSED: CRUICKSHANK CANT BURRELL
HAMBURGER SV: KARGUS KALTZ RIPP BLANKENBURG (WINKLER) BJØRNMOSE ZACZYK MAGATH
BERTL EIGL STEFFENHAGEN (SPERLICH) REIMAN. SUBS UNUSED: HIDIEN SPINCKE ETTMAYER

So Hearts were out of a European competition once again, but there could be no denying that they had been beaten by a very good side, as John Haggart conceded after the game. 'They were far too good for us it's as simple as that,' he said, adding, 'I am not saying that they will win the trophy, but it will take a pretty good side to put them out.' John's words proved to be prophetic when six months later Hamburg went on to win the trophy, beating Anderlecht 2-0 in the final in Amsterdam. There is no doubt that the game against Leipzig at Tynecastle remains long in the memory of fans and players alike. However, for both Roy Kay and Scott Wilson it was other ties that have abiding memories. It was Roy Kay's goal that sparked the revival in the famous game, but for him the games against Hamburg stand out due to the quality of the opposition:

I still get asked about *that* game. It really was a special night. Despite being behind by a couple of goals, there was a great belief in the side that we could at least take the game into extra time. My goal came as a bit of a surprise, not just because I didn't really score that often but because I received a pass from Rab Prentice! Rab liked to beat defenders, which he could do with ease, but this time he played the ball inside, I stretched out a foot and it ended up in the net.

There were some wild celebrations at the end of the game, both on and off the park. For me, though, it was a bit of a strange night as I went to a party being held for my niece Lindsay's second birthday. Quite rightly she was the centre of attention and no one really bothered too much about the Hearts result.

Anyway, the win set up the games against Hamburg, a real quality side.

In the game in Hamburg, although we did not play that well, when Donald Park snatched our second goal the look on the German players' faces was as if they had lost the game. They were probably thinking about the 'away goal' rule, and after our result in the previous round who could blame them.

As we know, the second leg did not turn out to be a happy night. Our game plan was to get the ball to Rab Prentice and let him inflict the damage. However, he was up against such a classy full back in Manny Kaltz, and ended up chasing him more the other way.

Sadly these were the only European ties I played in during my time at Hearts, but they gave me some happy memories, particularly of that night in September.

For Hearts stadium announcer Scott Wilson, it is the Leipzig game that remains with him today – not, as might be expected, the home leg, but the away game in East Germany.

To a fanatical 15-year-old Hearts fan, it seemed a good idea at the time – a coach trip from Edinburgh, followed by a ferry across the North Sea, then another coach journey through European countries I had only read about in geography lessons at school, all to see my team play in the Cup Winners Cup. Fantastic!

That was back then when I was not just as worldly-wise as I am today and I was not prepared for the bum-numbing boredom that a two-day coach trip each way entails. My excitement lasted as far as the ferry crossing to Holland, then it was a case of looking at miles and miles of motorway.

When we eventually reach the border to make the switch from West to East Germany, or GDR as the border guards were fond of telling us, we began to wish for the tedium of the autobahn. It was a traumatic experience and we were held up for the best part of three hours.

With a coach full of half-asleep, half-pissed Jambos, it didn't make for a particularly good atmosphere. I think there was also a breakdown in translation, as the bus convenor had to come around all of us with a plastic bag asking for 'donations' to speed our way through customs. I'd love to say that we all told them in unison to sling their hook, but when faced with the potential of a further three-hour delay, we soon loosened our wallets. The communist border guards had certainly embraced capitalism, 13 years before the fall of the Berlin Wall!

The transition from the free West to the communist East was quite marked. The buildings, people, cars and shops all looked drab and I actually felt sorry for these people, despite the border guards having relieved me of half of my intended spending money. Anyhow, we arrived in plenty of time to have a look around before kick off and it was as well that I didn't have lots of spending money as there was nothing in the shops to buy.

The match was a hard-fought affair, and if I remember correctly, not particularly well refereed. People who know me are aware that I view most matches through maroon-tinted specs, but even so this one was appalling. Despite the best efforts of the referee we only lost 2-0, so as we trooped out of the ground, even with the thought of that horrendous return journey, we were still confident of getting a result back at Tynie.

As it turned out, we did it in style and as I invaded the pitch at the end. It seemed to make that tedious journey all worth while.

CHAPTER 7

1984–85 UEFA Cup

NOT MANY OF those who trooped out of Tynecastle at the end of the Hamburg game expected that they would have to suffer greater disappointment by the end of the season. A disastrous run of results from February saw Hearts suffer the indignity of relegation to the First Division. For the next six seasons the Gorgie men were the 'yo-yo' side of Scottish football, gaining promotion one season only to be relegated the next. The only 'glamour' ties in this period came in the form of participation in the Anglo-Scottish Cup. However, first-round defeats at the hands of both Partick Thistle and Airdrieonians were hardly a match for European ties.

In season 83–84 Hearts, now managed by Alex Macdonald and Sandy Jardine, finished in fifth spot, not only retaining their place in the top flight, but gaining a place in the following season's UEFA Cup.

When the draw for the first round took place in Geneva, the fates conspired against Hearts once again. While Scotland's other representatives, Rangers and Dundee United, drew relatively weak opposition in Bohemians (Ireland) and AIK Futbol (Sweden) respectively, Hearts were paired against crack French outfit Paris Saint-Germain with the first leg due to take place in Paris in the Parc des Princes, a stadium more closely associated with rugby than football, something unthinkable in the Scottish capital but an arrangement that was readily accepted by the Parisiens.

Their manager, George Peyroche, had put together a side that contained both experience and skill in abundance. Players such as Domenique Bathenay, Richard Niederbacher, Gerard Janvion and Domenique Rocheteau were all French internationalists. However, it was the Yugoslavian Safet Susic that Alex MacDonald had already identified as the man that could cause the danger to Hearts.

Hearts flew to the French capital on the Tuesday before the game and based themselves in the luxurious Trianon Palace Hotel in Versailles. They did so on the back of a 1-0 defeat at Parkhead, which had been witnessed by seven representatives from PSG. The group had an unexpected early encounter when assistant manager Sandy Jardine, in no uncertain terms,

Tom Heaney Jnr (front left), Graham Clark, 'Coky' White and friends get ready to leave for Paris, September 1984

stopped the camera crew attached to the French deputation from filming Hearts' pre-match warm-up. PSG themselves had also lost at the weekend and had a record of only one win in seven outings. Despite the relatively poor form of both sides, it was a clash that was eagerly anticipated in both Scotland and France.

PARC DES PRINCES – WEDNESDAY 19 SEPTEMBER 1984
PARIS SAINT-GERMAIN: 4 (SUSIC 23 & 57; ROCHETEAU 35; NIEDERBACHER 65)
V
HEARTS: 0
REFEREE: E SOSTARIC (YUGOSLAVIA)

Perhaps wary because Rangers supporters had once again dragged the reputation of Scottish football through the mud the previous day in Dublin, over 1,000 CRS (French riot police) were deployed to watch over the Scottish contingent. They had little to worry about, as the estimated 3,000 from Edinburgh were determined to prove that they could enjoy their European outing without causing the same havoc as those from the West of Scotland.

In a detailed, one-hour team talk before the game, Alex MacDonald outlined his plan to negate the threat of the French outfit. Brian Whittaker was to play alongside Craig Levein in the middle of defence and Walter

Kidd was given the unenviable role of trying to pin down the elusive Safet Susic, with Sandy Jardine playing behind the trio ready to sweep up any danger. However, Doddie had not reckoned with the introduction into the PSG line-up of 'the black Flash', Nambetingue Toko. The giant forward from the Republic of Chad caused problems from the outset and it didn't take long before Davie Bowman was withdrawn from midfield in an effort to restrict his runs at the Hearts back line. Toko, though, was not the only danger, with Rocheteau, Fernández, Niederbacher and Susic all proving elusive. Hearts were struggling to remain on level terms and it did not help their cause that

The author and friends in Paris before the game, 1984 (author's collection)

Egon Sostaric, the Yugoslavian referee, seemed to be favouring the home side. Midway through the half he awarded a rather dubious free kick after Brian Whittaker was adjudged to have fouled Domenique Rocheteau on the edge of the box. Up stepped Susic to send the ball over the defensive wall and into the net before Henry Smith could move.

It was a setback, and Hearts then survived several close things before Gary Mackay had a chance to draw the sides level after 28 minutes. Although he beat three defenders before finding himself with only the keeper to beat, his final effort was poor and he sent the ball sailing high over the bar.

The referee continued to make some baffling decisions, none more so than when he pulled up Alex MacDonald for being offside but then noticed a French defender on the line beside the goalkeeper. He restarted the game with a drop-ball, but the chance had gone.

The game began to slip further from Hearts grasp on 35 minutes when Susic and Toko combined to present Rocheteau the easiest of chances to double PSG's advantage.

Two down at the interval, Alex MacDonald was now faced with the dilemma of either trying to tighten the defence in the hope of not losing another goal or pressing forward in order to try to snatch a goal that could make all the difference for the second leg.

The answer was the latter and Hearts continued to battle hard, with battle being the appropriate word as Jimmy Bone traded blows with Philip Jeannol and Dave Bowman suffered from an attack by Alain Couriol.

Walter Kidd began to maraud down the left-hand side as often as possible. However, this left that man Susic with more room and 12 minutes into the second half he tucked away the third goal after a cross from Toko had only been half-cleared.

The goal was the signal for Alex MacDonald to make way for Willie Johnstone and for a while it looked as though he could be the architect of a vital away goal. First he created a chance for John Robertson and then Jimmy Bone, but the home side stood firm and were able to add a fourth goal with 25 minutes left.

It was a great goal by any standards. Richard Niederbacher waltzed through the centre of the Hearts defence before playing a one-two with who else other than Safet Susic – before blasting home the return pass.

With time running out, Brain Whittaker, John Robertson and Sandy Jardine all tested Dominique Baratelli, the veteran French keeper, but in the end PSG ran out worthy winners.

Despite the fact that Hearts had equalled their worst deficit in Europe to date, the fans continued to celebrate long after the final whistle. They refused to move until the team and Wallace Mercer had taken a bow. It was a gesture that the chairman described as 'fantastic' and led the Prefecture de Police Commissaire, Paul Roche, to say, 'The Scottish fans were very good, great ambassadors for their country.'

PARIS SAINT-GERMAIN: BARATELLI LEMOULT JEANNOL (BACCONNIER) JANVION BATHENAY COURIOL NIEDERBACHER FERNÁNDEZ ROCHETEAU (LANTHIER) SUSIC TOKO. SUBS UNUSED: CARDINET N'JOLEA MOUTIER
HEARTS: SMITH KIDD WHITTAKER JARDINE (S) LEVEIN MACKAY(G) BOWMAN (D) BLACK BONE MACDONALD (A) (JOHNSTON) ROBERTSON. SUBS UNUSED: WESTWATER COWIE O'CONNOR PARK

When PSG arrived in Edinburgh on the Tuesday before the second leg, the fortunes of the two sides since the first meeting could not have contrasted more. While the French outfit had remained unbeaten and were climbing steadily up Ligue 1, Hearts had suffered at the hands of both Dundee and Aberdeen in the league and Dundee United in the semi-final of the League Cup. The team had slumped to second-bottom of the division only just ahead of Morton on goal difference.

George Peyroche stated that he would field what was basically the same side that had taken Hearts apart in Paris, then confirmed that they would not sit back and defend their lead. Things did not look good for the home side. Hit by several injuries, Alex MacDonald was also hampered in his team selection by the fact that Roddie McDonald was still serving a European suspension picked up from his time at Celtic when he was sent off against Politehnica Timisoara in 1980.

TYNECASTLE PARK – WEDNESDAY 3 OCTOBER 1984
HEARTS: 2 (ROBERTSON 27 & 86)
V
PARIS SAINT-GERMAIN: 2 (NIEDERBACHER 10; JEANNOL 45)
REFEREE: L ERIKSSON (SWEDEN)

As the teams lined up, only midfielder Luis Fernández was missing from the PSG team that had ruthlessly exposed Hearts' frailties in Paris. Hearts, on the other hand, started with three changes from their Parisien starting 11. Missing were Craig Levein, Gary Mackay and Alex MacDonald, who were replaced by George Cowie, Donald Park and Willie Johnstone respectively.

As expected, the home side went straight into attack in the opening minutes, searching for the early goal that was vital if they were to have any chance of getting back into the contest. However, PSG were quick to take advantage and it was the big hitman Richard Niederbacher who put the tie beyond doubt with a superb goal after only ten minutes. Safet Susic created the chance when he took on the Hearts back line before clipping a neat ball through to the Austrian, who wasted no time in stroking it into the far corner of Henry Smith's net.

The contest was over but Hearts, and John Robertson in particular, were not prepared to go down without a fight. He forced Dominique Baratelli to throw himself full length to keep out a typical rasping drive, then he pulled the sides level after 27 minutes. Jimmy Bone laid off a cross from Kenny Black and there was Robbo ten yards out to sweep the ball past the French keeper.

The goal lifted the crowd and Kenny Black and Davie Bowman both tested Baratelli in quick succession. However, with seconds remaining in the half, once again it was Susic who caused more damage when he whipped in a cross that was met by Philippe Jeannol who knocked the ball behind Henry Smith.

Susic was quickly into his stride after the break: he linked well with Toko who, after beating Walter Kidd, crossed to Dominique Rocheteau whose thunderous shot just shaved the crossbar.

From that point on, it became the Nambetingue Toko show as the big winger proceeded to run rings round the home defence. It was not surprising that Walter Kidd's name ended up in the referee's book after yet another illegal attempt to contain the man from Mozambique. His finest moment came when, after a spot of 'keepy-uppy', he lobbed the ball goalward, but Henry Smith did just enough to keep it out at the second attempt.

PSG took their foot of the pedal slightly, doing just enough to contain Hearts. Even the introduction of Alex MacDonald and Derek O'Connor for Donald Park and Jimmy Bone did nothing to turn the tide. But just when it looked as if PSG would end up worthy winners, a typical piece of John Robertson magic salvaged a draw when his lob beat Baratelli all ends up with only a couple of minutes left on the clock.

HEARTS: SMITH COWIE WHITTAKER JARDINE (S) KIDD BLACK BOWMAN (D) BONE (O'CONNOR) PARK (MACDONALD (A)) ROBERTSON JOHNSTON. SUBS UNUSED: WESTWATER MCLAREN GAULD
PARIS SAINT-GERMAIN: BARATELLI LEMOULT JEANNOL (TINMAR) JANVION BATHENAY COURIOL NIEDERBACHER BACCONNIER ROCHETEAU (LANTHIER) SUSIC TOKO. SUBS UNUSED: CARDINET N'JOLEA MOUTIER

If the adventure had been brief, Hearts had still left their mark on European football, with the travelling fans gaining praise from the local authorities in Paris and the UEFA observer at Tynecastle, Belgian Victor Lamaux, stating that the game had been well organised and the fans' behaviour exemplary. He would be putting in his 'best ever report of a European match'.

Almost from the moment Willie Johnston scored the goal against Celtic that ensured qualification, diehard supporter John Fairbairn began penning what has now become known as 'The European Song'. Little did John know quite how prophetic the line 'we travelled far by bus and car and other times we went by railway' would be by the time Hearts walked out in the Parc des Princes. Supporters young and old sought any method possible to be in the French capital for Hearts' first European tie in eight years. Among them was MSP David McLetchie. Whether he was one of the hundreds that took part in impromptu football match under the shadow of the Eiffel Tower he won't say, but he does recall the 'other' game in Paris:

> The game against Paris Saint-Germain in 1984 stands out as my all-time favourite European tie. Having followed the team faithfully during the 'yo-yo' years when we spent four seasons in the First Division visiting grounds like Gayfield, Links Park, Boghead and Cappielow, it was a real thrill to be in the Parc des Princes watching us take on PSG, one of the top teams in European football. For me, it marked the end of the dark days and the revival of Hearts as a major Scottish club for which Wallace Mercer, Alex MacDonald and Sandy Jardine take enormous credit.

As we know, the 4-0 scoreline did not flatter PSG and the game will never rank as one of our better European performances, but being there was what counted. It was our reward for loyalty, for sticking by the team through thick and thin, and that support never wavered throughout the game even as the goals rattled in.

After all, we were in what is arguably the second finest city in Europe (behind Edinburgh of course) and we were there on merit, thanks to some sterling performances the previous season when we finished fifth in the table following our return to the top flight.

Two stories in particular stand out from that trip. The first was of the Hearts fan that went into a patisserie, bought a croissant, sunk his teeth into it and then complained loudly to his friends, 'There's nae meat in this bridie.'

The second involved Andrew Kyle, the young man who was severely injured in a Metro station accident which led to an amputation, but who philosophically told his hospital visitors that, just like Hearts, he had 'lost an away leg'.

That sums it up for me. We may have been lacking sophistication but we were never lacking in spirit and the team who took on PSG that night developed two years later into the finest Hearts side I have witnessed in nearly 50 years of supporting the club. We were back in the big time... that night in Paris said it all.

CHAPTER 8

1986–87 UEFA Cup

THERE IS NO NEED to go into the circumstances which saw Hearts participate in the 86–87 UEFA Cup, as there are some things that even the passage of years does not help. However, along with Dundee United and Rangers, Hearts' name was in the hat when the draw was made at the UEFA HQ in Geneva. Once again 'the luck of the draw' saw the Gorgie men handed the toughest task after being paired with Dukla Prague, with the first leg to be played at Tynecastle. Originally, Hearts had been drawn away but it was agreed to swap the tie because Dukla's neighbours, Sparta, had also been drawn at home.

With strong links to the Czech army, Dukla had rarely missed a season in Europe since the late '50s and had reached the semi-final of the Cup Winners Cup the previous season, being eliminated by eventual winners Dynamo Kiev. Their squad included seven current full internationals and Günter Bittengel who had been gaining rave reviews for the Under-21 side.

Despite their strength in depth, Dukla had started the season badly, so when coach Walter Borthwick and second-team boss John Binnie were dispatched to Czechoslovakia, they saw them thumped 5-0 by Sparta.

The Hearts pair also took in a 1-0 defeat against Vitkovice as Dukla slumped to the bottom of league with only one point from four games. Their form improved slightly in the week before they arrived in Edinburgh when they beat Trnava 1-0 in a game also watched by Borthwick and Binnie.

By contrast, Hearts had started the season well and after seven games were sitting second top, one point behind Dundee United. In the lead-up to the Dukla game they had beaten Aberdeen 1-0 and were then whisked away to the Marine Hotel in North Berwick, where the team watched videos of Dukla in action – although with the Czechs playing so poorly it was hardly a true indication of how dangerous they could be.

For the game, manager Alex MacDonald had a full squad to pick from while Dukla boss Jiří Lopata would have to do without right back Ales Bazant and striker Stanislav Korejeik, who was suspended.

TYNECASTLE PARK – WEDNESDAY 17 SEPTEMBER 1986
HEARTS: 3 (FOSTER 1; CLARK 66; ROBERTSON 78)
V
FK DUKLA PRAHA: 2 (FITZEL 44; KLUCKY 65)
REFEREE: A VAN VOLCEM (BELGIUM)

Despite the fact that Wallace Mercer had taken the decision to raise the prices for the game by around 33 per cent (Stand £8/£6; Enclosure £4; and Terracing £3) a healthy crowd of nearly 19,000 turned out to see if Hearts could do better than against PSG two years earlier.

Dukla, playing in their 'away' kit of all yellow, were still absorbing the unique atmosphere of Tynecastle when they fell behind in the first few seconds. From the kick off Hearts gained a throw-in on the right-hand side. Ian Jardine took it quickly to Sandy Clark who nodded into the path of Wayne Foster whose left-foot shot bulged the net. Time on the clock... 40 seconds.

Despite the early setback Dukla slowly began to work themselves into the game, prompted by Luboš Urban in midfield and with Günter Bittengel showing exactly why he was so highly thought of. Bittengel created a couple of chances for himself as the Prague men sought to bring the tie level, but it was his pass to Stanislav Griga that saw the Dukla number seven waste their best opportunity when it looked easier to score.

Hearts were by no means being overrun and a few minutes before the end of the half Wayne Foster had a great opportunity to double their lead, courtesy of the referee. A pass from Brian Whittaker hit off the official and straight to the Englishman, but a tremendous block by Petr Kostelnik kept the visitors in the game.

With one minute to go the score was level after a goal that the visitors play probably merited. Milan Luhovy did well to turn just inside the box before sliding the perfect pass to Dusan Fitzel, who slipped the ball past Henry Smith with ease.

Alex MacDonald sent on John Robertson for John Colquhoun after eight minutes of the second half as Hearts sought to put pressure on Dukla, who looked to defend in depth and rely on hitting Hearts on the break. It was from one of these fleeting raids that the Czechs went close to going ahead. Bittengel started it off with a great run and shot that Henry Smith did well to turn away for a corner which was then only half cleared to Josef Klucky on the edge of the penalty area. The Hearts defence could do nothing as he thundered in a drive which rattled the crossbar before bouncing clear. But a few minutes later Klucky got lucky.

On 65 minutes a cross from Petr Rada, wide on the right, eluded the

Hearts defence that looked to have moved out quickly enough to leave Klucky in an offside position. Neither the linesman nor the Belgian referee saw any infringement and allowed him to blast the ball home.

It was a hammer blow to Hearts' hopes, but only a minute later another dubious goal brought them back into the tie. Dukla keeper Kostelnik went up to deal with a cross into the box, but under pressure from Sandy Clark he dropped the ball, allowing the Hearts number nine to poke it into the net. The Czechs were incensed that the goal was allowed to stand and the name of Luboš Urban entered the referee's book for being over-zealous with his protests.

Andy Watson came on in place of Ian Jardine and within four minutes of his appearance Hearts were ahead for the second time in the game. Sandy Clark flicked on a long ball out of defence by Sandy Jardine and there was John Robertson to nip in to make it 3-2. It was a trademark Clark/Robertson goal and it nearly worked again with minutes to go. This time, though, Robbo blasted the ball over and Hearts had to settle for a one-goal advantage.

HEARTS: SMITH KIDD WHITTAKER JARDINE (S) BLACK LEVEIN COLQUHOUN (ROBERTSON) JARDINE (I) (WATSON) CLARK MACKAY(G) FOSTER. SUBS UNUSED: BRUCE MCADAM MACDONALD (R)
FK DUKLA PRAHA: KOSTELNIK KLUCKY NOVAK (J) FIALA RADA GRIGA BITTENGEL URBAN GAJGER LUHOVY FITZEL. SUBS UNUSED: VADURA NOVAK (P) NOTIN VODICKA

After the game, assistant manager Sandy Jardine pronounced himself happy with winning the game although he did recognise that with the quality of player available to Dukla, they would have to alter their tactics for the return leg. 'We wanted a lead of any kind and we got it. It will be a different game over there with less space for Dukla to make passes,' he said.

In the two weeks between the first and second legs, Hearts continued their good form, thrashing Motherwell 4-0 and drawing 0-0 at Dens Park. Ironically, if the same result had been achieved the previous season, it would have seen them competing in the European Cup. As it was, it kept them one point behind leaders Dundee United, although last season's nemesis, Celtic, had joined them on 14 points.

Hearts departed Edinburgh on Tuesday 31 September but soon regretted Wallace Mercer's decision to fly on scheduled flights. The original plan had been to charter a flight then sell seats to fans wishing to travel to the Czechoslovakian capital. This idea was abandoned when the support for the overpriced two-day trip proved limited. It was Hearts that were left to pay the price when the flight from Edinburgh to London was delayed which resulted in the journey taking a gruelling eight hours. As a consequence the players were left exhausted by the time they reached the Intercontinental Hotel in the centre of Prague, so plans for an evening training session were abandoned in favour of a workout on the afternoon of the game only a few hours before the 4.30PM kick-off.

Ian Jardine had picked up an ankle injury before leaving Scotland, with Jimmy Sandison coming in as a late addition to the squad. In the end the only change to the team that had drawn against Dundee was the inclusion of Gary Mackay in favour of Andy Watson. Dukla were without the services of the scorers of their goals in Edinburgh, Klucky and Fitzel. However, they were strengthened by the return of their top striker, Stanislav Korojick.

STADION DUKLY PRAHA NA JULISCE – WEDNESDAY 1 OCTOBER 1986
FK DUKLA PRAHA: 1 (GRIGA 53)
V
HEARTS: 0
REFEREE: H KOHL (AUSTRIA)

Perhaps inspired by the cost of the Czechoslovakian beer, Hearts supporters had made the journey in numbers and easily made up one third of the 3,000 crowd that basked in brilliant sunshine. The question was, would they see a Hearts side that would defend their one-goal advantage, or a team that would seek to become the first to beat Dukla at home in seven years?

It took only a couple of minutes before they got their answer when Petr Kostelnik did well to hold on to a low cross from John Colquhoun. The big goalie denied Colquhoun again in the sixth minute when he reacted quickly after stopping a volley from Wayne Foster.

Hearts were certainly the better team and it took the home side nearly

20 minutes to pose their first serious threat. Milan Lihovy sent the ball into the goal area and both Henry Smith and Stanislav Korojick rose for it, with the Czech hitman coming off worse. After receiving lengthy treatment for his head knock, he had to be carried off and replaced by Stanislav Griga in a move that was to work out well for Dukla.

The author and friends outside the Stadion Na Julisce in Prague (author's collection)

Brian Whittaker was showing that he had the measure of danger man Günter Bittengel and was also able to set up some good attacking moves down the left. It was from his cross that Wayne Foster came close to opening the scoring but unfortunately his header was brilliantly tipped away by Kostelnik.

At the other end, Henry Smith was called on to produce some heroics to keep Hearts ahead on aggregate after 33 minutes when he held on to a great shot from Tomaz Kris. It was an important save but it was to be the only thing he was called to do in the half and the sides went in all square.

At the restart John Robertson replaced Wayne Foster who had suffered a groin strain, but Robbo had little chance to get into the game as Dukla began the half in determined mood. They dominated the opening exchanges and stunned Hearts with a goal that all but ended their hopes after 53 minutes. Luboš Urban began the move on the right before slipping the ball to substitute Griga. He made space for himself by turning Craig Levein cleverly before firing a right-foot shot to the near post. Henry Smith did well to get a hand to it but could not stop the ball crossing the line.

Hearts thought they had earned a chance to bring themselves back into the game when Ales Lausman crashed into John Robertson in the box. It looked a clear penalty to everyone except Austrian ref Helmut Kohl, who waved away the appeals. By pressing forward, they were leaving gaps at the back which left opportunities for Dukla to exploit. Günter Bittengel, now free from the shackles of Brian Whittaker, had two chances to end the game as a contest but failed to take either.

John Robertson was doing everything he could to turn the game round but on one occasion he was a bit too exuberant and was booked after a clash with Kostelnik. The Dukla goalkeeper was then involved in a mix-up with Josef Novak that almost allowed Robbo a chance, but he recovered just in time to clear the danger.

With time running out, Alex MacDonald sent on Andy Watson for Walter Kidd, who had battled on well after having his leg strapped at half-time. Watson had the ball in the net moments after coming on, but he offered little complaint when the goal was ruled out for offside.

The home side were content to protect their advantage and brought on defender Jiří Vadura in place of Kriz in an effort to run down the clock. It was a tactic that worked well for them and the referee blew for time as soon as the stadium clock showed that 45 minutes had been played. It was an action that certainly angered Sandy Clark and he remonstrated long and hard with the whistler all the way off the park.

FK DUKLA PRAHA: KOSTELNIK LAUSMAN NOVAK (J) FIALA RADA VODICKA BITTENGEL URBAN KOREJCIK KRIZ LUHOVY. SUBS UNUSED: VADURA NOVAK (P) NOTIN VODICKA
HEARTS: SMITH KIDD (WATSON) WHITTAKER JARDINE (S) BERRY LEVEIN COLQUHOUN BLACK CLARK MACKAY (G) FOSTER (ROBERTSON). SUBS UNUSED: BRUCE MACDONALD SANDISON

Despite going out on goal difference, the games had proved that Hearts had made excellent progress in European terms in the two years since being humbled in Paris. On that occasion the travelling support had stayed long after the whistle, cheering the team, and it was the same this time round. Perhaps some were wondering if things might have been different had the club not given up home advantage for the second leg.

Dukla progressed to third round of the competition after beating Bayer Leverkusen, again on 'away' goals, before being eliminated by Inter Milan in a tournament best remembered for Dundee United being beaten in the final by IFK Goteborg.

It was a disappointing way to exit the competition but now, many years later and after many hours of reflection on the whole adventure (which were mainly spent in the Staggs in Musselburgh with my great friend Tom Heaney), for me the trip to Czechoslovakia was the epitome of what following Hearts in Europe is all about:

> They say that you always remember your first girlfriend but in the majority of cases the first one never works out the way you thought it would as you make a lot of mistakes before it comes to a sad end. So it is with following Hearts in Europe.
>
> My first away trip had been two years earlier, to Paris, a journey I made in the company of John Fairbairn, the guy that famously composed 'The European Song'. I'm sure he based the line 'we travelled far by bus and car and other times we went by railway' on our itinerary to the French capital. Perhaps he couldn't find anything to rhyme with 'hovercraft', or perhaps he has tried to wipe from his memory one of the stormiest English Channel crossings in maritime history. It's certainly one neither I nor a stewardess called Tracey will ever forget in a hurry!
>
> If our choice of transportation was our first mistake the second came along shortly after when our hotelier decided to say *au revoir* after some amongst our group decided on a spot of late night hi-jinks. Homeless on the streets of Paris, and still over 36 hours before kick off!
>
> No relationship can survive after getting off to a bad start and so it was with this European adventure. I will skip how I spent a night on a hotel room floor where the true occupant decided to let some air into the room about 2AM by throwing his shoe through the closed window. I won't linger on the game itself as it has been covered in detail earlier, but it's fair to say the whole thing ended in tears. However, again much like girlfriends, you learn from your mistakes and so it was when I decided to follow Hearts to Prague.

When Callum Anderson announced that he was going to run a bus from the Auld Worthies pub in Gorgie Road, my past experience told me that it was not for me, so instead I went to other end of the spectrum and booked on the club's official flight. Wallace Mercer ensured that I had to pay handsomely for the privilege but it was worth it, as back in 1986 the Velvet Revolution was still three years away and Prague was not quite the open, stag-do-friendly place it is today.

The communist regime imposed many restrictions on anyone wanting to travel and being included in the official party seemed likely to ease the sort of problems I could imagine Callum's Auld Worthies bus would encounter. Visas were applied for and approved and I'm sure I even caught one of the armed military actually smiling as we trooped through Prague-Ruzyne airport. On reflection, he was probably thinking of the 30-minute journey to our hotel we would have to endure in a bus of a type I had once seen in a photograph of Hearts bringing the League Cup back to Edinburgh in 1954.

Included in the trip were the services of an official government tour guide, Marek, who was to take us on a trip round the city. Before we set off, he warned us of some 'dos and don'ts' while staying in Prague, number one of which was not to exchange money illegally.

We had not been allowed to bring any Czech crowns into the country and had been told that there would be plenty of opportunity to change our cash at the official bureau de change. What they didn't tell us was that the locals were desperate to get their hands on foreign currency and would offer an exchange rate far in excess of the official one. Everywhere you went, they were all at it, illegal or not – taxi drivers, lift attendants and even tour guides called Marek were offering you a deal.

Forewarned, we started our walking tour of the city where we took in the historic sights such as the castle, Wenceslas Square and Charles Bridge. Interesting though they were, our group were getting a little bored with this activity when Marek pulled his master stroke by taking us to U Fleku, one of Prague's oldest beer halls. Now he was talking our language! Not even the old man in the corner playing tunes (and I use that word reservedly) on his accordion could spoil our enjoyment. After our third our fourth pint of the excellent Czech beer an attempt was made to get the old guy to play the Hearts song, but the old adage is true, you can't teach an old dog new tricks. By now Marek had realised his mistake and was frantically trying to get us out of this fine establishment and back to the hotel. A fifth round was ordered before he could bring some sort of semblance of order to proceedings and we all rather reluctantly agreed that this pint would be the last.

I was still trying to get to grips with the currency to pay my share until one individual in our midst shouted up 'This one's on me, boys.' With around 20 of us in the group, all having five or more beers, there were over 100 pints to be paid for. I was still shell-shocked with such generosity when someone else yelled, 'Ach, it's only 10p a pint!' – making the total bill about a tenner.

Back at the hotel, I had my first encounter with typical Czech cuisine at the official dinner hosted by commercial manager Charles Burnett and Craigie Veitch. The first course of soup set the standard when we were presented with a bowl of liquid with some dubious brown substance in the middle. It's safe to say the highlight of the whole event was an amusing speech from the redoubtable Mr Veitch. This was followed by the raffle for a rather 'interesting' first prize, which sadly I didn't win.

The buffet breakfast the following morning offered a more edible selection although the range fell into the 'continental' category rather than the artery-hardening 'fry up' style I was used to. In the queue I found myself behind the Swedish tennis ace Stefan Edberg who was in town to play in a Davis Cup semi-final a couple of days later. Somewhere amongst my souvenirs I have a photograph of the two of us, breakfast in hand. Although we share questionable hairstyles, Stefan seems quite happy with his choice of croissant and fruit, while I have the look of a man who has just realised there is no square sausage or Ayrshire bacon on offer.

In the free time before the game a couple of us decided to take another wander round the town. It soon became apparent why the locals were so anxious to get their hands on foreign currency. There was next to nothing available to buy in the local shops. The only 'luxury' goods were available in 'tourist only' shops where the dollar and pound were king. I tried to buy some Dukla Prague-branded merchandise in a sports shop, but to no avail. Their entire stock seemed to consist of a basketball (?), a beer mug with an unidentified logo and a t-shirt from an over-35s international rowing event that had been held in Prague a few weeks earlier. For some reason, I bought the t-shirt.

We did know that beer was available, so, armed with the only word in Czech I knew, we went in search of 'pivo'. We didn't have far to look. As anyone who has been to the city will testify, there are bars on every street corner. In the first one we tried we were welcomed with open arms, the owner realising that he had two thirsty tourists with money to spend in his establishment. However, he overstepped the mark when he tried to charge us an exorbitant 20p a pint, a 100 per cent mark up. Enraged, we walked out.

Later, getting on the coach that would take us to the stadium for the 4.30PM kick off, we were issued with a ticket for the game which turned out to be the most expensive thing available in Prague. We did not get the luxurious facilities we might have expected for our money, more the opposite. However, the magical pivo was freely available and we were now quite happy to pay 20p a pint. Anyone wanting to buy more than two or three glasses of the stuff was given a metal carrier that was reminiscent of those used by milkmen when delivering the morning pinta, a truly wonderful system.

Once again I was left disappointed at the end of the 90 minutes. All that was left was a trip to the airport and a flight home. However, I had enjoyed the experience immensely.

Along with several conversations with the late Tom Heaney Jnr in the Staggs in Musselburgh, this trip gave me the motivation for writing this book, as to me it encompassed everything that following Hearts abroad should be. Although I have been on many other European trips since, the visit to Prague in 1986 always remains with me as the best ever.

CHAPTER 9

1988–89 UEFA Cup

FOR THE SECOND TIME in three seasons Hearts finished as SPL runners-up to Celtic, an achievement that allowed them participation in the UEFA Cup. The club had been able to announce a trading profit of £308,824, which had only been possible through the sale of popular striker John Robertson to Newcastle United for £625,000. Robertson's departure was universally condemned by the fans and the purchase of Ian Ferguson from Dundee United for £325,000 did little to appease the support.

Without Robertson Hearts struggled at the start of the season and had only collected three points from four games before they took on Irish opponents St Patrick's Athletic in Dublin. Although a part-time outfit, Hearts' managerial team of Alex MacDonald and Sandy Jardine left nothing to chance and travelled to Dublin to watch St Pat's in their first league game of the season against Cork City on the Sunday. The Irish side got off to a winning start with a narrow 2-1 victory.

Hearts travelled to Ireland on the Tuesday morning and based themselves in Killiney on the outskirts of Dublin. With the game having been switched from St Pat's home pitch of Richmond Park to Tolka Park, the squad trained at the bigger ground on the Tuesday evening with only Wayne Foster, who was suffering from a chest complaint, giving any cause for concern.

TOLKA PARK – WEDNESDAY 7 SEPTEMBER 1988
ST PATRICK'S ATHLETIC FC: 0
V
HEARTS: 2 (FOSTER PEN. 13; GALLOWAY 41)
REFEREE: H KING (WALES)

By the time of the kick off, Foster had declared himself fit enough to make his 100th first-team appearance, with the more experienced Eamonn Bannon starting on the bench. Just under 9,000 turned up (having paid £15,400 in gate receipts) and many of them were wearing Celtic shirts, with an estimated 3,000 having made the journey from Edinburgh, the atmosphere inside the ground was tense.

The visitors got off to the perfect start when they were awarded a penalty after 13 minutes. Dave Henderson, the big St Pat's goalie, made a mess of a cross from Ian Ferguson and could only push the ball out to Kenny Black. His first-time shot was handled on the line by John McDonnell and Wayne Foster stepped up to slam the ball home from the spot.

The goal settled the side and they played with a visible confidence, controlling the game for long spells. They got further reward four minutes before the break when Mike Galloway was left unmarked and Gary Mackay fired over a corner from the left. His powerful header was nestling in the back of the net before Henderson could move.

In the second period Hearts seemed content to hold on to their two-goal advantage, which allowed the home side to create a couple of opportunities and Henry Smith had to look lively to prevent Mark Ennis from reducing the leeway.

With ten minutes of the half gone, the already dark mood inside the ground took a turn for the worse when an air-horn was thrown from a group of supporters standing behind a banner bearing the legend 'Dublin & District Celtic SC'. The referee brought the game to a halt before consulting the UEFA observer from England, David Smith. The incident led to a loudspeaker announcement appealing for calm.

When play resumed Hearts continued to dominate with Ian Ferguson missing an easy opportunity to seal the tie when he was left clear with only the keeper to beat, but his shot was easily blocked by Henderson.

With only eight minutes remaining, Hearts suffered a blow when Henry Smith had to be carried from the pitch. A free kick from Robbie Gaffney was nodded down by Maurice O'Driscoll and Smith clashed with Damian Byrne in an effort to get to the ball. The stopper came off worst and ended up with a deep gash in his right shin that required several stitches. His injury left the way clear for Murray McDermott to make his European debut at the age of 38, although his services were rarely called upon as Hearts ran out worthy winners.

ST PATRICK'S ATHLETIC FC: HENDERSON FLEMING KELTCH MCDONNELL BYRNE (D) GAFFNEY FENLON O'DRISCOLL MOODY (MEAGAN) BYRNE (P) (REID) ENNIS. SUBS UNUSED: GREGG TRACEY FORAN
HEARTS: SMITH (MCDERMOTT) KIDD BERRY WHITTAKER BLACK MCPHERSON COLQUHOUN MACKAY(G) FERGUSON GALLOWAY FOSTER (BANNON). SUBS UNUSED: JARDINE BURNS GAVIN

Rather strangely, there was nearly a month between the first and second legs, in which time Hearts' stuttering league form continued with draws against both clubs from Dundee and defeats at the hands of Aberdeen and Rangers. Indeed, they had been beaten twice by the Glasgow club within the space of four days, with the loss in the SPL being followed up with a 3-0 reverse in the Skol Cup semi-final.

St Patrick's had also been in poor form, suffering three defeats in a row until they managed to arrest the run with a 3-0 win over Cobb on the Sunday before travelling to Scotland. For some unknown reason they chose to fly to Glasgow instead of the capital and then based themselves in the west of Scotland. They arrived without their first-choice keeper, Dave Henderson, who had to stay behind in Dublin to complete his shift as a fireman before making his own way across the Irish sea on the morning of the game.

Once again Hearts' only injury doubt was Wayne Foster, who had picked up a calf muscle strain. On this occasion it was decided not to risk him and the Englishman had to settle for a place on the bench with the experienced Eamonn Bannon starting.

TYNECASTLE PARK – 5 OCTOBER 1988
HEARTS: 2 (BLACK 24; GALLOWAY 67)
V
ST PATRICK'S ATHLETIC FC: 0
REFEREE: T PRESBERG (NORWAY)

As might be expected, both teams started the game cautiously, Hearts not wanting to give away an early goal and the visitors playing as though they didn't want to lose the goal that would surely end the tie.

The first opening came Hearts' way after 23 minutes when Damien Byrne's attempted clearance flew backwards towards his own goal. Eamonn Bannon and Henderson both challenged for the ball with the Hearts man winning the race, but his header somehow managed to miss the target from point-blank range.

The opener was not far away, though. Two minutes later Kenny Black blasted an unstoppable left-foot shot past Henderson after being set up by John Colquhoun. The goal all but killed the tie as a contest, but the away side continued to battle for a consolation goal and Hearts were thankful to Dave MacPherson and Walter Kidd for clearing the danger in quick succession before the end of the half.

Hearts suffered a blow after only ten minutes of the second half when Eamonn Bannon pulled up sharply with a hamstring injury. His place was taken by Wayne Foster who quickly made his mark in the 67th minute when his cross from the left reached Mike Galloway, whose left-foot shot squeezed in low between Henderson and the near post.

The goal was the signal for the Irishmen to lose their discipline before the Norwegian referee finally lost patience and booked Damien Byrne after a particularly robust challenge on Wayne Foster. With the game won, it was clear that the home side did not need to take any risks with injuries and the tempo dropped considerably. This allowed the Irish side more possession, which they took advantage of when Mark Ennis finally got the ball in the net. His joy was short-lived as the goal was chalked off for an infringement that only the referee spotted.

At the final whistle Hearts were in the second round of the competition for the first time since 1976 and for only the third time in their European history they had won both legs.

HEARTS: SMITH KIDD BERRY WHITTAKER GALLOWAY MCPHERSON COLQUHOUN MACKAY(G) FERGUSON BLACK BANNON (FOSTER). SUBS UNUSED: MCDERMOTT JARDINE (1) MCLAREN MOORE ST PATRICK'S ATHLETIC FC: HENDERSON FLEMING KELTCH (BYRNE P) MCDONNELL BYRNE (D) GAFFNEY FENLON O'DRISCOLL TRACEY (REID) MOODY ENNIS. SUBS UNUSED: MEAGAN OSAM FORAN

When the draw for the next round was made in Zurich two days later, Hearts were put in the unusual position of still not knowing their next opponents, being paired with either Austria Vienna or Žalgiris Vilnius from Russia. The second leg of their first-round tie was scheduled for the Friday evening after the original game had been postponed on the Wednesday evening due to the weather conditions in Austria.

The concern for Hearts secretary Les Porteous was that the side from Lithuania held a 2-0 lead after the first leg and if they managed to hold onto their advantage it would pose all sorts of travel problems for the Edinburgh side. His worries were allayed when Vienna triumphed 5-2 on the night, ensuring Hearts a more comfortable trip in the next round.

As well as sending second-team coach John Binnie on a spying mission to Austria to watch Vienna play out a 2-2 draw with Innsbruck, Alex MacDonald turned to a rather unusual source for information on their next opponents. Gordon Smith had been a team-mate of MacDonald's at Rangers but had also played for Admira Wacker under Vienna's manager Gustl Starek. By the time Hearts headed up to Dunkeld for their pre-match get-together, the management team had built up a substantial dossier on their opponents. As well as reports from Binnie and Smith, the squad watched a video of the Austrians' win over Vilnius. They were a quality side with over half a dozen internationals, the most famous being the great Herbert Prohaska.

Vienna had also watched Hearts in action in a league game against Celtic at Tynecastle. Assistant coach Fritz Fehler looked on as the Gorgie men went down 2-0 after another lacklustre performance. Diplomatically,

Fehler expressed his surprise at the physical nature of Hearts' play and his satisfaction that the second leg was to be played in the Austrian capital, which he thought would ensure his club's progress into the next round.

TYNECASTLE PARK – WEDNESDAY 26 OCTOBER 1988
HEARTS: 0
V
FK AUSTRIA WIEN: 0
REFEREE: I VAN SWIETEN (HOLLAND)

The tie had generated a great deal of interest with 14,000 packing into Tynecastle to watch a game that had been sponsored by Teachers whisky, something that was almost unheard of. In something of a surprise move, Gary Mackay was omitted from the starting line-up, with the manager at pains to point out that it was not through injury.

From the first whistle, Hearts went on the attack and almost opened the scoring in the second minute when a cross from Alan Moore on the right was missed by Attila Sekerlioglu and fell to Eamonn Bannon. After a couple of strides Bannon let fly but Franz Wohlfahrt in the Austrian goal somehow managed to block his shot from point-blank range.

Dave McPherson was next to go close when he got on the end of a cross

Austria Vienna arrive at Edinburgh airport ahead of the UEFA Cup clash in October 1988
© The Scotsman Publications Ltd. Licensor www.scran.ac.uk

from John Colquhoun, but this time it was Vienna captain, Manfred Zsak, who managed to clear the danger. Although Hearts continued to dominate, the visitors managed to show that they could be dangerous on the break, with Andreas Ogris and Argentinean international José Percudani both going close.

As they had in the first half, Hearts went close in the opening minutes of the second period. Eamonn Bannon fired in a free kick which John Colquhoun managed to direct into the path of Wayne Foster, but his shot was cleared on the line.

The Austrians were struggling to contain the home side and Anton Pfeffer had to resort to illegal tactics to stop Allan Moore in an act that brought the first booking of the game. With an hour gone the booking count was evened up when Hearts captain Dave McPherson was overly robust in stopping Andreas Ogris, and at that point Alex MacDonald decided to send on Gary Mackay in place of Wayne Foster.

Mackay's impact was immediate. He unleashed a shot from the left-hand side which Wohlfahrt did well to fingertip over the bar. There was no stopping Hearts and Allan Moore had three chances to grab the opening goal, but he was foiled on every occasion by Wohlfahrt.

Again the Austrians hit back, Ogris finishing a neat run by testing Henry Smith with a rasping drive that the Hearts keeper did well to hold. Hearts hit back through Gary Mackay, whose fine effort went inches over the bar.

The game ended with Hearts still on top but unable to break the deadlock as the Viennese side held on for a result that would make them firm favourites to qualify for the next round.

HEARTS: SMITH KIDD BERRY WHITTAKER GALLOWAY MCPHERSON COLQUHOUN MOORE FOSTER (MACKAY (G)) BLACK BANNON (FERGUSON (I)). SUBS UNUSED: MCDERMOTT JARDINE MURRAY
FK AUSTRIA WIEN: WOHLFAHRT SEKERLIOGLU OBERMAYER DEGEORGI ZSAK PFEFFER OGRIS (PLEVA) PROHASKA PERCUDANI STÖGER (FRIND) KÜNAST. SUBS UNUSED: FISCHER PROSENIK FURTNER

After an encouraging display against the Austrians, it was hoped that the same level of performance could be carried into their league games, but a draw against Aberdeen followed by a 3-0 midweek defeat at Ibrox saw the club drop to third-bottom of the SPL. Despite their lowly position no one expected that at 10.30AM on Thursday 3 November an announcement would be made that they had parted company with co-manager Sandy Jardine, Wallace Mercer stating that he thought that it was time to revert to the more traditional 'one man in charge' set-up.

The move predictably sparked controversy, which was further added to the following day when former director Douglas Park announced that he was going to head a consortium in an effort to mount a takeover of the club. Park had only resigned from the board 24 hours prior to the announcement of Jardine's sacking, so the latest development seemed to confirm the rumours of a power struggle within the club that had been circulating for some time.

For his part, Wallace Mercer firmly rejected the idea that he was willing to sell his stake in the club. However, when he made a hasty exit from Edinburgh to Vienna 24 hours ahead of the official party, the jungle drums went into overdrive.

By the time the squad joined the chairman in Austria there were several players giving the manager cause for concern with injuries. Definitely out was Ian Ferguson with a flu virus, Neil Berry was suffering from a twisted ankle, Dave McPherson had a thigh strain and Walter Kidd could take no part in the Tuesday evening training session held in sub-zero temperatures at the stadium and stayed inside the dressing room, receiving treatment for a foot injury. Interestingly, the away team room had been had been labelled 'Heard of Midlothian' an obvious spelling error, but by the end of the 90 minutes all of Vienna had certainly heard of the team from Scotland.

Vienna had a full squad to choose from, plus they were going into the game holding a 12-game unbeaten record at home (including the recent 4-0 win over Sportsklub, which had a 10:30AM kick-off time on Sunday), and so it was little wonder that the bookies back in Scotland were offering odds of 6-1 for Hearts to qualify.

PRATERSTADION – WEDNESDAY 9 NOVEMBER 1988
FK AUSTRIA WIEN: 0
V
HEARTS: 1 (GALLOWAY 57)
REFEREE: J-M NEGREIRA (SPAIN)

As Hearts lined up at the start, all three players with injury doubts were pronounced fit enough to be included in the side, with Jimmy Sandison being handed the important role of marking the ever dangerous Herbert Prohaska.

A crowd of less than 15,000 were inside the vast stadium on a bitterly cold night as Hearts swept into attack, with Wayne Foster going agonisingly close after he got on the end of a through pass from Gary Mackay on the edge of the box. The home side were not slow to recognise the danger that Foster posed and Manfred Zsak was fortunate to escape punishment for a crunching tackle on the Englishman after only four minutes. Foster required lengthy treatment before carrying on but was clearly struggling with the injury. His handicap allowed the Austrians the opportunity to

88

exploit their advantage and Michael Künast had the ball in the net on the nine-minute mark, only to see the linesman flag for offside. A minute later, Hearts made the change needed with Foster leaving the park and John Colquhoun taking his place.

Hearts then had the ball in the net themselves a couple of minutes later, after Mike Galloway latched onto a pass from Jimmy Sandison, but he was rightly flagged for being offside as both sides struggled to gain the upper hand.

José Percudani was proving troublesome to Hearts and twice he created good shooting opportunities for himself, but on both occasions the Argentinian's efforts went narrowly past Henry Smith's left-hand post. The Hearts keeper had to be alert, though, when he tried a snap shot from just outside the box – but Smith was down quickly to clear the danger.

With 57 minutes gone, Hearts eventually beat the Austrians' offside trap when Eamonn Bannon, just inside the Viennese half, lofted a ball over the defence with Walter Kidd and Mike Galloway both looking yards offside on the right, but the Spanish referee allowed play to continue. Kidd controlled the ball, then played it into the middle where Galloway nipped in ahead of Franz Wohlfahrt to break the deadlock with a well placed header at the near post. The goal deflated the home side and Hearts nearly scored again through Jimmy Sandison when Wohlfahrt was at full stretch to push away his strike, on the end of a flowing move that had started in their own half. At the end Hearts were in total control as the small travelling support celebrated what had to be one of Hearts' greatest results in the European history.

FK AUSTRIA WIEN: WOHLFAHRT HÖRMANN (SEKERLIOGLU) OBERMAYER DEGEORGI ZSAK PFEFFER OGRIS PROHASKA PERCUDANI KÜNAST PLEVA (CHANCELS). SUBS UNUSED: FISCHER STÖGER FURTNER
HEARTS: SMITH KIDD BERRY MCPHERSON WHITTAKER SANDISON GALLOWAY MACKAY (G) (JARDINE (I)) FOSTER (COLQUHOUN) BLACK BANNON. SUBS UNUSED: CAIRNS MOORE MURRAY (M)

After the team and fans came under attack from some disgruntled locals, the party headed back to Edinburgh in the early hours of the morning, leaving behind Les Porteous, who was to take the 350-mile trip to Zurich for the third-round draw. Teams such as Inter Milan, Bayern Munich, Juventus and Maradona-inspired Napoli were all left in the competition, each guaranteeing a sell-out crowd at Tynecastle. But in the end Hearts were paired with Velež Mostar, a little-known outfit from Yugoslavia, with the first leg to be played in Edinburgh in under two weeks.

The date did not allow Alex MacDonald any opportunity to watch Mostar in action as they had no games lined up before the sides met.

The Velež Mostar players relax at Edinburgh airport after arriving for their UEFA Cup third round clash at Tynecastle, November 1988
© The Scotsman Publications Ltd. Licensor www.scran.ac.uk

Velež general manager Enver Maric did make the trip to Scotland to take in Hearts' 0-0 draw with Dundee United as the Maroons continued to struggle in the SPL.

With their lack of match practise, the Yugoslavs arranged a friendly against the Malaysian national side which they convincingly won 5-0 on the Sunday before flying to Edinburgh. Their unusual build up to the game continued on Monday night when they chose to hold a training session at the Gyle rather than at Tynecastle. Hearts were more traditional in their preparations, heading to their usual retreat in Dunkeld on the day before the game, then having a light workout at Muirton Park the morning before.

Scorer of the all-important goal in Vienna, Mike Galloway, had been missing due to suspension against Dundee United but he was brought back for the European tie, with Jimmy Sandison being unlucky and dropping to the bench.

TYNECASTLE PARK – WEDNESDAY 23 NOVEMBER 1988
HEARTS: 3 (BANNON 18; GALLOWAY 56; COLQUHOUN 90)
V
FK VELEŽ MOSTAR: 0
REFEREE: E FREDRIKSSON (SWEDEN)

On a chill evening that left the partially frozen pitch with a light covering of snow in places, 17,500 packed into Tynecastle hoping that Hearts could build a lead that would take them into the last eight of the competition. Ian Ferguson almost gave them a first-minute lead in spectacular fashion when he tried his luck with an overhead kick that went just wide.

The visitors were finding it difficult to cope with Hearts' front three of Colquhoun, Ferguson and Galloway and it was perhaps a surprise that it took nearly 20 minutes before the Gorgie side went ahead. Gary Mackay played the ball out to Ian Ferguson on the right, who then put in a superb cross to the back post which was met perfectly by Eamonn Bannon to volley home, making it 1-0.

Hearts threatened to run riot as they controlled the game but both Ian Ferguson and John Colquhoun spurned gilt-edged chances to increase the lead before the break. However, their rhythm threatened to be upset when Eamonn Bannon did not reappear after the interval because of a hamstring injury. His place was taken by Jimmy Sandison who lined up in central defence with Neil Berry moving forward into midfield. However, the change did not affect the pattern of the game and Hearts continued to press.

Eammon Bannon puts Hearts 1-0 ahead against Velež Mostar
© The Scotsman Publications Ltd. Licensor www.scran.ac.uk

Ten minutes into the half they got their reward when Brian Whittaker's cross from the left was headed on by Mike Galloway. Ian Ferguson went up with Velež goalkeeper Vukasin Petranović, but the ball broke back to Galloway who prodded in his fourth goal in the competition.

Gary Mackay kept the pressure on when a few minutes later he blasted the ball goalward from fully 25 yards. Petranović did well initially, but let the ball squirm from his grasp and was relieved to see it slip past the post. The keeper was in action again in the 69th minute when he made a fine double save from a Kenny Black header followed by a shot from Dave MacPherson. Mostar were beginning to show signs of frustration, with the aptly named Ivica Barbaric and Ibro Rahimić being shown yellow cards before a terrible tackle on John Colquhoun by Ismet Šišić resulted in the centre half being shown a straight red card.

With the game into stoppage time, Hearts made their numerical advantage tell when Gary Mackay slipped a ball through to John Colquhoun, who wasted no time in blasting in number three despite the despairing dive of Petranović.

HEARTS: SMITH KIDD (JARDINE (I)) BERRY MCPHERSON WHITTAKER BLACK COLQUHOUN MACKAY (G) FERGUSON (I) GALLOWAY BANNON (SANDISON). SUBS UNUSED: MCDERMOTT CRABBE MCLAREN
FK VELEŽ MOSTAR: PETRANOVIĆ HADŽIABDIC GOSTO (JURIĆ (S)) RAHIMIĆ ŠIŠIĆ REPAK GUDELJ KAJTAZ BARBARIC TUCE (KODRO). SUBS UNUSED: PUDAR TUFEK ČAVAR

Despite another outstanding display in Europe, Hearts' poor run of form continued in the league when a defeat by fellow strugglers Motherwell was followed up by a 1-1 draw against Dundee. The lack of success prompted the chairman to sanction a move for Tosh McKinlay, who signed in a £300,000 transfer from Dundee – ironically, having played his last game against Hearts at the weekend.

Although ineligible to play, McKinlay joined the squad that left Edinburgh on Tuesday 6 December on the specially chartered plane to Yugoslavia. Missing from the travelling party was Wayne Foster, still troubled by the ankle injury he had sustained in Vienna. Wallace Mercer remained at home due to 'business reasons'.

The flight to Split on the eastern shore of the Adriatic was followed by a four-hour bus journey through the mountains to the historic town of Mostar. Sandy Clark had made the same journey 48 hours earlier to take in Velež' game against Dinamo Zagreb, which ended in a 1-1 draw. However, the home side gained the victory after a penalty shoot-out as no draws were allowed in the Yugoslavian league. He was also able to check on the facilities that were available and immediately recommended that the club should take their own food and water.

After the gruelling journey, the team still managed to find time to train at the compact Gradski stadium in the evening. Neil Berry took no part due to a swollen ankle. The pitch was in terrible condition with large areas covered by mud rather than grass, which led Henry Smith to describe the goal areas as *swamps*.

Hearts' opponents, lacking the influential trio of Šišić, Barbaric and Rahimić, all suspended after their indiscipline in the first leg, were boosted by the return of star striker Predrag Jurić, on special leave from national service in the army.

GRADSKI STADIUM – WEDNESDAY 7 DECEMBER 1988
FK VELEŽ MOSTAR: 2 (TUCE 31; GUDELJ 89)
V
HEARTS: 1 (GALLOWAY 65)
REFEREE: G LONGHI (ITALY)

There was a less than welcoming atmosphere inside the stadium at kick off, with Alex MacDonald and his team being pelted with fruit and toilet rolls as they took their seats in the away dugout. Playing in a 'candy stripe' strip, Hearts refused to be intimidated and coped well in the opening exchanges, getting men behind the ball and giving the home side little opportunity to reduce the deficit.

There was a scare in the 28th minute when Zijad Repak went down in the box after clashing with Neil Berry. It looked as though the Italian referee, Carlo Longhi, had given the award, but then he allowed play to continue. Three minutes later Mostar went ahead when Walter Kidd failed to deal with a free kick into the box. The ball dropped to Semir Tuce who lashed a left-foot shot past the helpless Henry Smith.

Just before half-time the referee spoke to Alex MacDonald when the manager came out to complain about a nasty tackle by Predrag Jurić on Walter Kidd. Amazingly, the official took no action when a glass was thrown from the stand aimed at the Hearts manager. The UEFA observer, Romanian Constantin Dinulascu, was later reported to have told MacDonald, 'There is no problem.' During the interval MacDonald was summoned to the referee's room and warned about his 'future conduct'. Adding insult to injury, a flare was thrown in the manager's direction as he emerged from the tunnel for the start of the second period. Luckily physio Malcolm Colquhoun was on hand to extinguish the pyrotechnics – while the match officials stood idly by.

Things were better on the park. Hearts resolutely defended their advantage as Velež struggled to add to their total. Although doing well in defence, Alex MacDonald's men were rarely seen as an attacking force but with 66 minutes played, Mike Galloway popped up to continue his remarkable scoring record when he snatched his fifth goal of the competition. Eamonn Bannon played a short free kick to John Colquhoun who beat a defender before crossing the ball perfectly for Galloway to loop a header over Petranović and into the net.

The Yugoslavs now needed to score another four to stay in the competition, a task which always looked beyond them. They did, however, grab a winner in the last minute when a mistake by Gary Mackay allowed Vladimir Gudelj a clear run on goal before beating Henry Smith from close range. The goal was of little consolation as the referee brought proceedings to a close moments later and Hearts were in the last eight of the tournament.

FK VELEŽ MOSTAR: PETRANOVIĆ HADŽIABDIC GOSTO JURIĆ (S) ĐURASOVIĆ JEDVAJ REPAK (KODRO) GUDELJ JURIĆ (P) KARABEG TUCE. SUBS UNUSED: PUDAR ČAVAR TUFEK BIRJUKOV
HEARTS: SMITH KIDD JARDINE (I) MCPHERSON WHITTAKER BERRY GALLOWAY (MOORE) MACKAY COLQUHOUN BLACK BANNON. SUBS UNUSED: MCDERMOTT FERGUSON (I) SANDISON MURRAY (M)

After the game the small band of Hearts supporters and the team came under attack from disgruntled home fans but managed to return to their hotel without injury. It was there that news started to filter through that the 'business reasons' which had prevented Wallace Mercer from travelling to Yugoslavia were that he was brokering a deal with Newcastle United for the return of Gorgie's favourite son, John Robertson.

Robertson's time on Tyneside had not gone well and with new manager Jim Smith in place, the Geordie club were prepared to listen to offers for the striker. Despite interest from both Rangers and Dundee United, the Hearts chairman was able to put together a package, with the help of businessman Ramez Daher, that would bring Hearts' spending to over £1 million in a week.

These were heady times at Tynecastle, now the sole representative from the UK in European football, and everyone was elated after being paired with European aristocrats Bayern Munich when the draw was made in Zurich on the Friday. With the competition taking a winter break, it was over two months before the Germans visited Tynecastle and in the intervening period Hearts' league results improved markedly, although they still lay in the lower half of the table.

By comparison, Bayern were heading the Bundesliga but had recently suffered a 4-3 defeat by lowly Karlsruhe at home in the cup. There were reports that the Germans were struggling to find the form that they had

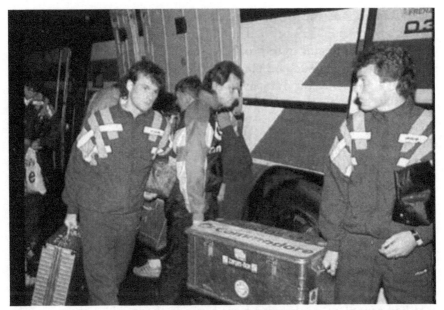

Bayern Munich arrive in Edinburgh

shown before the 11-week league shut-down over the winter months. Again, they failed to impress when they avenged the cup defeat to Karlsruhe in their league clash just before travelling to Scotland.

The Bayern assistant coach watched on as Hearts went down 3-0 at Pittodrie in a game that saw John Colquhoun add to a list of injury worries – he had to be carried off after a clash with Aberdeen keeper Theo Snelders. He joined first-team regulars John Robertson (pelvic injury), Gary Mackay (hamstring) and Craig Levein, who had recently returned to the team after 13 months out, all receiving treatment from physio Alan Rae. Definitely missing from the squad that headed to their North Berwick base was Brian Whittaker, who had suffered a broken leg after playing an important part in the clubs run to the quarter-final.

Jupp Heynckes, however, had a full squad to choose from when the Bavarians flew into Edinburgh on Monday. On hand at the airport to greet them was Wallace Mercer, who was amazed to see the official Bayern team bus that had been driven from Munich just to transport their stars when in Scotland.

Mercer had brought in PRO, a team of consultants, to maximise the income the club could expect from the glamour tie. They had to be convinced that moving the game either to Murrayfield or Hampden would not be tolerated, but had managed to secure sponsorship worth £15,000 with Commodore, the German computer company that happened to be Bayern's main sponsor. They had also signed a deal with cable TV company RTL+ to allow the game to be broadcast live in Germany. The contract was worth an additional £80,000 but meant that the match had to be brought forward 24 hours to the Tuesday night, a move that would come back to haunt the club in weeks to come.

TYNECASTLE PARK – TUESDAY 28 FEBRUARY 1989
HEARTS: 1 (FERGUSON 55)
V
FC BAYERN MÜNCHEN: 0
REFEREE: H KOHL (AUSTRIA)

While Robertson and Mackay were only considered fit enough for a place on the bench John Colquhoun had recovered sufficiently to take his place in a side that included 18-year-old Alan McLaren, making his European debut.

Despite admission prices being raised to £10 and £20, almost 27,000 packed into Tynecastle to see if Hearts could overcome a Munich side that had scored 12 goals away from home in the previous three rounds, including three in the San Siro against Inter Milan. However, from the first whistle Hearts paid little notice to their visitors' reputation and were a match for the Germans in the opening period, although neither side could create an opening to bother the keepers.

With 13 minutes played, Bayern gave an illustration how dangerous they could be on the break when Ian Ferguson lost possession to Olaf Thon just inside the Hearts half. His precise pass found Swedish international Johnny Ekstrom, who knocked it onto Hans Flick, but his effort went inches wide of the far post.

Bayern's cause was not helped by the playing surface, which had been heavily sanded before the game and was now cutting up quite badly, something that affected their normal passing game. Hearts, on the other hand, took a rather more direct route, but the long balls forward did not allow either Mike Galloway or Ian Ferguson many opportunities to worry the German rearguard. They did manage to get the ball in the net after half an hour when Raimond Aumann could only punch clear a cross from Eamonn Bannon. The ball fell to Tosh McKinlay, who lashed it home, only to see his effort ruled out by referee Kohl for a previous infringement. It had been the overweight Mr Kohl that had angered the Hearts team the previous season with a rather inept display in their defeat in Prague, but on this occasion his decision brought few protests.

Hearts' next opportunity came within three minutes of the restart when

96

Raimond Aumann can do nothing to stop Ian Ferguson putting Hearts 1-0 up against Bayern Munich at Tynecastle, 1989
© The Scotsman Publications Ltd. Licensor www.scran.ac.uk

a long pass found Mike Galloway, whose cross just eluded Ian Ferguson before reaching Eamonn Bannon. Unfortunately, he rushed his shot which hit a defender before being cleared.

Alex MacDonald's men were dominant. Bayern, struggling to contain them, conceded a number of fouls in quick succession. One, in the 54th minute, was within striking range for Ian Ferguson and Aumann did well to stop his well hit drive from giving Hearts the lead. He could do nothing a minute later when a foul on Kenny Black on the left saw Tosh McKinlay play the free kick short for Ferguson to lash the ball, right-footed, high into the net from 25 yards.

It was a stunning goal by any standards and worthy of winning any game, and despite the Germans putting plenty of effort into scoring an equaliser, Henry Smith did not have a save to make in the remaining 35 minutes. The nearest threat to his goal came when Klaus Augenthaler tried an audacious drive from fully 50 yards that went inches over the bar. Indeed, it was Hearts who went closest to scoring when, with eight minutes left, Dave MacPherson charged forward, beating the offside trap, only to fire his shot straight at Aumann.

HEARTS: SMITH MCLAREN MCKINLAY MCPHERSON BERRY LEVEIN GALLOWAY FERGUSON (1) (MACKAY G) COLQUHOUN (FOSTER) BLACK BANNON. SUBS UNUSED: MCCLOY SANDISON ROBERTSON
FC BAYERN MÜNCHEN: AUMANN GRAHAMMER PFLÜGLER JOHNSEN AUGENTHALER FLICK KÖGL (ECK) REUTER WOHLFARTH (WEGMANN) THON EKSTRÖM. SUBS UNUSED: CHEUER KASTENMAIER

After one of the most memorable victories in the club's history, most of the players were rewarded with a week off due to the SPL taking a break for Scotland's World Cup qualifier against France. On returning to league action they narrowly lost 1-0 to Celtic at Parkhead, but it was off the park that problems had begun emerge.

The West German FA had received a complaint from VfB Stuttgart, whose quarter-final against Real Sociedad had been played on the same evening that the game from Tynecastle was broadcast live in Germany and in a highlights package by Thames TV in England. Under new laws introduced in an attempt to curb the number of live games shown on TV, clubs had to get the permission from the football associations involved before they could go ahead. In Hearts' case, it seemed that authorisation had not been obtained from the German FA. Hearts' initial defence was that they had informed the broadcasting company of the decision but they still went ahead with transmission, something outwith the club's control. Nevertheless, there was a case to answer and both Hearts and the SFA were invited to provide written submissions to the UEFA disciplinary committee.

The only headache for Jupp Heynckes was an injury to star player Olaf Thon, who was unable to take part in the training session at their Sabener Strasse complex. The head coach was at pains to point out that the loss of Thon was a blow that would not weaken his side due to the quality of the player they had as a replacement. The coach's confidence in getting the result that would see them qualify was shared by the club, who were offering half-price tickets for the semi-final to any member of the Munich public that attended the clash against Hearts.

Alex MacDonald remained unconcerned and hinted that he would take the 'same again' approach to the away leg that had served them so well in the past. This meant there would be no place in the starting line-up for Ian Ferguson or John Robertson. Ironically, Robertson was one of only two players in the Hearts squad who had actually played in Munich's Olympic Stadium when years earlier along with Gary Mackay he had played for Edinburgh Under-15 schoolboys against their German counterparts. The game had resulted in a 7-0 trouncing by the Scots, with Robertson and Mackay grabbing three of the goals. A repeat scoreline would be virtually impossible, but any sort of win would do.

OLYMPIASTADION – TUESDAY 14 MARCH 1989
FC BAYERN MÜNCHEN: 2 (AUGENTHALER 16; JOHNSEN 69)
V
HEARTS: 0
REFEREE: E ALADRÉN (SPAIN)

The vast stadium was only at a quarter of its capacity despite a sizeable contingent of travelling support that made every effort to encourage their favourites from the start. Hearts seemed content to contain the threat of the West Germans by competing in midfield, a tactic that left Bayern trying shots from distance, with Norbert Nachtweih going close after seven minutes. Hearts responded a few minutes later when a corner kick by Kenny Black caused panic in the Bayern rearguard, who looked relieved when the Spanish referee blew for a foul by Mike Galloway.

Just when it looked as if Hearts had done everything required to snuff out their hosts' early threat, disaster struck – or at least, Klaus Augenthaler did. Bayern's captain was allowed to stride forward, leaving both Gary Mackay and Kenny Black trailing in his wake, to unleash an unstoppable shot past Henry Smith from 25 yards.

Now on level terms, it looked as though Munich would take control but it was Hearts that went closest to scoring when a neat move between Tosh McKinlay and Dave McPherson in the 23rd minute allowed Mike Galloway to release John Colquhoun through Bayern's defence. Raimond Aumann raced from his line and did just enough to close down the angle, and the little forward's right-foot shot drifted just wide of the target.

After having lost a goal to a long-range effort, it seemed that Hearts had not learned their lesson when Norbert Nachtweih was once again allowed to shoot from 20 yards. His attempt looked goal-bound until Henry Smith brought off a magnificent fingertip save at the expense of a corner.

There was another scare shortly before the end of the half when Dave McPherson halted Hans Flick's progress on the edge of the area. The referee decided the infringement had taken place outside the box and waved away the German's claim for a penalty.

At the start of the second half, both Roland Wohlfahrt and Erland Johnsen went close to increasing Bayern's lead before Hearts went agonisingly close to grabbing a vital away goal. With 57 minutes played, John Colquhoun got his head to a cross from Kenny Black and with Aumann beaten, watched in disbelief as the ball crashed against the post. Dave McPherson was quickest to the rebound but Hans Pflügler threw himself in the way and Bayern survived. Hearts were eventually undone with 21 minutes left when Stefan Reuter was allowed time and space to whip in a cross from the right-hand side. Henry Smith barely got his fingertips to the ball as it dropped onto the head of Erland Johnsen and into the corner of the net.Both John Robertson and Ian Ferguson were introduced into the action, but neither could grab the vital goal that would see Hearts through to the semi-final and Bayern finished the game the stronger side.

FC BAYERN MÜNCHEN: AUMANN NACHTWEIH PFLÜGLER JOHNSEN AUGENTHALER FLICK KÖGL
REUTER WOHLFARTH ECK (EKSTRÖM) WEGMANN. SUBS UNUSED: SCHEUER GRAHAMMER
KASTENMAIER SCHMIDT
HEARTS: SMITH MCLAREN MCKINLAY (ROBERTSON) LEVEIN BERRY MCPHERSON GALLOWAY
MACKAY COLQUHOUN BLACK BANNON (FERGUSON (I)). SUBS UNUSED: MCCLOY KIDD SANDISON

Long after the final whistle the estimated 3,000 travelling support stayed on the terracing singing the praises of the team forcing the players to re-emerge from the dressing room to take the applause. Although they had been beaten, they had given everything. Alex MacDonald summed it all up after the game when he said, 'We went very close, but Lady Luck was not on our side. We played well and nearly caused an upset.'

In the semi-final Bayern were knocked out by a star-studded Napoli side that included Diego Maradona, so Hearts had come very close to having the then world's greatest player gracing Tynecastle Park. As it was, it had taken a spectacular goal by one of Europe's best sides to eliminate the team from the competition, so it is little wonder that the 1988–89 season is well remembered as the club's best run in European football.

Although the run in Europe had come to an end, the saga of the television broadcast rumbled on. After a meeting in Berne, UEFA sent a telex to Tynecastle on Friday 24 March informing them that the club had been found guilty of a breach of the rules. The punishment was threefold: a fine of 100,000 Swiss francs (approximately £36,000) was imposed, plus an order to pay Stuttgart compensation and a ban on selling transmission rights to any ties the next time they qualified for a UEFA tournament.

As Wallace Mercer considered that the fault lay with the agents he had employed, it was no surprise that the club lodged an appeal. The chairman, along with secretary Les Porteous and legal representative David McLetchie, travelled to Geneva to present their case. After an hour of listening to Hearts' submission and then two hours of deliberation, the appeals panel, headed by Ludwig Straessle of Switzerland, announced that as 'no new evidence had been produced that could have been favourable to the club', the appeal had failed. In their own inimitable fashion they also raised the original fine to £93,285 – plus £3,732 costs, as they had now taken into consideration the sum Hearts had received from the broadcasting company.

It was a sad end to what had been Hearts' best run in a European competition to date.

For most of the players involved it was to be their greatest achievement on the European stage, but Eamonn Bannon had already played in the final of the competition as well as a semi-final of a European Cup with Dundee

United a few years previously. There were many highlights from his 14 appearances in Europe for the Hearts:

I always used to enjoy playing in European games, whether it was with Hearts or Dundee United. Not only were they special nights for the fans, it was special for the players too. Back then it was a ten-team league and you soon got used to playing against the same opponents week in, week out. They got used to your tricks and turns and vice versa, so coming up against someone different was a breath of fresh air.

You also had to adapt to the different styles of football. What you have to remember is that back then there was not the same football coverage on TV that there is today – SKY Sports was in its infancy and coverage was restricted to the English Premiership. Not only that, but we didn't have the Internet, so information about players wasn't as readily available as it is these days. People would laugh now but I remember that Alex [MacDonald] Sandy [Jardine] and Walter [Borthwick] would show us photographs of our opposite number so that we could recognise them. That was the only preparation we had. After that, it was really up to you to go out and win the battle.

As for the games themselves, it's hard to recall now because as a player you don't really have the time to sit back and admire what's going on around you. There are certain incidents that still stick out, like the time we played Velež Mostar over there. It was quite a hostile atmosphere from the start but we had built up a three-goal lead from the first game in Edinburgh and we thought we could keep the crowd quiet by containing Velež. It worked well and even when we went one down we were still confident we could see out the game.

Things changed when Mike Galloway scored to make it 1-1 not long into the second half. We had grabbed an important away goal and the crowd knew it. I was out on the wing and at one stage I felt something whiz by my head, and out of the corner of my eye I spotted a guy in the crowd with a catapult, firing marbles – and I was his target! Needless to say, I started to drift into midfield despite Alex and Sandy constantly shouting at me to 'go wide, go wide'.

Later the same season we played Bayern Munich. I have good reason to remember the tie over in Germany, and not only because it was the quarter-final of a major competition. Firstly, I can't forget the look on Kenny Black's face when Klaus Augenthaler fired in their equaliser. The big guy had broken out of their half and was midway inside ours, with Kenny trying to get back at him to make the tackle. Then for some reason Kenny shouts out '*Shoot*'. I don't know how good Augenthaler's command of English was but that is exactly what he did, and the ball sailed passed Henry Smith. Bayern got another one and despite the fact that John Colquhoun had a chance late on, we were out. It was a huge disappointment, but for me at least this was tempered by the fact that after the game I heard that I had become a father again – my wife had just given birth to our baby boy.

We had beaten Bayern at Tynecastle in the first leg and everyone that was there will remember Ian Ferguson's goal. Who wouldn't, it was a great strike. But for me, the goal I remember most was Glynn Snodin's against Slavia Prague. We were 1-0 down from the first leg, so although we were 3-2 ahead on the night, we were heading out of the competition. There were about ten minutes to go and we were throwing everything at them. Craig Levein was pushing forward when he was brought down about 25 yards out. Up stepped wee 'Snodgrass' and hammered the ball into the top corner. Fantastic!

My one real regret was our defeat by Bologna. After gaining a good result against Dnipro, we let ourselves down against the Italians. I know everyone thinks that Serie 'A' sides are good, but really Bologna were very poor. Having beaten them 3-1 at Tynecastle, we should have been good enough to progress to the next round. But it was not to be.

European football is great for all concerned. It certainly gave me an opportunity to travel to places like the Dnipropetrovsk that I probably wouldn't have seen otherwise.

CHAPTER 10

1990–91 UEFA Cup

QUALIFICATION FOR THE 90–91 UEFA Cup came via a respectable third place finish in the SPL, behind champions Rangers and runners-up Aberdeen. However, prior to participation in the first round, Hearts had made a stuttering start to the new season, with only one point from three games. Wallace Mercer relieved manager Alex MacDonald of his duties on the Monday following a 3-1 reverse at Ibrox.

It was a decision that was unpopular in many quarters, with John Robertson describing it as 'scandalous, shocking' and 'pandering to the whims of a few hundred fans'. MacDonald's assistant, Walter Borthwick, had also been shown the door and Sandy Clark was put in temporary charge of the side. He opened his managerial account in the best possible fashion, with Robbo bagging a double and Craig Levein getting the other in a convincing 3-0 win over Hibs at Easter Road, a game best remembered for the some idiot trying to attack Robbo after he opened the scoring. Only a week after taking charge, Sandy led Hearts into the unknown on the club's first visit to the Soviet Union after the draw for the UEFA Cup paired them against FC Dnipro Dnipropetrovsk.

For the trip to Dnipropetrovsk, Hearts chartered a plane from Aeroflot at the cost of £35,000 and offered supporters the chance to travel at the exorbitant cost of just over £500 per person. The 28 well-heeled souls who took up the offer found themselves on a flight that got them to Kiev – after which they had to complete the trip with a 450-mile bus journey.

Despite Dnipro having first qualified for European competition six years earlier, Hearts were one of the first foreign sides to play in the Ukrainian city. A vital industrial centre, it housed many nuclear, military and space installations – all top secret in pre-glasnost times, with foreigners being unwelcome. It was one of Russia's 'closed cities' and as such the football team were forced to play their games at alternative venues.

The squad trained in the Meteor stadium hours after their arrival and both Jimmy Sandison and Gary Mackay gave the manager cause for concern, having picked up knocks in the win against Hibs. Mackay

Stadium Meteor, Dnipropetrovsk (author's collection)

had a swollen knee and Sandison a groin strain, putting their places in the starting line-up in doubt. Clark was also missing the suspended Dave MacPherson and Derek Ferguson, who had an ankle injury.

Another important figure that was not in the travelling party was Chairman Wallace Mercer, who had remained in Edinburgh to continue the search for the next Hearts manager. News from back home suggested that this would be the then Bristol City manager Joe Jordan, although all the relevant parties were denying the suggestion.

STADIUM METEOR – WEDNESDAY 19 SEPTEMBER 1990
DNIPRO DNIPROPETROVSK: 1 (GUDIMENKO 55)
V
HEARTS: 1 (ROBERTSON (22)
REFEREE: W FOECKLER (GERMANY)

Sandy Clark only needed to make one change to the team that had played so well against Hibs. With Gary Mackay failing a fitness test, Irishman David McCreery took his place in an attack-minded side, captained for the day by 19-year-old Alan McLaren.

McLaren was called into action almost immediately when he produced a terrific tackle to prevent Evgueni Shakov making an early breakthrough. It was an indication of things to come as the Hearts defence had to be at their best to prevent them from falling behind. Henry Smith distinguished himself with a fine save from a low drive by Nikolai Kudritshy before Yuri

Gudimenko missed the target when handily placed.

Hearts had to reshuffle the pack when Neil Berry was hurt after putting in a tackle and had to be replaced by Davie Kirkwood. After the change, and against the run of play, Hearts went ahead on 22 minutes when John Robertson placed a powerful header behind Dnipro goalie Valeriy Gorodov. George Wright began the move after the defence had repelled yet another attack from the home side. He made a great run down the wing before sending the ball into the middle, where Wayne Foster headed the ball to Robertson, who dived in to make it 1-0.

The goal clearly rattled the home side, but they were soon back in their stride and Vladimir Guerachenko had the ball in the net but not before the linesman had correctly raised his flag for offside. Not long after, Eduard Son had a gilt-edged chance to equalise when Jimmy Sandison failed to deal with a cross from the right but with the Ukrainian almost standing on the goal line, he sent his header over the bar.

Sandison distinguished himself minutes into the second half when his magnificent tackle prevented Yevhen Shakov from scoring a certain equaliser. However, Dnipro were not to be denied and after 55 minutes Gudimenko volleyed home a cross from Kudritsky. It was by any standard a great goal but it had to be to beat a well organised Hearts defence where every man was playing superbly. Henry Smith was the hero eight minutes later with an acrobatic save that prevented Andrei Sidelnikov making it 2-1.

In a rare attack, the visitors had a legitimate penalty claim turned down by the German referee when John Robertson was barged off the ball in the box. It was about the last time Hearts threatened as Dnipro now took a stranglehold on the game. Time and again they were thwarted as the clock ticked down, but Hearts held firm to produce one of their finest results away from home in a European competition.

DNIPRO DNIPROPETROVSK: GORODOV YUDIN BESHENAR SIDELNIKOV GUERACHENKO KUDRITSKY BAGMUT BENKO (YAROVENKO) SON GUDIMENKO SHAKHOV. SUBS UNUSED: ZHIDKOV EDWARDSON DERIAVKO MANTUR
HEARTS: SMITH MCLAREN MCKINLAY LEVEIN BERRY (KIRKWOOD) WRIGHT ROBERTSON MCCREERY (KIDD) FOSTER SANDISON COLQUHOUN. SUBS UNUSED: WALKER BANNON FERGUSON (I)

When the team arrived back in Edinburgh, Wallace Mercer was at the airport to congratulate them on achieving such a good result, having concluded the deal that would see Joe Jordan become the new man in charge at Tynecastle.

Jordan's reign did not get off to the most auspicious of starts, with a 3-0 defeat at Parkhead, but on the Saturday before the return leg an Eamonn

Bannon goal was good enough to beat Dundee United at Tynecastle. For the Dnepr game Jordan would have to do without Neil Berry, David McCreery and Scott Crabbe, all ruled out through injury or illness.

The Ukrainians also had injury problems with their highly rated captain, Viktor Tischenko, who was unable to travel to Scotland. Despite his absence Dnipro had still managed to win their last three games comfortably and were sitting in fifth place in the Russian championship. Their coach, Yeugene Koucherevski, unsurprisingly predicted that his side would progress to the next round but, strangely, only on the away goals rule; he forecast a 2-2 scoreline.

TYNECASTLE PARK – WEDNESDAY 3 OCTOBER 1990
HEARTS: 3 (MCPHERSON 19; ROBERTSON 22 PEN & 42)
V
DNIPRO DNIPROPETROVSK: 1 (SHAKOV 41 PEN)
REFEREE: E HALLE (NORWAY)

With television coverage banned from Tynecastle after the indiscretion against Bayern Munich, a crowd of just under 19,000 gathered on a cold October evening to see if Hearts could take their place in Friday's second round draw.

Dave MacPherson won the toss and elected to kick with the assistance of the strong wind blowing from the Gorgie Road end. The advantage almost helped them get off to the perfect start. Ian Ferguson had the ball in the net in the first minute after John Robertson dummied a pass from Tosh McKinlay, but his joy drained away when he noticed that the stand-side linesman had his flag raised. It was a tight decision and one that many in the crowd did not agree with.

Hearts got the breakthrough they were looking for 20 minutes into the half, with the goal coming from the head of Dave MacPherson. As Tosh McKinlay prepared to take a free kick, Vladimir Gudimenko seemed more concerned about wrestling with the Hearts captain and as a consequence lost the flight of the ball, letting MacPherson nod Hearts in front.

Two minutes later more indiscipline from the visitors allowed Hearts to double their advantage – they were awarded a penalty after John Robertson was sent sprawling in the box. The little striker took the kick himself and did his usual efficient job to make it 2-0. The Soviets were now in disarray and showed little of their normally slick, passing game as more indiscipline crept into their play. At 35 minutes a crude tackle by Vladimir Gerathsenko on George Wright caused Wright to be replaced by Gary Mackay. Dnipro were still dangerous and fashioned a great chance for Yevhen Shakhov, but Henry Smith proved to be his equal with a fine save.

John Robertson puts Hearts 3-1 up against Dnipro at Tynecastle © SNS Group

Four minutes before the break Dnipro were thrown a lifeline when Tosh McKinlay tripped Vladimir Bagmut in the box. This time the Hearts keeper could do nothing to stop Shakhov making it 2-1 from the spot.

Far from letting their heads drop, Hearts stormed up the park and restored their two-goal advantage two minutes later: John Colquhoun sent in a corner that was headed on by Alan McLaren and once again there was John Robertson to knock the ball past Valeriy Gorodov. In doing so, he overtook Mike Galloway as Hearts' top scorer in European competition.

The second half started in the same manner as the first, with Ian Ferguson putting the ball in the net but once again being flagged for offside. This time, though, virtually no one disagreed with the decision. The Russians tried to play themselves back into the game but Hearts stood firm. Few chances presented themselves for either side but both Ian Ferguson and John Colquhoun came close to settling the issue. At the other end and with time running out, Henry Smith bravely saved at the feet of Yuriy Gudimenko after the forward had been put through by Andrei Sidelnikov. It was the last clear chance Dnipro created and Hearts ran out worthy winners.

HEARTS: SMITH MCLAREN MCKINLAY LEVEIN KIRKWOOD MCPHERSON COLQUHOUN (FERGUSON (D)) WRIGHT (MACKAY(G)) ROBERTSON FERGUSON (I) BANNON. SUBS UNUSED: WALKER SANDISON FOSTER
DNIPRO DNIPEROPETROVSK: GORODOV YUDIN GERASTHENKO SIDELNIKOV BEGENAR KUDRITSKY

BAGMUT MANTUR SON GUDIMENKO SHAKHOV. SUBS UNUSED: YAROVENKO SMOLSNIKOV BENKO YUDKOV KRAKOVSKI

Hearts were represented by club secretary Les Porteous at the second round draw in Zurich on Friday 5 October. He was 'satisfied' when the Tynecastle side were paired with Bologna, observing that travel arrangements would not provide such a headache as in the previous round.

There was also another reason to be pleased, as on the playing front the Italians were certainly not one of the 'big hitters' of Serie A. In fact they had only recently won their way back into the top division after many years languishing in Serie B and even lower. They had not started the current season particularly well and by the time they arrived in Edinburgh they were anchored at the foot of the league. Following their latest defeat (a 1-0 loss to Cesena) Francesco Scoglio paid the ultimate price and was replaced as manager by Gigi Radice who was making his second spell in charge of the club.

Hearts' form had also been poor – they had taken only one point from games against Motherwell, St Johnstone and Aberdeen. Going into the game, they were now second bottom of the SPL, only a couple of points ahead of St Mirren.

Wallace Mercer made the match an all-ticket affair and decided to raise the prices considerably. Given the side's poor results, there had been disappointing sales. Even promotions such as a prize draw and a £2 discount on a match ticket to anyone that bought a programme for the St Johnstone game were not enough to turn the tie into the financial windfall it could have been. With the TV coverage ban still in place, Hearts had managed to turn it into something of a commercial disaster.

On the playing side, John Robertson was suffering from a hamstring injury he had picked up playing for Scotland and was a major doubt. However, Scott Crabbe could be considered for the first time since suffering from a bout of food poisoning seven weeks earlier. In the end, Robertson was not risked and Crabbe was given a place on the bench, with Wayne Foster getting the nod to play up front.

TYNECASTLE PARK – WEDNESDAY 24 OCTOBER 1990
HEARTS: 3 (FOSTER 6 & 23; I FERGUSON 39)
V
BOLOGNA FC 1909: 1 (NOTARISTEFANO 61)
REFEREE: J-M NEGREIRA (SPAIN)

Slightly over 11,000 turned up to witness Hearts get off to a confident start. They took the game to a clearly nervous Italian side and their endeavours were rewarded after only eight minutes when the former Dundee United double act of Eamonn Bannon and Ian Ferguson carved open the Bologna defence to set up Wayne Foster, who hit a left-foot shot from 15 yards into the corner of Nello Cusin's net.

The Bologna keeper did not look likely to inspiring confidence in his team-mates when eight minutes later he made a mess of dealing with a corner from John Colquhoun. Dave MacPherson nodded the ball on to Ian Ferguson, but with the goal at his mercy the striker couldn't manage to get anything behind his shot and it was scrambled off the goal line.

With Hearts dominant, it was only a matter of time before the second goal arrived and once again it was Dave MacPherson who provided the opportunity with a surging run down the left-hand side. Davie Kirkwood received his pass but mis-hit his shot, giving the Italians defence time to clear the danger. However, the ball was allowed to run through to John Colquhoun on the right, then was immediately whipped back into the danger area – and there was Wayne Foster to send an angled header behind Cusin via the base of the post.

The goal was the signal for the small band of travelling supporters situated in the wing stand to voice their displeasure. The disturbance prompted a plea for good behaviour to be broadcast in Italian over the stadium PA. When this was ignored some of Lothian and Borders' finest went in to settle the unrest.

The visitors' mood darkened further six minutes before the interval when they saw their side fall further behind. Eamonn Bannon sent in a cross from the left that Ian Ferguson managed to head goalward. Cusin tried to turn the ball over but only succeeded in tipping it onto the bar and Ferguson reacted the quickest to nod the rebound into the net.

It would have been difficult for Bologna to get any worse and they did begin the second half in brighter fashion. Hearts, on the other hand, seemed to have taken their foot of the pedal and did not manage to fashion as many chances as they had in the first period, although they contained the Italian threat quite easily.

With just over an hour played, the referee, José Maria Negreira, made a baffling and ultimately crucial decision when he penalised Henry Smith for time-wasting – standing with the ball in his hands waiting to clear it up the park; it did not seem that he held on to it any longer than normal, but the Spanish official thought otherwise and awarded an indirect free kick 16 yards from goal. There then ensued one or two minutes of jostling in which Dave MacPherson saw his name go into the book, before Massimo Bonini touched the ball to Egidio Notaristefano whose low effort beat

Smith at his right-hand post after taking the slightest of deflections.

Any thoughts Bologna might have had of a comeback were extinguished two minutes later when their German striker, Herbert Waas, was shown the red card after a wild lunge at Craig Levein, leaving them to play out the remaining time with ten men. All in all it was a satisfying result for the home team, although the loss of an away goal under such controversial circumstances took the edge off a fine display.

HEARTS: SMITH MCLAREN MCKINLAY LEVEIN KIRKWOOD (FERGUSON(D)) MCPHERSON COLQUHOUN BERRY FOSTER FERGUSON(I) BANNON. SUB UNUSED: WALKER SANDISON MACKAY CRABBE
BOLOGNA FC 1909: CUSIN MARIANI VILLA DI GIÁ ILIEV TRICELLA VERGA BONINI (BIONDO) WAAS NOTARISTEFANO LORENZO (CAMPIONE). SUBS UNUSED: VALLERIANI NEGRO TRAVERSA

If that had been a good result, what followed in the league certainly was not. By the time the squad flew out to Italy, Hearts sat firmly at the bottom of the SPL. A defeat to St Mirren and a draw with lowly Dunfermline had seen them drop to tenth place.

Joe Jordan and his newly appointed assistant manager, Frank Connor, also had an injury crisis to deal with as the club sought to continue their journey in Europe. As the team trained in the Stadio Dall'Ara on the evening before the game, Scott Crabbe was the only recognised forward who was able to take a full part. John Robertson (hamstring), John Colquhoun (leg injury) and Ian Ferguson (ankle injury) all sat out the session, while the hero from the first leg Wayne Foster confined to his room in the Hotel Molino Rosso with a cold. Bologna also had a list of players that would not take part, with Galvani, Di Giá, Poli all injured and Waas suspended after his dismissal at Tynecastle. They were, however, boosted by the inclusion in their squad of Hungarian striker Lajos Détári, a recent £3million purchase from Olympiakos.

STADIO RENATO DALL'ARA – WEDNESDAY 7 NOVEMBER 1990
BOLOGNA FC 1909: 3 (DÉTÁRI 19; VILLA 73; MARIANI 84)
V
HEARTS: 0
REFEREE: I VAN SWIETEN (HOLLAND)

On the bright but chilly afternoon of the match a reasonable contingent from Edinburgh were present in the Renato Dall'Arro Stadium, although most had spurned the opportunity to travel with the official party. Once again, the asking price was over £500 a head – the club seemed determined to try to milk every penny from the European games. Some had spotted Bologna officials wining and dining the match officials in the elegant

Grande Hotel the previous evening and now there was concern amongst the support that Hearts might be subject to some dubious decisions akin to the one at Tynecastle that had cost them dearly.

In a mirror image of the first leg, it was the away side that made a jittery start to the game, with the home side playing confidently. Détári showed why Bologna had paid such a high fee for his services as early as the fifth minute when he created a good shooting opportunity for himself, only to thrash the ball into the side netting from close range. It was a let-off, but Hearts did not heed the warning and the opening goal went the way of the Italians after 19 minutes. Craig Levein attempted to cut out a through ball from Rufo Verga, but it dropped into the path of Détári, allowing him to run in on goal before rounding Henry Smith to smash the ball into the net.

Hearts were not functioning as an attacking force and goalkeeper Nello Cusin did not have to make a save of any note in the first 45 minutes, whereas on several occasions his opposite number was called upon to maintain Hearts' overall lead, with fine saves from both Pietro Mariani and Renato Verga.

In the second period John Colquhoun started to see more of the ball and began to pose a threat to the home side's dominance. The Italians reply was to revert to type and employ illegal methods to nullify the danger, with one of his runs being halted by an elbow to the face from Antonio Cabrini. It was a tactic that was also used on Neil Berry and John Robertson by Fabio Poli and Rosario Biondo respectively – the only player to be punished being Robbo, presumably for time-wasting!

With 25 minutes to go, Joe Jordan replaced Eamonn Bannon with Alan McLaren as he sought to hold on to the aggregate advantage. However, Bologna continued to pile pressure on the Hearts defence.

Henry Smith had been the hero with two outstanding saves, the first from Poli and the second from a header by Bonini, but he was eventually beaten in the 73rd minute by a low drive from six yards by Renato Villa.

Hearts, now staring elimination in the face, pushed forward to get the vital away goal that would put them through. Once again, the spoiling tactics of the Italians came into play, with Détári eventually being able to trot off the pitch unaided after going down with an injury that initially looked as if it might end his playing career. Antonio Cabrini became the first Bologna name to go into the referee's book for yet another assault on John Colquhoun, but as if by way of an apology to his hosts of the previous evening, Mr van Swieten took the name of Craig Levein for an innocuous foul on Cusin.

Pressing forward in numbers meant that there were plenty of gaps in

Hearts' rearguard and this was ruthlessly exposed by Pietro Mariani with just over five minutes left when he scored Bologna's third with a fine solo effort.

BOLOGNA FC 1909: CUSIN BIONDO CABRINI VERGA VILLA TRICELLA MARIANI BONINI CAMPIONE (POLI) DÉTÁRI (LORENZO) NOTARISTEFANO. SUBS UNUSED: NEGRO VALLERIANI ILIEV
HEARTS: SMITH MACKAY (G) MCKINLAY LEVEIN KIRKWOOD MCPHERSON COLQUHOUN BERRY ROBERTSON (CRABBE) FERGUSON(I) BANNON (MCLAREN). SUBS UNUSED: WALKER KIDD FERGUSON (D)

It was a disappointing end to a campaign that had the potential to match or even better the run two years earlier. Bologna matched Hearts' achievement of reaching the quarter-final, and were eliminated by Sporting Lisbon. For former player and manager Craig Levein, in the four games Hearts had produced their best and worst performances:

> I have been involved in some memorable European occasions with Hearts, both as a player and later as manager. Wins against the likes of Bayern Munich, Braga and Bordeaux are obviously highlights, but for me the best team performances seemed to be reserved for drawn games away from home.
>
> The 2-2 result in Portugal against Braga was a great achievement – they were a quality side, as was proven in subsequent seasons. It meant we qualified for the next round and that brought in over £1million to the club. Another one that springs to mind is the 0-0 draw in Sarajevo, which was achieved in difficult circumstances. Again it meant qualification to the next round after getting a good result at home. Both these games came when I was in charge, but as a player it's the away leg in the Ukraine against Dnipro that sticks with me. It was a great battling display and it's just a pity it was seen by so few Hearts fans.
>
> We had not been playing well in the league and, as happens, it was the manager that carried the can. Just before the European game, Sandy Clark was put in temporary control. He was certainly thrown in at the deep end as his first game happened to be against Hibs. Anyway, we got a result and as I remember it I scored our second. I never got too many goals in my playing career but I always seemed to get one against Hibs, which kept the fans happy.
>
> Although we didn't know very much about Dnipro, we were pretty confident we could get a result over there and then have the chance to finish the tie at Tynecastle.
>
> The thing that I remember most was when we first arrived in the city – the only word to describe it would be 'depressing' – everything seemed so dull and grey, really just as you would imagine an Eastern Bloc town to look like back then.
>
> The stadium was an open, run-down affair with steep concrete terracing. On the day of the game the crowd seemed to be made up of lots of military personnel, but we were always aware of the handful of

fans that had made it from Edinburgh.

Dnipro turned out to be a very good side with superb technical ability and we were on the back foot from the start. We did manage one attack through George Wright and – as he seemed to be able to do regularly – up popped Robbo to put us ahead. The rest of the game was spent defending as a team and they did get an equaliser. On reflection, it was probably daylight robbery, but I still think it was one of the best defensive displays in Europe.

We thought we would be in for a real test in the second leg, but they didn't travel well and it was a different side that turned up at Tynecastle a couple of weeks later. We won quite easily, as we did against Bologna in the next round, but in that game we lost a silly goal which proved to be crucial.

The Italians were an ordinary side and nowhere near as good as Dnipro, but in the return leg in Bologna we got our tactics all wrong. We were all given man-marking duties and the guy I was supposed to shadow was all over the place. I even found myself having to follow him when he started playing in the right back position! Anyway, we paid the price and went out. So after one of the best performances in the first round we produced one of the worst in the second, which was frustrating for everyone.

CHAPTER 11

1992–93 UEFA Cup

BY THE END of the 90–91 season Joe Jordan had steered the club into a reasonable mid-table position, but the fifth-place finish was not good enough to see them qualify for Europe. However, the following season they once again split the Old Firm and finished as runners-up in the SPL, an achievement that allowed them to become one of Scotland's representatives in the UEFA Cup, along with Celtic and Edinburgh rivals Hibernian (due to their victory in the League Cup final against Dunfermline).

The draw saw Hearts make a return to Prague, where seven years earlier they had exited the competition at the hands of Dukla. On this occasion they were paired with Salvia Prague, a club with a strong Scottish connection. Founded in 1892, they were for some years in the shadow of neighbours Sparta. This changed in 1905 on the arrival as manager of former Celtic and Scotland forward John Madden. For the next 25 years 'Jake' brought success to the club, his reign becoming known as the 'golden age' of Slavia. Madden's achievements made him a legend in Prague where he stayed until his death in 1948. A statue was erected there in his honour.

From the '30s the club's fortunes were mixed and they went through a particularly bad period during the '50s and '60s. In 1990 America-based Czech businessman Boris Korbel invested heavily, bringing in talented players such as Patrik Berger and Vladimir Smicer who, along with manager Vlastimil Petrzela in his second spell in charge, had begun to get Slavia back to the level they had once enjoyed.

With the first round of the UEFA Cup competition not starting until the middle of September 1992, by which time the Scottish season was well under way. With Celtic being the only team that had managed to beat them so far, when the Hearts squad stepped on the plane to fly to the Czech capital, they were joint top of the SPL along with Rangers.

Slavia were also in fine form as Joe Jordan and chief scout John Calderwood knew, having taken in their recent matches against Dukla and Sparta. Slavia had won both comfortably, scoring seven goals in the process, with striker Pavel Kuka grabbing four over the two games.

Preventing Kuka from adding to his impressive tally was not the only worry for Joe Jordan. UEFA rules allowed for only three non-Scots to take part in the tie, meaning that of the four Hearts first-team regulars Peter Van de Ven, Wayne Foster, Glynn Snodin and Ian Baird, someone would have to miss out. Injury also narrowed the manager's choice: both Craig Levein and Alan McLaren were ruled out, leaving problems in the defence.

VELKY SRAHOVSKY STADION – WEDNESDAY 16 SEPTEMBER 1992
SK SLAVIA PRAHA: 1 (TATARCHUK 85)
V
HEARTS: 0
REFEREE: S HUSAJNOV (RUSSIA)

Eden stadium, Slavia's ground, was considered inadequate to accommodate UEFA Cup ties, and so the game went ahead in the council-owned Velky Srahovsky stadion. There was a sparse crowd of fewer than 5,000 inside for the 6.00PM kick off. Hearts made only one change to the team that had beaten Aberdeen at Tynecastle four days earlier, Neil Berry, who had only just returned after 18 months out with cruciate damage, taking the place of Craig Levein in a makeshift back line.

The home side were soon in their stride and their slick passing movements gave the Tynecastle men some problems. Graeme Hogg had been handed the duty of keeping Pavel Kuka under control but he could do nothing when the Czech international found space for himself in the box with 15 minutes gone. His shot from 12 yards beat Henry Smith but cannoned back off the post and was booted clear.

In a rare attacking move, Hearts created a chance for their danger man John Robertson after 23 minutes. Derek Ferguson started the move when he got the ball to the little striker eight yards out; unfortunately, Robbo sent his left-foot drive inches over the bar. This turned out to be Hearts' only opportunity of the half and Slavia continued to control the game.

Their constant pressure almost brought the opener with ten minutes left of the half when Russian international Vladimir Tatarchuk managed to escape the attentions of Peter Van de Ven inside the box. With only Henry Smith to beat, he somehow managed to screw the ball wide from only six yards out.

The second half continued in the same vein, with the visitors having to thank Henry Smith for keeping the scores level when he did well to stop Patrik Berger, and then Jiří Lerch, from putting Slavia ahead. However, ten minute into the half, Henry could only stand and watch as a free kick from Radim Necas hit his left-hand post then bounced along the line only to hit the other post before being cleared. The Czech was frustrated again when another of his free kicks looked goal-bound before Smith pulled off yet another save from the top drawer.

Scott Crabbe came on to replace the injured John Robertson and with eight minutes left he was inches away from getting a precious away goal in Hearts' first meaningful attack of the second period. But minutes later it was Slavia that broke the deadlock through Vladimir Tatarchuk after Hearts conceded a free kick almost on the touchline. With everyone expecting a cross into the box, the Russian international smashed in an unstoppable shot from fully 30 yards into the net.

It was a disappointing end to what had been a battling performance, but Joe Jordan was still upbeat after the game when he said, 'It was a bad goal to lose. I wasn't surprised by Slavia. I knew they were a good team but I still think we can go through.'

SK SLAVIA PRAHA: JÁNOŠ PETROUŠ SUCHOPÁREK ŠILHÁVY BERGER TATARCHUK LERCH (BEJBL)
PENICKA KUKA NECAS NOVAK. SUBS UNUSED: PRAZENICA RUSNAK VAHALA
HEARTS: SMITH HOGG MCKINLAY BERRY MACKAY(G) VAN DE VEN ROBERTSON (CRABBE)
FERGUSON (D) BAIRD MAUCHLEN FOSTER (BANNON). SUBS UNUSED: WALKER WRIGHT WILSON (T)

Between the two ties Hearts' form took a dip. A 2-0 defeat at Ibrox was followed by a 1-0 reverse against lowly Airdrie, these results seeing them slip to fourth in the SPL. By coincidence, Airdrie were also involved in Europe in midweek, travelling to Prague to take on Slavia's rivals Sparta in the Cup Winners Cup. After the game at Broomfield, it looked as if it would be the Diamonds and not the Hearts that would have the better chance of turning up trumps.

In Hearts' favour was the knowledge that in the seven previous European ties Slavia had played away from home, they had yet to register a win. However, if they were to overcome the one-goal deficit, Joe Jordan would need a full squad to choose from and there were injury worries over John Robertson, Alan McLaren, Neil Berry, Gary MacKay and Ally Mauchlen.

Prior to the game the players were taken away to their normal base in North Berwick where the bracing east coast air worked wonders and only Neil Berry and Ally Mauchlen could not be considered for the game.

TYNECASTLE PARK – WEDNESDAY 30 SEPTEMBER 1992
HEARTS: 4 (MACKAY 11; BAIRD 21; LEVEIN 43; SNODIN 79)
V
SK SLAVIA PRAHA: 2 (SILHAVY 15; KUKA 65)
REFEREE: R LARSSON (SWEDEN)

The game started at a hectic pace, both sides creating chances in the opening minutes. Firstly, Michal Petrouš charged forward to cross for Pavel Kuka, but the forward mistimed his run and the danger was cleared. John Robertson and then Eamonn Bannon responded for Hearts, but again their threat was snuffed out by the visitors' defence.

Zdenek Jánoš in the Slavia goal had to be at his best after eight minutes when Ian Baird put him under pressure with a diving header from a cross from Tosh McKinlay. The opening goal was only delayed for three minutes when the keeper was well beaten after a flowing move involving Ian Baird, Glynn Snodin and John Robertson was finished off with a crisp strike by Gary Mackay from the edge of the box.

Tynecastle went wild as Hearts drew the tie level, but the euphoria was short-lived when Slavia made it 1-1 four minutes later. When the game restarted, Slavia forced their first corner but before it could be taken Vladimir Tatarchuk fell to the ground in apparent agony. The source of his discomfort was unknown as nobody seemed to be near him at the time and the Swedish referee annoyed the home support by allowing treatment on the pitch for several minutes. The interruption obviously distracted the Hearts defence as Jaroslav Silhavy was allowed to nip in front of Henry Smith to give the Czechs a vital away goal. It was a goal that Archie MacPherson famously likened to 'being kicked in the groin at

Zedenek Jánoš tries in vain to stop Glynn Snodin's free kick giving Hearts a late winner against Slavia Prague © SNS Group

your birthday party' – and it certainly was a sore one!

It left Hearts now needing to score at least twice to qualify and they responded in the best possible fashion with 21 minutes gone. Eamonn Bannon played a quick one-two with John Robertson on the right before swinging in the perfect cross for Ian Baird to send a powerful header behind Jánoš to restore their advantage on the night.

Despite Slavia still holding the upper hand on aggregate, they were clearly rattled and they resorted to some robust tackling to stop Hearts from finding any rhythm. Foul after foul went unpunished before Martin Penicka tested the referee's patience once too often and had his name taken for yet another crude foul on John Robertson.

With two minutes of the half remaining, Hearts' pressure paid off when a corner kick from Eamonn Bannon was met perfectly by Craig Levein eight yards out to make it 3-1.

Within minutes of the start of the second half, Jaroslav Silhavy twice quite literally made his mark on John Robertson with challenges that went unpunished. Then with just under an hour played, Slavia were reduced to ten men when Penicka, who had already been booked in the first half, was shown a red card for an alleged tackle from behind on Ian Baird – a case of mistaken identity, as the tackle had actually been made by Vladimir Tatarchuk, but the decision stood.

Hearts continued to dominate but, as often happens, they were caught out by a quick counter-attack with disastrous consequences. Radim Necas was allowed to hit a speculative ball upfield from midway inside his own half. Craig Levein's defensive header was pounced upon by Pavel Kuka, who played a one-two with Jiří Lerch on the edge of the box. Seeing Henry Smith advancing, the 24-year-old international striker took advantage by lobbing the ball expertly into the far corner of the net.

With the aggregate score now 3-3 the crowd fell silent, realising that the Czechs also had the advantage of two away goals. However, there were still 25 minutes left and Hearts piled forward in search of the goal they required. This left them exposed at the back and they were almost caught by Kuka again, but this time he lifted his shot over the bar from only six yards.

Then, with ten minutes left, Slavia paid the ultimate price for their undisciplined display when Jiří Lerch was punished for a foul on Craig Levein 30 yards from goal. With the penalty area full of players jostling for position, Glynn Snodin stepped up and sent the ball past the defensive wall and high into the net. It was a goal worthy of winning any game. Tynecastle erupted – and then once again at the final whistle as Hearts completed a memorable victory in one of the most exciting European games ever seen in Gorgie.

HEARTS: SMITH HOGG MCKINLAY LEVEIN MACKAY(G) VAN DE VEN ROBERTSON MCLAREN
(WRIGHT) BAIRD SNODIN (WILSON) BANNON. SUBS UNUSED: WALKER FERGUSON (I) CRABBE
SK SLAVIA PRAHA: JÁNOŠ PETROUŠ SUCHOPÁREK ŠILHÁVY JURESKO TATARCHUK BINIC (BERGER)
PENICKA KUKA NECAS (NOVAC) LERCH. SUBS UNUSED: BEJBL PRAZENICA VAHALA

A crowd of almost 17,000 had been attracted to the game, encouraged by the fact that Hearts had actually dropped their normal prices by £1 to £6 for a terracing ticket. As they drifted off into the night, they were unaware that a transfer that would see the popular Scott Crabbe leave Tynecastle for a fee of £215,000, plus Allan Preston moving in the opposite direction in a part-exchange deal with Dundee United. On the same day the move was concluded, the draw for the second round saw Hearts once again paired with Standard Liège, the first team they met when they made their European debut 34 years earlier.

The transfer of Crabbe did not sit well with many Hearts supporters and fewer than 8,000 turned out a few days later to watch the team draw 1-1 with St Johnstone at Tynecastle. That draw was followed by another 1-1 scoreline in midweek against Celtic when new boy Preston was on the mark. Despite the goal, it was former favourite Scott Crabbe, who got the biggest welcome when he made his return to Tynecastle with Dundee United the following Saturday. Although Hearts won the game 1-0, they failed to impress Liège's assistant coach, Leon Semmeling, who expressed the view that his side would be too good for the Gorgie men.

Hearts also had Liège 'watched' in their league game against Beveren, in which the Belgians ending up 3-1 winners. Managed by former Dutch international Arie Haan, Standard were a young side and sat at the top of the league having been beaten only once since the start of the season. Their international forward Marc Wilmots underlined his danger by scoring all three goals in the win over Beveren.

TYNECASTLE PARK – WEDNESDAY 21 OCTOBER 1992
HEARTS: 0
V
ROYAL STANDARD DE LIÈGE: 1 (BETTAGNO 7)
REFEREE: G KAPL (AUSTRIA)

Once again the lure of European competition brought the crowds back to Tynecastle, with over 16,000 passing through the turnstiles, almost double the number that had turned up for the Dundee United game.

The Belgians immediately impressed with their swift, accurate passing movements as Hearts tried hard to keep on terms. With only seven minutes gone, Craig Levein did well to break up an attack at the expense of a corner. The kick was taken by Patrick Vervoort as the Hearts defence switched off and allowed the unmarked Alain Bettagno to place a powerful header past Henry Smith.

Hearts' reply was instant. Ian Baird guided a header into the path of John Robertson, but his shot went inches over the bar. He went even closer after 16 minutes when he was first to react after Gilbert Bodart could only parry a drive from Gary Mackay. With the goalkeeper helpless, Regis Génaux came to his rescue and managed to make a last-ditch goal-line clearance.

Hearts dominated the play but could not find a way through the superbly organised defence, but the Belgians needed a slice of good fortune when a rasping drive from Gary Mackay looked goal-bound until it took a deflection that saw the ball go inches over.

For the second half the home side sprung something of a surprise, with Alan McLaren replacing Craig Levein. The young defender had been out of the side through injury since the home tie against Slavia Prague and had been rated highly doubtful before the game.

Despite the change Hearts still could not find a way through for the equaliser. Ian Baird let his frustration show and his name went into the Austrian referee's book for barging into Bodart after the goalkeeper had easily gathered a cross.

Glynn Snodin almost reproduced his heroics of the previous round after 67 minutes when he lined up another free kick. Unfortunately for him, the Liège wall stood firm as the ball took a deflection to go behind for a corner.

Joe Jordan's last throw of the dice was to replace Derek Ferguson with his namesake, Ian, but to no avail. In fact it was the away side that found the back of the net when Marc Wilmots stuck the ball behind Henry Smith. However, the referee had already blown for offside and it was an action that saw the Belgian become the fourth player of the game to be booked.

HEARTS: SMITH HOGG MCKINLAY LEVEIN (MCLAREN) MACKAY(G) VAN DE VEN ROBERTSON FERGUSON (D) (FERGUSON (I)) BAIRD SNODIN BANNON. SUBS UNUSED: WALKER MILLAR WILSON (T) ROYAL STANDARD DE LIÈGE: BODART GÉNAUX VERVOORT DEMOL CRUZ (PISTER) BETTAGNO HELLERS GOOSSENS LÉONARD VAN ROOY WILMOTS. SUBS UNUSED: MUNARON BISCONTI ASSELMAN QUARANTA

The defeat prompted predictable newspaper headlines such as 'Hearts Below Standard' and 'Belgians Set Their Standard High', and it is true to say that their performance had not matched that of the game against Slavia Prague. There was no doubt, however, that the Belgians were a very competent side and the task of beating them on their own turf would be a difficult one.

When they trained in the Stade de Sclessin on the evening before the game, the squad were in confident mood, boosted by two wins in the SPL, against Motherwell and Dundee. They were still smarting from comments made by Liège manager Hann, who had compared them to a rugby team, something that irked Henry Smith. 'We're not here to get into a war of words,' he responded. 'The best thing we can do is to beat Standard then smile in their faces.'

STADE MAURICE DUFRASNE – WEDNESDAY 4 NOVEMBER 1992
ROYAL STANDARD DE LIÈGE: 1 (WILMOTS 63)
V
HEARTS: 0
REFEREE: M LEDUC (FRANCE)

Despite the game being televised live and it being a bitterly cold evening, a reasonable crowd of 17,000, including a sizable away support, turned out to watch Hearts make their return to the scene of their first ever European game.

Ian Baird's booking at Tynecastle had been his second of the tournament, which earned him a one-game suspension. Joe Jordan had natural replacements in Ian Ferguson and Wayne Foster, with the former getting the nod. Perhaps more surprising was the managers' decision to start with Ally Mauchlen instead of the more experienced Eamonn Bannon.

With the backing of a noisy support, it was the home side that were first to threaten. Alain Bettagno escaped the attention of Ally Mauchlen to create a shooting opportunity, but he failed to trouble Henry Smith as the ball flew inches over the bar. Full back Regis Génaux was next to try his luck and Smith had to look lively to get down at his left-hand post to prevent Standard from taking the lead.

It took Hearts ten minutes before they created their first chance when John Robertson outsprinted the home defence on the left before playing the ball into the path of the onrushing Tosh McKinlay. Gilbert Bodart in the Liège goal rushed off his line and bravely threw himself at the feet of the Hearts man, deflecting the ball away to safety.

Hearts created another good chance when Gary Mackay and John Robertson combined well to set up John Miller, but his firm, low shot just scraped the right-hand post. It was to be the last clear-cut chance of the half, but after a quick break from their own half Liège came close to going in front when Marc Wilmots was inches away from connecting with a low cross from the right, with Henry Smith rooted to his line.

The crowd were treated to a performance from a pipe band at half-time and no sooner had the strains of 'Scotland the Brave' evaporated into the night than the teams reappeared for the second half. Gilbert Bodart had obviously come off worse in his clash with Tosh McKinlay and stayed in the dressing room. His replacement, Jacques Munaron, was put under pressure immediately as Hearts stepped up the search for the goal that would level the tie. Twice André Cruz was forced into making desperate clearances, booting the ball high into the stands. His next action was to attempt the same thing, but this time with John Robertson and not the ball. Amazingly, the outrageous foul went unpunished by the French referee as Standard battled to hang onto their one-goal advantage.

Then with Hearts dominant, John Millar lost the ball in midfield to Partick Vervoort, who immediately played it through the middle of the Hearts defence. With Tosh McKinlay and Craig Levein chasing back, Marc Wilmots nipped in between the two and slipped the ball underneath the advancing Henry Smith.

Joe Jordan reacted by introducing Glynn Snodin for the tiring John Millar, with the team set up to play long balls from the back for the forwards and midfield to run onto. The tactic almost worked when a ball from Craig Levein was nodded on to John Robertson. But with only Munaron to beat, he slammed the ball against the substitute keeper's legs and the chance was gone.

As Hearts pushed forward, large gaps started to appear at the back. With minutes remaining Marc Wilmots almost exploited the space when he found himself free, with only Henry Smith to beat, but the normally deadly striker fluffed his attempted chip shot and the ball drifted wide as the game ended with the Belgians on top.

ROYAL STANDARD DE LIÈGE: BODART (MUNARON) GÉNAUX VERVOORT DEMOL CRUZ LÉONARD HELLERS BETTAGNO GOOSSENS VAN ROOY WILMOTS. SUBS UNUSED: LASHAF QUARANTA PISTER ASSELMAN
HEARTS: SMITH MCLAREN MCKINLAY LEVEIN MACKAY(G) (FOSTER)VAN DE VEN ROBERTSON FERGUSON (D) FERGUSON (I) MILLAR (SNODIN) MAUCHLEN. SUBS UNUSED: WALKER HOGG BANNON

As had happened in their first outing in Europe back in 1958, Hearts had been defeated by Liège. Standard's own challenge only lasted another round when they were eliminated from the competition at the hands of French side AJ Auxerre.

It had been an unremarkable campaign for Hearts, but the win against Slavia Prague at Tynecastle is still well remembered by many, one of whom is lifelong Hearts fan and former player Scott Crabbe:

Although I have been to many European games as a supporter, I have also been fortunate enough to play in a couple. It was the game that I didn't get to kick a ball that still lives with me to this day.

I had a place on the bench that night against Slavia. It was a great win for the team, but I couldn't enjoy any of it as I already knew that I had played my last game for Hearts as earlier in the day I had agreed terms with Dundee United, a move that I didn't want to happen.

The story really starts the previous season when Alex Totten the manager of St Johnstone made an enquiry about my availability. It might seem crazy now, but I didn't have an agent so I more or less had to deal with everything myself, and as a young lad I felt obliged to listen to what St Johnstone had to say. When I got back to Tynecastle some of the older lads like John Robertson and Gary Mackay asked me what I was thinking about. They told me I was under contract at Hearts and I didn't have to do anything I didn't want to.

A move to Perth, or perhaps it's more accurate to say a move away from Tynecastle, was the last thing on my mind, so I said a polite 'No thanks' and that was the end of it.

When Joe Jordan called me into his office the following season to say that Dundee United were interested in taking me to Tannadice, nothing had changed for me and again it was a case of 'Thanks but no thanks'. However, it wasn't as simple this time as the manager made it quite clear that he wanted the move to go through and if it didn't my opportunities in the first team would be *limited*.

So while the rest of the boys relaxed in the Marine Hotel before the Slavia game, I really had no alternative but to go up to Dundee and talk to Jim McLean. The trouble was, I still didn't have anyone to offer me advice, nor, for that matter, any transport to make the journey. That's when a couple of my friends stepped in.

Gordon Lockerbie was a lawyer and he was the best person I could think of to keep me right... well, on the legal technicalities of the contract at least. Then Tom Heaney offered me the use of his car to get me up there. Tom was a salesman and was driving about in a BMW, something I wasn't used to, so I was delighted to accept.

I listened to what United had to say, but really I was flying at Hearts and was reluctant to move. Anyway, Mr McLean was great with me and allowed me time to think things over. I will always remember the look on his face when he showed me out and I got into Tom's car – he said something like, 'You're obviously doing all right at Hearts, I'm not sure we can afford you!'

On the drive back down the road all sorts of things went through my head, but in the end I knew that my time at Tynecastle was over and I had to move on. When I arrived back I was feeling terrible and couldn't bring myself to speak to the rest of the lads. To make things worse, for some reason Joe Jordan decided he wanted me to sit on the bench for the game, even although I was not in the right frame of mind.

The 90 minutes went by in a flash and at the end I made a beeline for Robbo and told him there and then that I was leaving. I asked him if I should go and throw my jersey into the crowd and I think it was then a lot of people realised that the rumours were true and this would be my last time on the pitch in a maroon shirt.

When I got back to the dressing room all the boys were celebrating but it was then that all the emotion came out and the tears started to flow. Wallace Mercer came over and took me back outside onto the park and was absolutely superb. He told me how badly the club were struggling for money and the £250,000 they would receive from United would go a long way to easing the problem.

Even although it was hard to accept that I was leaving, Mr Mercer made me feel a little better by making me realise that I had helped the club in some small way. For that reason, the Slavia game will always be the most memorable European game for me.

CHAPTER 12

1993–94 UEFA Cup

DESPITE A DISASTROUS RUN of results that saw them without a win since beating Hibs on 23 March, by the end of the 92–93 season Hearts had done enough to finish fifth in the league and qualified for the UEFA Cup for the second successive season.

As seems an old story, when the draw for the first round was made Hearts were handed an extremely difficult task, this time being matched with Atlético Madrid, the number three seeds in the competition, with the first leg being played at Tynecastle.

At times overshadowed by their city neighbours Real, Atlético had a proud record in both domestic and European football. They were probably best remembered for the infamous European Cup semi-final against Celtic in 1974 when they had three players sent off in the first leg. Despite the disadvantage they managed a 0-0 draw before winning the second leg 2-0 to reach the final, where they narrowly lost out to Bayern Munich after a replay.

Hearts had suffered a setback the previous Saturday when not only did they lose to a poor Motherwell side but also had John Colquhoun carried off on a stretcher during the game. Despite this he was still included in the squad that after a training session on Sunday headed down the coast to their base in North Berwick.

Atlético arrived in Edinburgh on Monday afternoon with no injury worries and fresh from a creditable 2-2 draw with Valencia, a game watched by Sandy Clark's assistant Hugh McCann and reserve team coach Walter Kidd. Their line-up would be weakened, as central defenders Roberto Solozabal and Jaun Jaunito were both out due to suspension. Their youth coach José Ogero had taken in the game against Motherwell and declared, 'Hearts are all physique and no technique. We are confident we will go through.'

What Señor Ogero had not seen, though, was the enigmatic Justin Fashanu whom he recognised as 'a powerful player' who 'could cause problems'. Fash was duly returned to the side after suspension, and also back in the starting line-up were Scott Leitch and Jim Weir, plus John Colquhoun had made a remarkable recovery and retained his place in an attack-minded team.

TYNECASTLE PARK – TUESDAY 14 SEPTEMBER 1993
HEARTS: 2 (ROBERTSON 70; COLQUHOUN 75)
V
CLUB ATLÉTICO DE MADRID: 1 (KOSECKI 77)
REFEREE: A FRISK (SWEDEN)

If the appearance of the 'Fash' was something the Spaniards might have expected, then the Scottish weather certainly wasn't. At kick off they were welcomed with the type of wind and driving rain that only Scotland can produce in September.

The weather may have played its part, but a solid performance from Hearts restricted the men from Madrid in an unremarkable first period. The only chance of any note came minutes from the end of the half when John Robertson took a pass from Gary Mackay before brilliantly turning his marker. Quick as a flash, he fired in a shot from 18 yards that looked destined for the top right-hand corner of the net, but Diego in the Atlético goal was equal to the task and pulled off a magnificent stop.

Soon after the restart, the home side should have had a penalty when John Robertson gathered a rebound from a free kick but was pulled back before he could get his shot away. It looked a simple decision for the Swedish referee, Anders Frisk, but to everyone's astonishment he didn't give the award. It was not his only controversial decision Mr Frisk, a last minute replacement for the more experienced Bo Karlsson, would make in his refereeing career.

With 20 minutes it was from another free kick left that Hearts eventually took the lead. Yet another foul on Robbo resulted in young Gary Locke floating in a ball from out on the right touchline. Diego could only push out Justin Fashanu's powerful, downward header. Robbo was the first to react and he knocked the ball into the unguarded net.

John Robertson was receiving some punishment from the Atlético defence and five minutes later a particularly crude lunge by the Brazilian international Moacir brought yet another free kick out on the left. The ball was worked across the park to Gary Locke midway inside the Atlético half and once again he swung in a delightful cross. This time it was met by John Colquhoun who controlled it on his chest before rifling it low into the far corner of the net.

It seemed nothing, not even the weather, could dampen the home

John Robertson opens the scoring against Atlético Madrid at Tynecastle © SNS Group

support's spirits now. The euphoria only lasted for two minutes, until Atlético substitute Roman Kosecki spun away from Alan McLaren 30 yards from goal. He brushed past Gary Mackay and before Craig Levein could get across to cover, he placed an accurate right-foot shot behind Henry Smith.

After being outplayed for most of the game Atlético had a vital away goal. It was a disappointing end to what had been one of the most memorable displays by a Hearts team in a European competition.

HEARTS: SMITH LOCKE MCKINLAY LEVEIN WEIR MCLAREN COLQUHOUN MACKAY FASHANU
LEITCH ROBERTSON (THOMAS). SUBS UNUSED: WALKER JOHNSTON BERRY HOGG
CLUB ATLÉTICO DE MADRID: DIEGO GÓMEZ GONZALEZ CAMINERO LÓPEZ MOACIR MANOLO
(SABAS) QUEVEDO GARCÍA (KOSECKI) PIRRI KIKO. SUBS UNUSED: ABEL JUANMA

If the first leg had been one of the best performances in Europe, then the second leg a fortnight later had to rate as one of the poorest.

As the team boarded the plane for the two and a half hour flight to Madrid on Monday morning, there was disquiet in the club. Dundee United had tabled what was described as a 'derisory' bid for John Robertson and Wallace Mercer was angered at Wheatsheaf Catering boss Chris Robinson's decision to make public his takeover plans for Hearts. The board of directors took the unusual step of holding an emergency meeting in Madrid, with the outcome being a firm 'no' to both offers.

The mood of the directors was in complete contrast to that of the players, as a John Robertson goal had been good enough to see them enjoy a morale-boosting win over Celtic at Tynecastle the previous Saturday. That game also saw Henry Smith notch up his 200th clean sheet for the club.

ESTÁDIO VICENTE CALDERÓN – TUESDAY 29 SEPTEMBER 1993
CLUB ATLÉTICO DE MADRID: 3 (PEDRO 35; MANOLO 72; GARCÍA 76)
V
HEARTS: 0
REFEREE: G GOETHALS (BELGIUM)

Coach Sandy Clark had no injury worries to concern him and in the end the manager stuck by the same 11 that had started against Celtic, with the only change from the first leg being a straight swap that saw Graeme Hogg replacing Jim Weir.

Straight from the kick off, the Spaniards went on the attack, seeking an early goal that would put them on top in the tie. Apart from an opportunity wasted by Monolo after five minutes, though, the Hearts defence stood strong, Craig Levein and Graeme Hogg were outstanding. Levein's contribution was all the more remarkable as it turned out that he was playing the game with a double fracture of his cheekbone after an accidental clash with Henry Smith early on.

Chances were few and far between for the visitors but the 1,000 strong away support thought that a tremendous volley by John Colquhoun had put them in front on the half hour mark. However, the near side linesman cut short the celebrations by rather belatedly raising his flag to signal for offside. It was to be the turning point of the game. Five minutes later the Spaniards went ahead, after getting the advantage from another offside decision. Atlético were awarded a free kick 30 yards out and Gómez played the ball to left back Pedro, who blasted a low shot past Henry Smith. The keeper seemed to be caught wrong-footed but there were three Madrid players in an offside position in front of him and he looked amazed that the goal was allowed to stand.

Hearts hit back almost immediately through Gary Mackay but sadly his drive was just wide of the mark. Justin Fashanu then forced Diago into great save but it was to be big Fash's last contribution as he was kept inside after the interval, Sandy Clark making the decision that he was in danger of being sent off after being booked in the first half.

Ian Ferguson took his place but failed to turn the shape of the game as Atlético continued to control play. However, despite their dominance the result remained in the balance until a horrendous error by Gary Mackay gifted them the game. With seemingly all the time in the world to clear it he dallied too long and allowed Manolo to rob him of the ball and the little Spanish international accepted the gift with ease.

Hearts were now up against it but still had nearly 20 minutes to get the goal that would see the game go into extra time. Unfortunately, another howler saw the game go Los Colchoneros' way. This time Henry Smith allowed a tame header from Luis García to bounce over his shoulder and into the net.

Despite Hearts trying hard to reduce the deficit, Atlético saw out the remaining 15 minutes with ease and Hearts' European campaign was over for another season.

CLUB ATLÉTICO DE MADRID: DIEGO GÓMEZ PEDRO CAMINERO LÓPEZ MOACIR MANOLO QUEVEDO GARCÍA KOSECKI PIRRI. SUBS UNUSED: JUANMA ABEL SOLOZABEL KIKO
HEARTS: SMITH LOCKE MCKINLAY LEVEIN HOGG MCLAREN COLQUHOUN MACKAY (G) FASHANU (FERGUSON I) LEITCH ROBERTSON (THOMAS). SUBS UNUSED: WALKER BERRY WEIR

Although going on to play many other games in European competitions, it was the games against Atlético that remain special in the memory for Hearts hero Gary Locke:

I had an early taste of European football with Hearts as I had travelled like thousands of others on a bus to Paris as a young lad. I was so young, I even got a bit of coverage in a Hearts fanzine at the time, the *Hearts Review,* where a picture of me in a woollen Hearts cardigan (no laughing, please) was published.

Just before the first game at Tynecastle I had been called into the Scotland Under-21 squad and although I didn't get a game it was great to be involved at that level. I felt the same way about the Atlético game as this was my first taste of European football as a player.

From being a fan, I knew what a European night was like at Tynie and this game was no different. With Hearts fans in every part of the ground there was a huge crowd and the atmosphere was buzzing.

The game itself was great and I had a hand in both goals, but it was the atmosphere that night that I will always remember. The fans were right up for it from the start and the Shed went mental at the goals. Having stood in there for years, I knew where my family and friends would be and at the goals it was brilliant to be able to run over and celebrate with them.

The second leg was totally different, though, as I had never experienced a crowd as hostile as Atlético's. We had a police escort from our hotel and when we arrived we had to go through a tunnel into the stadium, and that is where I first experienced their fans with scarves covering their faces. It still didn't stop them giving us dog's abuse. It was crazy.

Out on the park, rather than fencing there were clear plastic sheets all the way round the ground. When we came out for our pre-match warm-up, they began banging on them and giving us pelters, but it was what I enjoyed and I couldn't wait to get started.

The game itself is a bit of a blur, but I remember John Colquhoun scoring a goal that would have put us one up. Unfortunately, the ref chopped it off for offside, which was a shocking decision, but after that Atlético played well. At their goals I remember the fans running up and down the terracing throwing flares and fireworks making an atmosphere almost as incredible as at Tynecastle!

It was very emotional at the end as I felt we had let the fans down, but having been in Paris in '84, I knew the thousands that had made the journey to Madrid would still have loved the experience. It was great to see them all stay behind after the final whistle and for us to go out and applaud them.

Despite the defeat I looked at it as an incredible experience and couldn't wait to play in Europe again.

CHAPTER 13

1996–97 Cup Winners Cup

THE 93–94 SEASON ENDED with Hearts in mid-table and also having reached the quarter-final of the Scottish Cup. In comparison to other seasons, this could be looked upon as a reasonable achievement. Wallace Mercer, though, had grander ambitions for the club and brought in Tommy McLean to replace Sandy Clark as manager before the start of the 94–95 campaign.

McLean's tenure was short-lived, only lasting the season, and results showed little improvement. Mercer then turned to former Hearts stalwart Jim Jefferies to lead the club, with Jim taking over in August 1995 after agonising over leaving Falkirk, where he had shown his managerial potential.

His arrival gave an instant boost to the team, which ended the season in a respectable fourth place in the SPL. However, the club's best achievement came in the Scottish Cup, where they reached the final for the first time for ten years. Despite having beaten Rangers 3-0 at Ibrox during the season, the Tynecastle men could not repeat the performance and lost 5-1 to the Glasgow club. With Rangers already having claimed the league title, being runners-up allowed Hearts entry into the 96–97 Cup Winners Cup.

For the qualifying round of the competition, Hearts were seeded 18th and when the draw was made in Geneva they were paired against Red Star of Belgrade, a daunting prospect. The name of Red Star was well-known throughout Europe. Although forever tragically linked with Manchester United back in 1958, as recently as 1991 they had won the European Cup. War had raged in the Balkans for several years and a ceasefire had only been brokered a year earlier, making the first leg something of a trip into the unknown for Hearts.

Jim Jefferies had made the journey a week earlier, missing Hearts' 'friendly' against Porto to take in Red Star's cup tie against third division Podgorica, a game Red Star comfortably won 4-0. He could not have been failed to be impressed by their big forward, Zoran Jovicic, who scored all four goals.

STADION CRVENA ZVEZDA – THURSDAY 8 AUGUST 1996
RED STAR BELGRADE: 0
V
HEARTS: 0
REFEREE: H ALBRECHT (GERMANY)

As this was the qualifying round, the first tie came before the season had started in Scotland, Hearts only having played five 'friendlies' with mixed, but encouraging, results. Included in the starting line-up were recent signings Welsh international Jeremy Goss, and Davie Weir who had been acquired from Jim Jefferies' previous club, Falkirk.

Hearts kicked off on a balmy evening and were quickly into their stride, with John Colquhoun creating a shooting chance for himself after only six minutes, but his low shot drifted inches wide. Colquhoun continued to trouble the home defence and Darko Anikc was rightly shown a yellow card for bringing one of his runs to an abrupt end.

With 13 minutes played Red Star could do nothing to stop Jeremy Goss make a surging run down the right. He managed to cut the ball back from the bye-line to Colin Cameron, but with only the keeper to beat

Colin Cameron in action against Red Star Belgrade in Serbia ECWC August 1996
© mirrorpix

he snatched at the shot and the ball flew over the bar. That action was virtually the last time Hearts were seen as an attacking force. Although Radmir Petrovic's side began to dominate, Hearts defended superbly and on the occasions that Red Star did breakthrough they found Gilles Rousset in imperious form. He was first called into action on 18 minutes, when a great through ball from Miodrag Pantelic left Perica Ognjenovic through on goal. He shot low and hard but Rousset stretched out his leg to knock the ball clear. The young Yugoslav was again left bewildered 20 minutes later when Darko Anic created another chance. This time his right-foot drive from ten yards brought a marvellous diving save from Hearts' French goalkeeper.

The onslaught continued after the break and Ognjenovic was denied for the third time by another great save from Rousset after 53 minutes. The big keeper slightly blotted his copybook when he gave away a free kick inside the box after being penalised for taking too many steps, but once again the defence stood firm and the danger was cleared.

As time ran out, so did the home side's ideas, but with two minutes left Rousset had to produce a spectacular double save to keep the sides level. At the final whistle he led the team to acknowledge the small band of Hearts supporters in the stadium, who in turn showed their appreciation for what wad been a marvellous team performance. It was left to Jim Jefferies to sum it all up after the game, when he simply said: 'I'm delighted by the way we performed. Gilles was a different class.'

RED STAR BELGRADE: MILOJEVIC ZIVKOVIC DJOROVIC NJEGUS STANKOVIĆ (P)
MARINOVIC OGNJENOVIC PANTELIC (VULEVIC) JOVICIC STANKOVIĆ (D) (VANIC) ANIC. SUBS
UNUSED: JEVRIC BRATIC BOSKOVIC
HEARTS: ROUSSET FRAIL (MCMANUS) RITCHIE WEIR (D) MCPHERSON BRUNO MACKAY (G)
CAMERON COLQUHOUN GOSS POINTON. SUBS UNUSED: MCKENZIE FULTON ROBERTSON THOMAS

In the fortnight between the games both sides remained unbeaten, Hearts by virtue of a penalty shootout against Stenhousemuir in the League Cup and a 3-2 win against Kilmarnock in the first Premier League game of the season. Red Star had kept up their unbeaten start to their season with wins against Rad and Hadjuk Kula. Hearts' victories had come at a cost: there were injury doubts over Jeremy Goss, Pasquale Bruno and Neil Pointon. Dave MacPherson, who had been outstanding in Belgrade, had been suffering from a bout of pleurisy and it was hoped that he would recover sufficiently to take his place in the side. On the night only the Welshman, Goss, missed out. His place was taken by another recent recruit, Neil Mc-Cann. Red Star also made a change from the first leg, with Goran Boskovic being preferred to Miodrag Pantelic.

TYNECASTLE PARK – THURSDAY 22 AUGUST 1996
HEARTS: 1 (MCPHERSON 28)
V
RED STAR BELGRADE: 1 (MARINOVIC 59)
REFEREE: K NILSONN (SWEDEN)

In the opening exchanges neither side created any chances of note. They both made a nervous start, knowing that the first goal would be vital. It took over half an hour before the first real threat came on either goal, when 19-year-old Perica Ognjenovic managed to get himself free from the attentions of Pasquale Bruno and Dave MacPherson to send a great cross into the box. Zoran Jovicic looked favourite to get on the end of it before Neil Pointon somehow managed to get his head to the ball, sending it behind for a corner.

A few minutes later it was Hearts' turn to come close to opening the scoring. Neil McCann floated a free kick to the back post where Davie Weir rose to send a downward header goalward, but Zvonko Milojevic produced a terrific, diving save to keep the sides level.

With the half drawing to a close, Colin Cameron fired in a fierce shot that took a deflection off a defender before going behind for a corner. Neil McCann took the kick and Dave MacPherson met it perfectly, heading it high into the net.

Red Star hit back almost immediately through Dejan Stanković, whose strike brought out the best in Gilles Rousset. The sides went in with the home side ahead, much to the delight of the 15,000 inside the ground.

Ten minutes after the restart, another corner almost brought the second goal for Hearts. This time a kick from Colin Cameron was controlled by John Colquhoun at the back post. He smashed in a shot, but somehow Milojevic managed to pull off a superb, one-handed save from point-blank range.

It was another corner kick, with nearly an hour gone, that allowed Red Star to hit back. Vinko Marinovic was left unmarked, and although Gilles Rousset managed to get a hand to the ball, the Yugoslav's header had too much power behind it, and the game was all-square.

Hearts immediately started to press forward in numbers and the visitors responded by substituting Ognjenovic for the defensive-minded Nenad Sakic. With Red Star's danger man withdrawn, Jim Jefferies took off his marker, Pasquale Bruno, and sent on Kevin Thomas in an effort to snatch the goal they needed.

Despite pressurising for the rest of the game, the breakthrough would not come and even the introduction of top European scorer John Robertson

Dave McPherson celebrates putting Hearts 1-0 up against Red Star Belgrade in the ECWC at Tynecastle in August 1996 ©mirrorpix

with six minutes left was to no avail as Hearts crashed out of Europe on the 'away goal' rule.

HEARTS: ROUSSET WEIR (D) RITCHIE MACKAY (G) (ROBERTSON) MCPHERSON BRUNO (THOMAS) MCCANN (N) CAMERON COLQUHOUN FULTON POINTON. SUBS UNUSED: FRAIL MCMANUS
RED STAR BELGRADE: MILOJEVIC ZIVKOVIC DJOROVIC NJEGUS STANKOVIĆ (P) MARINOVIC OGNJENOVIC (SAKIC) ANIC JOVICIC STANKOVIĆ (D) (VANIC) BOSKOVIC (VULEVIC). SUBS UNUSED: JEVRIC PANTELIC

Although Hearts had lost only one of their last 12 home European ties, that was of little consolation to the manager. Obviously disappointed, he said, 'Red Star didn't put us out, we put ourselves out. The lads worked very hard but you can't give away free headers in the six yard box. We did enough to go through, but were out.'

Naturally, his opposite number saw it differently. Vladimir Petrovic was quoted as saying, 'I am happy we are through but we should have won in Belgrade.' After beating FC Kaiserslauten in the next round, Red Star were eliminated by eventual winners Barcelona in the second round.

Although it was a short sojourn in Europe, it was a memorable one for Jeremy Goss. He recalls:

I had only joined the club from Norwich City a few weeks earlier and had just played a couple of friendlies against Porto and Southampton, but before I knew it I was sitting on the plane heading to Belgrade to make my competitive debut in the Cup Winners Cup. For me that felt great.

I had spent my whole career at Norwich and played in some memorable games in Europe for them, although not as many as we should have, as although we qualified on another couple of occasions we suffered from the ban on English clubs that was in effect at the time. After leaving the Canaries I was looking for a new challenge and despite an attractive offer from Alan Curbishley at Charlton, I decided that my best move would be to sign for Hearts.

The reason I did that was that I had been sold on the club by Jim Jefferies, who immediately impressed me with his enthusiasm and ambition – and of course, he could also offer European football.

In Belgrade we were based in what I thought was a pretty basic hotel, but was told it was one of the best the city had to offer at the time. Nevertheless, I was excited just to be there, mixing with a new group of players. I wasn't alone as the new boy, as big David Weir and Neil McCann both joined the club about the same time. Neil Pointon was already at Tynecastle and I knew him from my time 'down south', and he was particularly helpful with advice about the Scottish game.

As for the match itself, my first thought was to get used to wearing a different colour jersey – I was so used to wearing the yellow and green of Norwich it somehow felt strange to be in the famous maroon strip. I settled in well and played on the right midfield. We were helped by the fact that it was a big pitch, which suited our game, and in the end we got a well deserved draw that gave us every chance of progressing to the next round.

I picked up a calf muscle injury in training before the second leg and although I was desperate to play, the manager told me he wasn't going to risk me, and I had to watch the game from the stand. Going out on the 'away goal' rule was a blow as I thought our performance over the two legs deserved better than that.

That was the start of what was to become an injury-plagued season for me. I had a persistent groin injury that limited my appearances, which was very frustrating. Like every footballer, I just wanted to play. I loved being at the club, there was a great squad of players with the correct leadership and everything felt good. I was staying in a beautiful city, but no matter how many times I ran up Arthur Seat nor how many hours I spent in the gymnasium in the old stand, I couldn't get to the level of fitness I wanted. Paul Hegarty was the reserve team coach at the time and he was very helpful, as were Jim Jefferies and Billy Brown, but by the start of the following season we all realised that my time at Tynecastle was at an end and we parted company, on the best of terms.

Looking back, it was an opportunity missed for me, as I felt I could have done well at the club. I am frustrated that the fans didn't get the chance to see the best of me.

But would I change anything? Absolutely not!

CHAPTER FOURTEEN

1998–99 Cup Winners Cup

FOR LONG SPELLS of the 97–98 season, Hearts ran the Old Firm close for the league championship, so much so that qualification for the UEFA Cup had been wrapped up with six weeks of the season left. Their title challenge ultimately fell short, but a memorable 2-1 win over Rangers in the Scottish Cup final meant that Hearts were entered into what was to be the last ever Cup Winners Cup competition.

Hearts were included in the qualifying round of the tournament and were drawn against FC Lantana. Based in the Estonian capital of Tallinn, Lantana were founded in 1994 when the influential Belov family 'bought out' Nikol Tallinn (who themselves had only been in existence for two years, having taken over from TVMK Tallinn). Having been beaten 3-2 in the Estonian Cup by local rivals Flora Tallinn, their participation in the Cup Winners Cup was due to Flora also having won the championship.

Despite having been in existence for such a short time, this was not their first outing in Europe – they had already played in all three European competitions and this was their second time in the Cup Winners Cup. Their first had ended in controversial circumstances. Paired with Latvian outfit DAG-Liepya, they won the first leg 2-1. It was later discovered that they had fielded an illegible player, the result was overturned and DAG were awarded a 3-0 victory which was good enough to see them through to the next round. In all the games they had played in European competitions, Lantana had in fact only one official win to their name, a 2-1 win against the Icelandic side IBV Vestmannaeyjar, in 1996.

With the game coming in the second week of August, Hearts had only played one game in the inaugural season of the SPL. In a repeat of the Cup final they had got off to the best of starts with a 2-1 victory over Rangers. As can only happen in Scottish football, despite the opening game of the season being on 1 August there were no SPL games played the following week, so rather strangely, Hearts' 'warm-up' to the European tie was a friendly against Charlton Athletic in a testimonial for their manager Alan Curbishley.

Despite playing their league games in the Viimsi Staadionil on the outskirts of Tallinn, Lantana moved the game to the larger Kadrioru Staadionil, scene of the infamous 'game that never was' World Cup qualifier against Scotland two year earlier and, ironically, Lantana's home ground before moving to Viimsi.

KADRIORU STAADIONIL – THURSDAY 13 AUGUST 1998
FC LANTANA: 0
V
HEARTS: 1 (MAKEL 21)
REFEREE: M BENES (CZECH REPUBLIC)

Admission for adults was the equivalent of £1.30 and free for kids, but even so it was a meagre crowd of little over 1,000 that turned out to see the game.

Hearts started brightly enough, with Stephane Adam and Neil McCann both passing up good chances to open the scoring. Despite Hearts controlling almost all of the play, it took over 20 minutes before the breakthrough came. Oleg Kolotsei was guilty of trying to be over-elaborate making a clearance in the box, and suffered the consequences when he was robbed by Lee Makel, who neatly curled the ball behind the despairing Sergei Ussoltsev.

Perhaps thinking that this would signal the start of a goal avalanche, Hearts seemed to lose concentration for the next few minutes. If they needed any indication that the result was not a foregone conclusion, Vitali Leitan was unlucky when his firm strike came back off the post four minutes later. For the rest of the half few chances came the way of either side, but with seconds remaining it was Hearts' turn to hit the woodwork when only the crossbar prevented Stephane Adam getting his name on the score sheet.

During the break the Hearts support were encouraged to sing 'Happy Birthday' to Miss Estonia on the occasion of her 20th birthday. The lovely lady was presented with a bouquet of flowers by Beatrice, described by the master of ceremonies Joel de Luna as 'one of Estonia's top models'. Joel also announced that after the game the Nimega bar in town would have a blues band providing live music, while the Nimeta bar would have some 'male entertainment'. It would be a tough choice for the few that had travelled from Edinburgh but either would be a better spectacle than what they had witnessed in the previous 45 minutes.

The second period began with Lantana danger man Leitan causing more trouble for the Hearts back line when he got the better of David Weir, only to waste the chance by firing his shot wide. It was the only excitement of an extremely dull half and the small away support amused themselves by singing less than complimentary ditties concerning CEO Chris Robinson.

The home side looked content to see out the game losing only one goal. Lee Makel was the only Hearts player who seemed likely to ruin their ambition and with eight minutes left he stung the hands of Lantana keeper Ussoltsev with a vicious shot from 20 yards.

Hearts did little to suggest they wanted to leave Estonia with more than their single goal advantage although Thomas Flögel should have doubled their lead in the last minute but he could not find the target after Ussoltsev had fumbled a cross from Neil McCann.

FC LANTANA: USSOLTSEV KRASNOPGROV KALIMULLIN KOLOTSEI BAHMATSKI MITJUNOV BORISSOV LEITAN VALUISKI (TSELNOKOV) GORJATSOV (KULIKOV) KOULITCHENKO SUBS UNUSED: KISELJOV JERSOIV

HEARTS: ROUSSET NAYSMITH WEIR(D) SALVATORI RITCHIE MAKEL LOCKE HAMILTON (J) (MURRAY (G)) ADAM (QUITONGO) FLÖGEL MCCANN(N). SUBS UNUSED: MCKENZIE (R) MCKINNON PRESSLEY MURIE HOLMES

Hearts continued their good form in the SPL, remaining unbeaten in a run that saw them heading the table by the time Lantana visited Edinburgh for the return leg. Their achievements were even recognised at international level, with Steve Fulton and Neil McCann being included in the Scotland squad to play Lithuania in a World Cup qualifier the following week. Both players were obviously included in Jim Jefferies' starting line-up, as were recent signings Steven Pressley and Rab McKinnon.

TYNECASTLE PARK – THURSDAY 27 AUGUST 1998
HEARTS: 5 (HAMILTON 18; FULTON 29; MCCANN 41; FLÖGEL 75; HOLMES 90)
V
FC LANTANA: 0
REFEREE: J WEGEREEF (HOLLAND)

Perhaps in part due to the good start to the season as well as the draw of European football, over 15,000 turned out to watch what was generally thought of as a formality against relatively unknown opposition. If the crowd came looking for goals they did not leave disappointed as Hearts eased themselves into the draw for the first round.

Lee Makel, the scorer of the goal in Tallinn, went close to opening the scoring again when he tried a shot from 20 yards as early as the third minute. It was marginally off target but it was a signal of Hearts' intention. Lantana knew they needed to score and went close through Andrei Mitjunov, whose header looked to be destined for the top corner of the net ,before Gilles Rousset produced a spectacular, one-handed save.

It was a warning that the visitors still posed a threat, but any doubts that Hearts would qualify were alleviated by Jim Hamilton after 18 minutes. Rab McKinnon charged down the left wing before cutting the ball inside to him on the edge of the area. The big striker took one touch to control before firing an angled drive into the far corner of the net.

Further chances came the way of both Steve Fulton and Stephane Adam, then the two combined for the second goal with half an hour gone. Adam opened up the fragile defence with a pinpoint pass for Fulton, whose delicate chip sailed over Sergei Ussoltsev to put the game beyond the Estonians.

The way Hearts were controlling the game it was inevitable that further goals would come. With four minutes left in the half, Neil McCann duly obliged when another good run and pass by Rab McKinnon presented him with the opportunity to blast the ball high into the net.

Lantana were certainly down but as if to prove they were not quite out, Sergei Koulitchenko was out of luck when his shot cannoned back off the post with Rousset beaten. The keeper then denied Vitali Leitan twice before Hearts once again took a grip of the game. They should have added to their tally with 74 minutes played after Sergei Ussoltsev could only parry an audacious David Weir header from 30 yards. The ball fell between Lee Makel and Thomas Flögel who contrived to get in each other's way before the danger was cleared.

Steve Fulton beats Lantana goalkeeper Sergei Usseoltsev to put Hearts 2-0 up in the ECWC tie at Tynecastle in August 1998

A minute later Flögel, on as a substitute for Stephane Adam, made amends when he pounced on another rebound, this time after a Neil McCann strike came back off the bar. His crisp drive from 15 yards finally snuffed out any challenge from the Estonians.

The goal was the signal for Jim Jefferies to take off Lee Makel – who had worked tirelessly – to allow 19-year-old Derek Holmes to make his European debut. He made the most of the opportunity, rounding off the scoring in the last minute when he swept home a cross from Neil McCann.

HEARTS: ROUSSET PRESSLEY LOCKE WEIR(D) RITCHIE FULTON MAKEL (HOLMES) HAMILTON
(J) (QUITONGO) ADAM (FLÖGEL) MCKINNON MCCANN(N) SUBS UNUSED: HOGARTH SALVATORI
MURRAY (G) MURIE
FC LANTANA: USSOLTSEV KRASNOPGROV KOLOTSEI BAHMATSKI LEITAN MITJUNOV VALUISKI
(TSELNOKOV) GORJATSOV KOULITCHENKO TJUNIN KULIKOV. SUBS UNUSED: KISELJOV
KALIMULLIN JERSOV

Having comfortably progressed to the first round (proper), Hearts were then drawn against Spanish side Real Mallorca, with the first leg to be played at Tynecastle. If Hearts were now competing in their 40th year of European competition, this was Mallorca's first.

Since being founded in 1916, they had languished in the lower divisions of Spanish football until being taken over by a Spanish TV company in 1995. Since then their improvement had been remarkable and they reached the final of the Copa del Ray for the first time in May 1997. They held Barcelona to a 1-1 draw but were eventually beaten 5-4 on penalties. However, Barca were also La Liga champions, therefore Mallorca became Spain's representatives in the Cup Winners Cup.

Unlike Hearts, they had not had to compete in the qualifying round; instead, they had been contesting the Supercopa de Espana with Barcelona and gained their revenge over the Catalans beating them home and away to lift the trophy. They had also started their season well and when they arrived in Edinburgh on the Tuesday evening they were fresh from a 2-0 win over Español. In the victory, though, influential Argentinean midfielder Ariel Ibagaza had broken his foot and was ruled out of the tie. He was Mallorca coach Hector Cuper's only injury concern.

For Jim Jefferies, however, the selection problems continued to mount. Already ruled out from the side were Thomas Flögel, Colin Cameron, Rob McKinnon and José Quitongo. Steven Pressley was considered doubtful and Stevie Fulton had now joined the injured list with a hamstring problem. In the end Pressley was passed fit, but Fulton joined the rest of the 'crocks' in the stand to watch the game. It all meant that the manager was forced to play Davie Weir in an unfamiliar midfield position, with Dave McPherson coming back into the side to play his first game since the Cup final back in May.

TYNECASTLE PARK – THURSDAY 17 SEPTEMBER 1998
HEARTS: 0
V
REAL CLUB DEPORTIVO MALLORCA: 1 (MARCELINO 17)
REFEREE: A TRENTALANGE (ITALY)

Paul Ritchie challenges for the ball in the ECWC tie first leg against Mallorca at Tynecastle
© mirrorpix

Tynecastle was near capacity at kick off, ensuring that special atmosphere unique to evenings of European football. Hearts responded straight away and within the first few minutes both Stephane Adam and Jim Hamilton tested Mallorca's keeper, Carlos Roa. It was the visitors, though, that created the best chance for the opener when after 11 minutes a cross from Lauren Bisan found Dani unmarked at the back post – but he should have done better than to send his header into the side netting.

The Spanish side went on to take the lead six minutes later, enjoying a huge slice of good fortune in doing so. Gilles Rousset seemed to have a corner from Jovan Stanković covered as he elected to punch the ball clear. Somehow he fluffed his effort, the ball hit the inrushing Marcelino on the chest and ended up in the back of the net.

Another corner from Stanković caused more panic in the Hearts defence five minutes later when his inswinger cannoned off the post. This time the ball was swept to safety but questions were again being asked about the marking at set-pieces.

For the rest of the half, the home side seemed to be unsure at what approach to take, whether to chase a goal or to continue with their original game-plan of holding the Spaniards and hitting them on the counter-attack. This resulted in a dearth of any real chances at both ends of the park and the once raucous crowd were now silenced as the whistle blew for the break.

In the second half Hearts upped the tempo of the game but could still not make the vital breakthrough. Stephane Adam came close to reaching a through ball, but was just beaten to it by Carlos Roa who had spotted the danger and rushed from his line to clear. In doing so, he caught Adam with his studs, which was the signal for some indiscipline to begin to creep into the game.

On the hour mark Dave McPherson had a great chance to pull Hearts level when a free kick from man-of-the-match Stefano Salvatori fell to him on the corner of the six yard box. Instead of blasting the ball goalward he tried a delicate side-foot shot. Carlos Roa had anticipated a powerful drive and spread his body in anticipation but was fortunate to get a foot to the ball to turn it round for a corner.

Minutes later Adam and Roa clashed for a second time when the Argentine goalkeeper clearly elbowed the Frenchman in the face. He was fortunate not to see a red card – astonishingly, Alfredo Trentalange, the Italian referee, let the incident pass without any punishment. The whistler was then forced to flash his yellow card in quick succession when both Marcelino and Stanković were booked for crude late challenges.

With 20 minutes to go Stanković, who Hearts had come up against a couple years earlier when he played for Red Star Belgrade, raised the level of his personal battle with Dave McPherson when he elbowed 'Slim' in the face, an incident that was 'missed' by the referee. Two minutes later the big defender took his own revenge with a well-aimed punch to the stomach as both men battled for the ball in the Mallorca box – yet another incident unnoticed by the ref, but not by the majority of the home support!

The ill-tempered game was played out without either side creating any further goal-scoring opportunities, with Mallorca content to waste time by feigning injury at every given opportunity, while Hearts and Jim Jefferies grew increasingly frustrated by the Spaniards behaviour.

HEARTS: ROUSSET PRESSLEY NAYSMITH WEIR(D) RITCHIE MCPHERSON SALVATORI LOCKE ADAM HAMILTON (J) (HOLMES) MCCANN(N) SUBS UNUSED MCKENZIE MAKEL MURRAY MURIE HORN
REAL CLUB DEPORTIVO MALLORCA: ROA SOLER(M) SIVIERO MARCELINO DANI STANKOVIĆ (CARRERAS) LAUREN OLAIZOLA ARPÓN (NINO) ENGONGA LÓPEZ (CARLOS). SUBS UNUSED: GALVEZ SOLER (F) PAVNOVIC BIAGINI

The acrimony between the clubs continued after the game when in the press conference Real manager Hector Cuper said, 'I think we deserved to win. They had a couple of opportunities to score but it all went as planned.' 'That's two more than you,' retorted Jim Jefferies, before bringing the proceedings to an abrupt close.

In the following weeks the manager's main concern was to bring in players to help improve Hearts' stuttering league form. While negotiations to bring in the likes of controversial Frenchman Vincent Guerin and Barcelona 'wonder kid' Juanjo continued, the team gained some good results, the latest being a creditable 1-1 draw at Parkhead. By the time they arrived on the sunshine island of Mallorca they were a respectable third in the SPL, behind joint leaders Rangers and surprise package Kilmarnock.

Hopes were high that the one-goal deficit could be overturned even although Flögel, Cameron, Quitongo and McKinnon were still sidelined. On the plus side, Gilles Rousset had recovered from the back injury that had kept him out of the side for two games, although, his stand-in, Roddy MacKenzie, had performed well, leaving Jim Jefferies with a tough decision to make.

For their part, Mallorca were also third in their league and had not conceded a goal since 18 August in the Super Cup against Barcelona. However, they had injury worries as goalkeeper Carlos Roa had dislocated his shoulder in training and had been ruled out, as had Ariel Ibagaza whose foot injury had not heeled.

The official ticket allocation for the game had been snapped up by 1,200 Hearts fans, but hundreds more travelled to the holiday resort, sparking fears there could be trouble on the island. Despite Chris Robinson's request that Mallorca restrict the sale of tickets, the Spanish club were happy to sell to anyone that turned up at their ticket office. Chairman Leslie Deans showed faith in the travelling support, taking out an advertisement in the local English language newspaper, the *Daily Bulletin*, that read, 'I know you will give the team the support they deserve on the night. I know that you will be ambassadors for Hearts and Scotland during your stay.' He was proved correct, with the only trouble at the game coming before the start from club and UEFA officials themselves.

ESTÁDIO LLUIS SITJAR – THURSDAY 1 OCTOBER 1998
REAL CLUB DEPORTIVO MALLORCA: 1 (LÓPEZ 49)
V
HEARTS: 1 (HAMILTON 76)
REFEREE: H ALBRECHT (GERMANY)

Despite having trained at the ground the previous evening, when they raised no objections to either the state of the pitch or the goals, as the players

Jim Jefferies, Billy Brown and Chris Robinson discuss the goalpost problem before the ECWC tie against Mallorca in October 1998 © mirrorpix

began their pre-match warm-up, Jim Jefferies spotted that there were discrepancies in the distance from the ground to the crossbar. As a guide, Dave MacPherson showed it was easier to touch the bar in the middle of the goal than at either end. Frantic discussions took place between officials of both sides and the Danish UEFA delegate, Knud Albertson.

A suggestion to have a replacement set of goals erected was ruled out because the originals were cemented in place. Then it was decided that the goalmouth could be levelled by lifting the turf and removing earth underneath, so with less than half an hour before kick off, the crowd were treated to the sight of a tractor appearing on the park. Before the groundsmen could begin the job, Jim Jefferies correctly argued that there would be a possibility of the goalkeepers slipping on the freshly re-laid turf, so this idea was also abandoned. The game did eventually go ahead on schedule, with Hearts making it clear they were only doing so under protest and after intervention from the British Consul on the island.

For the game, Gilles Rousset got the nod ahead of Roddy McKenzie and with Stevie Fulton failing a late fitness test, Lee Makel was introduced into the side. Dave MacPherson was on the bench in the only change to the starting line-up from the first leg.

It did not take long for the Spaniards to show they were quite prepared to continue the way they had left off at Tynecastle, with Javier Olaizola quickly getting his name into referee Albrecht's book. The German had officiated when Hearts took on Red Star in Belgrade and had shown his no-nonsense approach then, and once again he displayed his disciplinarian approach when Ariel López became the next player to be shown the yellow card, this time for dissent.

Hearts were by no way intimidated by the robust nature of Mallorca's play and looked prepared for the physical challenge. Lee Makel was perhaps fortunate that the referee only flashed a yellow card for a rash late challenge on Jovan Stanković. The persistent fouling did not allow either side to create any real openings and it was no surprise that it took almost 30 minutes before Hearts had their first clear chance. Second-choice goalkeeper César Galvez fumbled a free kick from Stefano Salvatori and dropped the ball at the feet of Jim Hamilton. Before the striker could react, the whistle had gone, with the referee adjudging that the keeper had been fouled.

Another chance came Hamilton's way seven minutes later, but his shot was deflected over by Miguel Soler after Stephane Adam made a superb run followed by a pinpoint cross.

Everything seemed to be falling to Hamilton and two minutes before the break he was denied once again. Neil McCann did well to dispossess Javier Olaizola on the right-hand side before playing the ball to Stephane Adam who cleverly laid it back to Hamilton. His fierce shot looked goal-bound and Galvez did well to push away his effort. The striker let his frustration show seconds before the end of the half when a clumsy challenge on Dani led to him being the fourth player to be booked.

The second half was only four minutes old when Mallorca doubled their aggregate advantage in the tie. Bisan Lauren was allowed to whip in a cross from the right-hand side and an unmarked Ariel López was able to bullet a header behind Gilles Rousset. It was undoubtedly a setback but it had not altered Hearts target, as they always knew they had to score twice to qualify and the goal had not altered the task in hand.

A real blow to their chances occurred a couple of minutes later when Neil McCann was the victim of a wild tackle by Javier Olaizola. Incredibly, the defender went unpunished as McCann was stretchered off the pitch. Derek Holmes was sent on as his replacement as Hearts reshuffled the pack, trying to find a formation that would enable them to play with two centre forwards but no winger to supply them.

With 15 minutes to go, the visitors were thankful for a tremendous tackle from Gary Naysmith that prevented Oscar Arpón getting the ball to either of two unmarked Real men who could not have failed to score. It was a crucial moment. Hearts swept up the park and Jim Hamilton got the goal that his endeavour deserved: Stephane Adam floated in a cross that Hamilton managed to get his head to before the outrushing César Galvez. Despite it hitting the left-hand post and a last ditch attempt at a goal-line clearance by Marcelino, the ball crept into the net, ensuring a frantic finish.

In the remaining minutes Real reverted to type, their players going down under the most innocuous of challenges. One by Paul Ritchie on Ariel López resulted in a mass brawl and Ritchie's name going in the book. Try as they might, the vital second goal would not come and all that was left was for Davie Weir to become the third Hearts man to be shown a yellow card.

REAL CLUB DEPORTIVO MALLORCA: GALVEZ SOLER (M) SIVIERO MARCELINO DANI (NINO) STANKOVIĆ LAUREN OLAIZOLA SOLER (F) (CARRERAS) ARPÓN LÓPEZ (BIAGINI) SUBS UNUSED: FRANCO CARLOS RUFETE PAVNOVIC
HEARTS: ROUSSET PRESSLEY NAYSMITH WEIR (D) RITCHIE SALVATORI LOCKE HAMILTON (J) ADAM MAKEL (MCPHERSON) MCCANN (N) (HOLMES). SUBS UNUSED: MCKENZIE MURRAY MURIE HORN SEVERIN

Although Hearts had been defeated, because of the controversy about the goalposts prior to the game they refused to accept they were out of the competition. It transpired that the UEFA delegate had informed club officials that they should play the game and submit an official complaint to UEFA headquarters *after* the match. It also emerged it was Mr Albertson himself who had brought the matter of the irregular goalposts to the attention of officials from both sides. To ensure UEFA would have the details first thing on Friday, immediately on their return to Edinburgh in the early hours of the morning, Hearts sent a fax to Geneva detailing their complaints.

There was good reason to be optimistic of a favourable response as a precedent had been set the previous season in the first round of the UEFA Cup when FC Sion of Switzerland had raised a similar complaint against Spartak Moscow. In that instance the ruling body had ordered a replay – and that was the very least Hearts were looking for now. However, the second round draw went ahead as scheduled that day, with Mallorca being drawn against Genk from Belgium.

By the time the appeal was heard the following Thursday, it appeared that UEFA had closed ranks. The Danish observer denied that he had stated that in his opinion the game should not take place, or that Hearts had told him that they were only going ahead with the game under protest. This was something easily disproved, as Hearts had a recording of the conversation which they hoped to present at the hearing in Geneva.

The club's representatives were originally given a meagre five minutes to present the case to the ten-man Control and Disciplinary Committee, but on appeal were allowed to return for a further 15 minutes to present photographic and video evidence. The German referee, Hermann Albrecht, and Knud Albertson also gave their version of events – although how much the Dane could remember was in doubt – there was a suggestion that he had enjoyed the 'hospitality' of the Spanish club enough to perhaps cloud his judgement!

After deliberation, it was announced that Mallorca did not have a case to answer and Hearts were informed that their protest should have been submitted in writing *before* the match began. Even if that had been possible, given the time constraints and the likelihood of the Spaniards co-operating by providing the facilities to do so, the paperwork would not have been seen by any UEFA official in Geneva any earlier than the documents they had submitted some ten hours later. Whatever the rights and wrongs of the case, Hearts were now officially eliminated from the competition . To add insult to injury, UEFA ruled that the club were to pay 5,000 Swiss Francs (approximately £2,250) in costs.

In the next round of the competition, ironically, Genk were ordered to play their first leg tie in Brussels as their ground did not meet UEFA standards. The second leg went ahead in the Estádio Luis Sitjar but the Belgians raised an official protest, claiming that the corner spots were not the regulation distance from the perimeter fencing. Unsurprisingly, their complaint was dismissed.

Mallorca were allowed continue to play their home games, including a semi-final clash with Chelsea, in the controversial ground and managed to reach the final. There they met Lazio of Italy at Villa Park, Birmingham, but were beaten 2-1 in the last ever Cup Winners Cup competition.

It certainly had been a unique European experience for Hearts A man who was caught up in the mayhem was their then chairman, Leslie Deans:

> Even although it was over 12 years ago, I still remember it well. It was wonderful, the weather was about 26 degrees and the morning before the game I had wandered round Palma's old town. It was good to see so many Hearts fans but it was a bit strange to see them wandering about wearing scarves in that heat. Old habits die hard!
>
> We were based in the Valparaiso Hotel and in the afternoon I was relaxing by the outdoor pool with Jim Jefferies when he told me that, despite being considered the underdogs, he thought we could win the game: 'I saw enough in the first leg to know that we have more than a good chance.' It was all I wanted to know and I told him that I was glad to hear it.

In the evening we met up with the Mallorca directors who were very hospitable and took us to the Palma Yacht Club, where I was introduced to Knud Albertson the UEFA delegate, but more about him later. We all enjoyed a pleasant evening with dinner on the terrace before we returned to the hotel.

The next day the manager took the players away for a light training session in the morning and when they returned they went to their rooms to rest. There was no lazing by the pool for them. It might be all right for supporters and directors, but not for the players! In the evening we went to the stadium and my first impression was it was a pretty run-down affair. We were told that they were building a new stadium – which I have subsequently seen. I understand they moved there a year or so after we played them – it was not a moment too soon.

Anyway, I was there about an hour or so before kick off so I ambled out into the stand, and down on the pitch I could see Jim Jefferies and Billy Brown with some official. Jim was gesticulating and from his body language I could see he was unhappy. I watched this for a few minutes but didn't know exactly what was going on so I decided to go down and find out.

As I wandered out of the tunnel, I saw that some of our support were already in the stadium and were also looking on, curious as to what was happening. When I reached the gaffer, his first words to me were, 'Look at it, it's that low you could touch it!' He was pointing at the crossbar and it was perfectly clear that it was considerably lower than it should have been. The ground was on a slope, not a major slope, but enough of a slope to make the difference.

Now the laws of football state that the dimensions of the goals must be standard – there is a bit of leeway on pitch measurements, but not the goals. So now I realised that we had the makings of a major incident on our hands and with the crowd growing we had to try and resolve it quickly.

The Mallorca officials did not deny there was a problem, they couldn't, it was so obvious. Jim Jefferies was adamant that if the matter was not resolved he wouldn't play the game. It was then that something happened that I am still angry about to this day. Someone from the British Consulate approached me and asked who I was and what the problem was. Once I explained the situation he said, 'There are thousands of people here and there could be trouble if the game does not start. If that happens I am going to hold you personally responsible.' I was lost for words.

The Mallorca representative was at pains to point out that it was the same for both teams, and I pointed out to him that I agreed – but it was not his side that needed to score. I also pointed out that the goals should be a standard size and his weren't. It was farcical at this stage.

Then the UEFA observer, who I had met the previous night at the yacht club, told us that we should go ahead with the game, then lodge an official complaint with UEFA HQ in Switzerland the next day. After a quick confab, myself, the manager and other club officials made it quite clear to him that we would do so, but under the strict understanding that we were doing it under protest.

The game went ahead and sadly it was a failure, a valiant failure, but we were out nonetheless. But that's not where the story ends, of course.

When we arrived back in Edinburgh it was straight back to Tynecastle to put our official protest in writing, as advised by Mr Albertson at the game. Then it was sent off to Geneva so it would be there in the morning as soon as the offices opened for business. We could not have been any quicker.

For the hearing we hired the services of a QC to put our case, but sadly UEFA decided not to take any action and we were out of the Cup. Various things were said to me after it all, one being that the Spanish FA held great sway in the corridors of power. While that might have been the case I don't know and can't state it categorically.

What I can state categorically is that, as I wanted to discuss the events that had gone on, I tried to engage the Danish observer in conversation immediately after the game. I saw him in a corridor leaning against a wall and his breath had a strong smell of drink; it was the last time I saw him and quite frankly I'm glad of that.

So that's the story of that night in Mallorca. You don't mind being beaten by a better team, you put your hands up and say 'Fine'. But that night I don't believe Hearts were beaten fair and square, and it was clear to all and sundry. Even as I talk now, all these years later, I still get very angry and still feel the sense of injustice.

CHAPTER 15

2000–01 UEFA Cup

A CRUCIAL 2-1 WIN over Hibs at Tynecastle on the last day of the season ensured the third place finish two points ahead of Motherwell that was good enough to see the club join Aberdeen and Celtic as Scotland's representatives in the qualifying round of the UEFA cup. The draw was kind to all three sides with Hearts being drawn against Icelandic outfit Iprottabandalag Vestmannaeyjar. A team with a long name but a short European pedigree (the only team to have been beaten by FC Lantana), it was generally considered that Hearts would have no difficulty qualifying for the first round of the competition.

Being drawn in the preliminary round meant an early start to the campaign with Hearts having to travel to Iceland after only two games in the SPL. Both matches had ended in draws, one a dull 0-0 affair against Hibs, but two late goals were needed against St Johnstone to secure a point at McDiarmid Park.

Because of the condition of IBV's home ground, the game had to be shifted almost 250 miles south to the Laugardalsvollur in Reykjavik, Iceland's national stadium. With a capacity of only 9,000 it was still easily capable of holding both sets of supporters with the crowd totalling about 800 at kick off.

LAUGARDALSVOLLUR – THURSDAY 10 AUGUST 2000
IPROTTABANDALAG VESTMANNAEYJAR: 0
V
HEARTS: 2 (SEVERIN 49; JACKSON 67)
REFEREE: S MOULIN (FRANCE)

Despite Hearts starting the game as firm favourites, it was the home team that looked the most dangerous in the opening exchanges, with Steingrimur Johannesson proving particularly troublesome for the Hearts rearguard. The big striker passed up an opportunity to give IBV a shock early lead when he just failed to connect with a low cross from Ingi Sigurdsson.

It took Hearts over quarter of an hour before they created their first opening, but even then it was more by chance than skill. Steve Fulton

Scott Severin raises above the IBV defence to put Hearts 1-0 up in Iceland © SNS Group

started the move with a cross to the back post where Colin Cameron took a wild swipe that fortuitously knocked the ball into the path of Robert Tomasheck. The startled Slovak was quick to react but couldn't control his shot, which went narrowly past.

Five minutes later Cameron was once again the provider, this time in a more conventional manner when he knocked down a cross for Gary McSwegan. His strike look goal-bound until Hlynor Stefansson stuck out his leg to make a desperate goal-line clearance. Another golden opportunity came McSwegan's way when he was on the end of another Steve Fulton cross, but this time he could only direct his header straight at IBV keeper Birkir Kristinsson.

At the other end Baldur Bragason was also wasteful with a header when Stefansson found him unmarked six yards out, but the Icelander's effort failed to trouble Antti Niemi and drifted wide of the upright.

It was not the type of performance Jim Jefferies had expected but a few well chosen words during the half-time break got the response he wanted. With the half four minutes old, Hearts went ahead when Scott Severin rose to head home a Steve Fulton free kick.

The visitors were now in complete charge and Steve Fulton, Darren Jackson and Colin Cameron all had excellent opportunities to increase the lead. However, it was another mis-kick from Colin Cameron that produced the second goal when his effort spun to Darren Jackson who made no mistake after 67 minutes.

The visitors were content to play out the rest of the game but had a scare when Johannesson had the ball in the net, only to see his effort ruled out for a foul by Johann Moller earlier, in the move that had led to the chance.

In the end it was a comfortable result to take back to Tynecastle and the club could feel confident about being in the ballot for the first round when it took place two weeks later.

IPROTTABANDALAG VESTMANNAEYJAR: KRISTINSSON GUDMUNDSSON (P) ALEKSIR STEFANSSON SIGURDSSON (I) (THORVALDSSON) BRAGASON JOHANNESSON VIDARSSON (SIGURDSSON (M)) JÓNSSON (MOLLER) MILETA ALMARSSON. SUBS UNUSED: GUDMUNDSSON (K) ANTONSSON JOHANSSON OLAFSSON
HEARTS: NIEMI FLÖGEL NAYSMITH SEVERIN PRESSLEY FULTON TOMASHEK CAMERON MAKEL (LOCKE) JACKSON (KIRK (A)) MCSWEGAN (O'NEIL). SUBS UNUSED: ROUSSET MURRAY (G) JUANJO SIMPSON

By the time IBV visited Edinburgh for the return leg, Hearts had slipped to mid-table in the SPL after managing only a draw with Aberdeen and being comprehensively beaten by a Henrik Larsson-inspired Celtic at Tynecastle. Despite these setbacks Jim Jefferies was confident that they could see off the threat of the Icelandic side, stating that it would be an opportunity for his forwards to significantly add to their goal tally.

TYNECASTLE STADIUM – THURSDAY 24 AUGUST 2000
HEARTS: 3 (MCSWEGAN 6; O'NEIL 19; TOMASCHEK 39)
V
IPROTTABANDALAG VESTMANNAEYJAR: 0
REFEREE: A COSTA (PORTUGAL)

It was a prediction that seemed to be shared by the Edinburgh public, who assumed that Hearts' passage into the next round was all but guaranteed. Just over 8,000 turning up to see the game. They didn't have to wait long for the first goal when Gary McSwegan headed home a Kris O'Neil cross in the sixth minutes after being left totally unmarked in the box.

He got another opportunity five minutes later after a great move involving Gary Locke and Juanjo had opened up a rather pedestrian IBV defence. This time, though, he just failed to meet the tempting cross put in by the little Spaniard.

IBV were struggling to keep up with the home side as Hearts stroked the ball about the park with ease and they contributed to their own downfall after 20 minutes when their dithering back line failed to clear a shot from Scott Severin. The ball only went as far as Robert Tomaschek on the edge of the area and his vicious strike flew into the net, leaving Birkir Kristinsson helpless.

Hearts' pressure was relentless and young Kris O'Neil squandered two opportunities before getting the goal his industry deserved after being set up by Robert Tomashek on 39 minutes.

Now 5-0 up on aggregate, and coasting, Hearts were guilty of taking their foot of the pedal in the second half, something that did not go unnoticed by the meagre crowd. The rumblings of displeasure were heightened when substitute Andy Kirk fell over rather than test the IBV keeper after a tremendous run from defence by Steve Fulton had set him up.

The Irishman's mistake was surpassed by that of Steingrimur Johannesson in IBV's first (and last) meaningful attack of the game after 83 minutes. A defensive error by Scott Severin allowed the Icelander in on goal and with only Antti Niemi to beat, he somehow managed to miss the ball completely and fall over. Perhaps to save his embarrassment, he was led from the park. IBV, having used their three substitutes, played out the remaining minutes with only ten men. It was a farcical end to what had been a completely one-sided encounter.

HEARTS: NIEMI LOCKE (MURRAY (G)) NAYSMITH SEVERIN PRESSLEY TOMASCHEK (FLÖGEL) FULTON MAKEL O'NEIL JUANJO MCSWEGAN (KIRK (A)). SUBS UNUSED: MCKENZIE JAMES CAMERON SIMPSON
IPROTTABANDALAG VESTMANNAEYJAR: KRISTINSSON GUDMUNDSSON (P) ALEKSIC STEFANSSON (I) SIGURDSSON (I) (MOLLER) BRAGASON JOHANESSON (M) SIGURDSSON (M) (JOHANSSON) JÓNSSON MILETA (VIDARSSON) ALMARSSON. SUBS UNUSED: GUDMUNDSSON (K) OLAFSSON EGILSSON THORVALDSSON

If the games against IBV had been mere formalities, Hearts knew that they were in for a tougher challenge when they were paired against German side VfB Stuttgart in the first round. Although not involved in the qualifying round, VfB had secured their place in the draw via the rather torturous route of the Intertoto Cup. Having had to play eight games, they were one of three 'winners' of the competition that allowed them entry to the UEFA Cup.

Managed by former player Ralf Rangnick, Stuttgart were heavily in debt and new president Manfred Hass had embarked on a cost-cutting exercise which saw the exit of the highly paid stars who had helped them reach the final of the Cup Winners Cup two years earlier. The club turned to their talented youth team to bring back the successes of previous years and only three players – Thomas Schneider, Zvonimir Soldo and Krassimir

Balakov – remained from the side beaten 1-0 by Chelsea. By the time the team left Edinburgh airport for Germany, Hearts were still in mid-table but were fresh from a 2-0 win over Dunfermline which was rather more convincing than the scoreline suggests. Stuttgart had also made a stuttering start to their season but had been boosted by a 2-1 win over giants Bayern Munich on the Saturday before the tie.

Jim Jefferies had a full squad to choose from but there was a slight doubt over Scott Severin, who had picked up an ankle injury in midweek playing for Scotland Under-21s in Latvia.

GOTTLIEB DAIMLER STADION – THURSDAY 14 SEPTEMBER 2000
VFB STUTTGART 1893: 1 (BALAKOV 35)
V
HEARTS: 0
REFEREE: C BOLOGNINO (ITALY)

At kick off Severin was passed as fit and took his place in the starting line-up. The most familiar face in the opposition was that of Sean Dundee, the South Africa-born forward who had been acquired after an unsuccessful spell with Liverpool. It did not take long for Stuttgart to show the threat they posed. After only three minutes Jochen Seitz flashed a header narrowly wide, with Antti Niemi rooted to his line. The Finn's goal next came under threat from one of his team-mates when Gary Naysmith miscued an attempted clearance, but once again the ball went inches past the post.

After 15 minutes a piece of magic from Fitzroy Simpson nearly saw Hearts unexpectedly take the lead. Cleverly beating Silvio Meissner, he then curled the ball towards the top corner of the net. It looked goal-bound all the way until Timo Hildebrand stretched out his left hand to turn it round the post.

It was Hearts' only real threat. The Germans continued to dominate, although they could do nothing with the possession as the visitors continued to defend stoutly. With 35 minutes gone, Stuttgart made the breakthrough that their play probably merited when Gordan Petric was penalised for a foul on Meissner 20 yards from goal. The veteran Bulgarian international Krassimir Balakov took the kick and floated the ball over the defensive wall into the net with

The scoreboard tells the story in Stuttgart © Davy Allan

Antti Niemi helpless.

At the start of the second half Hearts brought on Lee Makel in place of Scott Severin, who had shown signs that he had not fully recovered from the injury sustained while on international duty. The change did little to affect the run of play and the home side continued to seek the second goal that would make Hearts' task a lot harder at Tynecastle in a fortnight's time.

Hearts continued to be resilient in defence, which began to frustrate Stuttgart and their fans, who voiced their displeasure as attack after attack came to nothing. With the game almost over, the visitors suffered a blow when Colin Cameron went down injured after a clash with Pablo Thiam. The captain had to be carried from the field on a stretcher and was replaced by Robbie Neilson, who hardly had time to touch the ball before the final whistle sounded as Hearts completed what was a satisfactory night's work.

VFB STUTTGART 1893: HILDEBRAND MEISSNER THIAM BALAKOV CARNELL SEITZ (PINTO) SOLDO ENDRESS (SCHNEIDER) LISZTES HOSNY DUNDEE (GANEA). SUBS UNUSED: TRAUTNER BLANK TODT HLEB
HEARTS: NIEMI MURRAY NAYSMITH PETRIC PRESSLEY JACKSON (MCSWEGAN) SIMPSON CAMERON (NEILSON) SEVERIN (MAKEL) JUANJO FLÖGEL. SUBS UNUSED: MCKENZIE O'NEIL KIRK(A) JAMES

When Colin Cameron's injury was assessed on the return to Edinburgh it was discovered that it was not as bad as had first been feared. It was the only good news on the injury front as the list of players with knocks continued to grow.

Cameron had been able to take part in all three games Hearts played in the time between the two ties. The latest, a Sunday game in front of the Sky Sports cameras at Tynecastle against Kilmarnock, had ended in a disappointing 2-0 defeat and had also added to Jim Jefferies' lengthy injury list. By the day of the game the manager took the decision to introduce Kevin James into the starting line-up for the first time that season, plus to play both Gordan Petric and Gary Locke in unfamiliar midfield roles.

TYNECASTLE STADIUM – THURSDAY 28 SEPTEMBER 2000
HEARTS: 3 (PRESSLEY 16; PETRIC 62; CAMERON PEN 83)
V
VFB STUTTGART 1893: 2 (DUNDEE 37; BORDON 58)
REFEREE: B DERRIEN (FRANCE)

The makeshift nature of the side was exposed in the first few minutes when Hearts were forced to concede two corners in quick succession. From both, Marcelo Bordon had opportunities to open the scoring but he could not find the necessary finish required.

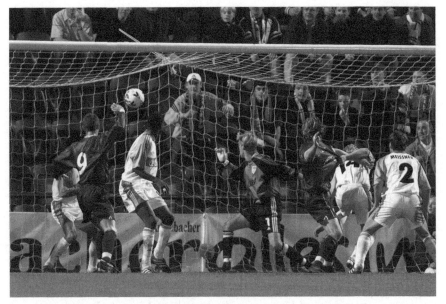

Steven Pressley heads Hearts level on aggregate against Stuttgart at Tynecastle
© SNS Group

Jim Jefferies' side slowly began to work their way into the game and forced their first corner after 16 minutes. Gary Naysmith took the kick which debut man Kevin James flicked on at the near post. It was flighted perfectly for the inrushing Steven Pressley who, despite the attentions of Thomas Schneider, sent a powerful header behind Timo Hildebrand. It was the signal for Tynecastle to erupt, evoking memories of a night against German opposition over 11 years earlier.

It was one thing being level on aggregate but it was still a difficult task to come away with a win as they had done against Bayern Munich. Stuttgart showed how dangerous they could be with a scintillating move ten minutes later when Sean Dundee and Kristzen Lisztes combined in a move that cut Hearts' makeshift defence apart. The ball was played to Jochen Seitz, whose shot from an acute angle flashed across Antti Niemi's goal when perhaps a cross would have produced a more profitable result.

That move had exposed the fact that pre-match injury doubt Gary Locke was clearly struggling, and Robbie Neilson was introduced in his place. The enforced change did not appear to disrupt Hearts' search for a second goal, in fact it was Neilson that came closest to adding to the tally when his powerful shot inside the box was only cleared after a desperate block by Timo Hildebrand.

Stuttgart continued to show that they were dangerous on the break, with the pace of Jochen Seitz a continual threat. His strike partner, Sean Dundee, required lengthy treatment after being brought down unceremoniously by Gordan Petric, but two minutes later he had recovered sufficiently to level the scores on the night.

Once again Hearts failed to stop Seitz as he made progress down the right-hand side, Antti Niemi could only parry his cross cum shot and the ball fell kindly for Dundee, who was able to hook the ball past the big Finn. It was a blow to Hearts' hopes and their plight could have got worse three minutes before the end of the half, when only a brilliant save from Niemi prevented Seitz putting the Germans in front.

In the second period Jochen Seitz continued to cause havoc for the Hearts back line but surprisingly it was Colin Cameron who found his name in the Swiss referee's book for an illegal challenge on the big forward.

After 12 minutes of the half the German pressure paid off when a drive by Silvio Meissner was deflect for a corner. In a set-piece almost identical to the one that had seen Hearts take the lead, Seitz's kick was flicked on at the near post by Ahmed Hosny for the Brazillian Marcelo Bordon to head home.

The goal looked to have won the tie for Stuttgart but Hearts refused to be beaten and within four minutes were back on level terms. Again the goal came from a corner, with Gary Naysmith once again finding Kevin James, whose knock-on was headed into the net by Gordan Petric.

Once again the 14,500 inside Tynecastle came alive and although the home side still needed two goals to go through, there seemed to be a belief amongst the team and the fans that it was not impossible to achieve.

With just over 15 minutes left, Gary McSwegan was introduced to the action in place of Andy Kirk, who was tiring. Within minutes of coming on he was involved in the incident that led to Hearts taking the lead when he pounced on a long clearance from Antti Niemi. As he was about to shoot just inside the box, he was grabbed from behind by Silvio Meissner. Although the referee blew for the infringement, he seemed to signal a free kick outside the area, until the mistake was pointed out to him by his assistant. With the award of a penalty it was obvious that Meissner had to be sent off, however Mr Derrien further confused matters when he flashed his red card at Pablo Thiam. For a second time the linesman corrected the ref and finally the correct man was sent for an early bath. The chaos did not affect Colin Cameron's concentration as he stepped up to bury the ball in the back of the net.

Now only needing one goal to qualify, Hearts poured men forward in numbers, reducing Stuttgart into some desperate defending. Thomas Schneider over stepped the mark when he scythed down Gary Naysmith with a tackle probably worthy of a straight red card. The referee chose instead to show him a yellow card, but having already been booked in the first half, justice was done and Schneider became the second German to receive his marching orders.

The resultant free kick was played into the box, only to be cleared to Robbie Neilson who cleverly lobbed the ball over the advancing Stuttgart defence to Gordan Petric. In the clear and with only Timo Hildebrand to beat, the big Serbian blasted the ball high over the bar.

It was a shocking and costly miss, as even with five added minutes Hearts could not find a way past nine-man Stuttgart, finally exiting the competition on the 'away goal' rule.

HEARTS: NIEMI MURRAY NAYSMITH JAMES PRESSLEY PETRIC LOCKE (NEILSON) CAMERON JUANJO FLÖGEL KIRK (A) (MCSWEGAN). SUBS UNUSED: ROUSSET JACKSON ADAM O'NEIL SIMPSON
VFB STUTTGART 1893: HILDEBRAND MEISSNER BORDON SCHNEIDER CARNELL THIAM BALAKOV (BLANK) SEITZ (PINTO) LISZTES (TODT) HOSNY DUNDEE. SUBS UNUSED: TRAUTNER GANEA HLEB AMANATIDIS

Stuttgart progressed to the fourth round of the tournament before being beaten by Celta Vigo in a competition eventually won by Liverpool. The miss by Petric is still remembered by all who were inside Tynecastle that night, leaving everyone once again thinking of what might have been. For Callum Anderson, well-known local publican and trustee of the Hearts former Players Association, the exit from the tournament is still fresh in his memory:

> I have worked in the pub trade for more years than I care to remember and for most of them I have been in the Gorgie/Dalry area. The Auld Worthies, Luckies and now Dickens have all had the reputation of being 'Hearts' pubs as I think that along with the club, bars are an important part of the community and I have tried to develop the links between the three wherever I have been.
>
> During my time there have been some great nights celebrating Hearts wins such as the two cup triumphs of course, but generally speaking 'European' nights are something special. Before the game there is always a real sense of anticipation and afterwards the conversations are more animated than usual as the thoughts turn to who we would get drawn against in the next round. Sadly, though, we have not had as many of those nights as I would have liked!
>
> I can still remember that night after the Stuttgart game. I was the manager at Luckies at the time and anyone that has been in knows it is

a big place, but there was only one topic of conversation – 'that' miss and how it spoiled our chances of another trip into Europe.

For me that was a bittersweet moment, as no matter where I have been I always arranged travel to the away ties from the pub, but that brings along its own problems.

One of the first trips I organised was a bus from The Auld Worthies in Dalry Road all the way to Prague in 1986. Czechoslovakia was still under a communist regime and the rules and regulations I had to follow were something else. I thought I had everything organised as we set off from Edinburgh and all went well on the long journey, at least that is until we reached Checkpoint Charlie in Berlin.

It was here we were going to cross from 'free' Europe into the East and as you could imagine controls were tight. Our bus-load of boisterous Hearts supporters attracted a fair bit of attention. We all had to get off the bus as it was searched (although I'm not sure what they were looking for) and our documents checked. It was only then that I discovered that one of the guys on the trip, Kenny MacDonald, had made it all the way to Germany without a passport. It wasn't that he had forgotten it, it was just that he didn't think he needed one! As a good bus convenor, there was only one thing for me to do. Yes, you've guessed it: kick him off and leave him behind. To this day I have no idea how he got back as it turned out that he had also left his money at home along with his passport.

If that was a problem for Kenny, it was me that ran into a spot of bother when Hearts were drawn against Lantana in Estonia. By then I was an old hand at organising travel to away games no matter where they were, but for this one the interest was so great I decided that I would charter my own plane to take my customers there. Everything went well and I had filled the plane that had by now been christened the 'Jambo Jet', when my scheme got a bit of attention from the press and the *Edinburgh Evening News* ran a story about my plans. Unfortunately, Chris Robinson the Hearts chairman at the time, saw the article and got in touch to tell me to cancel the flight as my trip was in competition against the official club flight – it was no surprise that what I was charging was far less than Hearts.

Things got a bit acrimonious, which was widely reported in the media. Mr Robinson threatened to report me to the BAA as he maintained that my plane was full of football hooligans, an allegation that was completely false – a few of the passengers were relatives of players. Things started to get out of hand. I wasn't going to back down and when the chairman decided to take legal action against me, my response was well reported at the time as being: 'See you in court, fat man.' In the end, though, the flight didn't take off as the company I had hired the plane from decided they didn't want to get involved with the dispute.

That bother didn't deter me, so when it came time to organise the trip to Stuttgart I decided that once again a flight was the only way to go. This time I had over 80 of my customers wanting to go, so I booked everyone on scheduled flights taking over the entire plane and effectively having our own flight, and there was nothing Mr Robinson or anyone else could do about it. The journey went without a hitch but it was in Stuttgart that one of the best funny moments that I have had happened.

When I go abroad I like to eat the local delicacies rather than find a McDonald's like a lot of the guys do. So a few of us found a restaurant before the game and decided to order the wienerschnitzel – everyone, that is, apart from Willie Hill. Not really recognised for being a man of the world, Willie's comment was 'Whit's that?', or words to that effect. When I gave him a description of the dish his response was, 'I'm havin' nane o' that foreign muck, I'm havin' spaghetti bolognese.' Priceless!

It's only on the foreign jaunts that you seem to get moments like these and I look forward to many more in the future.

CHAPTER 16

2003–04 UEFA Cup

CRAIG LEVEIN TOOK over from Jim Jefferies in December 2000 and two seasons later he guided the side to a third-place finish behind Rangers and Celtic. However, it took a late goal by Mark de Vries as Hearts beat Dundee 1-0 at Tynecastle on the last day of the season to ensure their return to the European stage for the first time since the Jefferies era.

The draw for the UEFA Cup saw them paired with the Bosnian cup winners FK Željezničar from Sarajevo. It was a tough draw as the Bosnians had a useful European pedigree, having qualified for the Champions League qualifying rounds for the previous two seasons.

However, they had made a poor start to their season and by the time they travelled to Edinburgh for the first leg they were lying in 11th position in the league with their defence of the cup already at an end after being put out the competition by second division outfit Kozara.

Hearts had made a much better start and were once again in third place behind the Old Firm, even although they had just suffered a heavy defeat to Rangers, losing 4-0 at Tynecastle. Another blow in the build-up to the game was that during the loss Phil Stamp picked up an injury that that ruled him out of the European tie. Steven Boyak took his place while Paul Hartley was preferred to Joe Hamill who dropped to the bench.

TYNECASTLE STADIUM – WEDNESDAY 24 SEPTEMBER 2003
HEARTS: 2 (DE VRIES 28; WEBSTER 58)
V
FK ŽELJEZNIČAR SARAJEVO: 0
REFEREE: J VAN HULTEN (HOLLAND)

It took Boyak under 30 seconds to make his mark on the game when straight from the kick off he floated a great cross into the Bosnian side's box. The ball was inch-perfect for Mark de Vries, but the big centre could only direct his header straight at Kenan Hasagic and the Zeljo keeper saved with ease.

Fifteen minutes later and again Boyak was at the heart of the action, but this time he received a head knock that saw him replaced by Jean Louis

Valois. The Frenchman himself was making his way back from injury so was well short of match fitness, having only played a few minutes the previous Saturday against Rangers.

With Željezničar packing the midfield, Jean Louis found himself in the thick of the action, but despite battling hard, chances for Hearts were few and far between. Some of the near-capacity crowd were getting restless when, after 28 minutes, a pinpoint through ball from Alan Maybury found Mark de Vries, who expertly turned his marker and shot into the net from 15 yards. Two minutes later Denis Wyness had an excellent opportunity to double the lead but his fierce shot was expertly dealt with by Hasagic. By contrast, Hearts stopper Tepi Moilanen was barely troubled until three minutes before the end of the half when he had to look smart following a short free kick by Almir Gredic was played to Sanel Jahec, who threatened to put the sides level.

The second period mirrored the majority of the first 45 minutes, with Hearts pressing forward in search of the vital second goal, but with the visitors having set their stall out to defend it was proving to be a difficult task. Scott Severin almost provided the answer when he set up Denis Wyness; once again, however, the chance went begging when he could only scoop the ball over the bar from a few yards out.

The vital second goal was only delayed by a minute when Mark de Vries got on the end of a cross from a Jean Louis Valois. As the ball thumped back off the crossbar, Paul Hartley was first to react to knock the rebound goalward. Some desperate defending from the Bosnians saw his effort blocked as the ball spun in the air, but Andy Webster was on hand to nod it over the line.

Despite continuing to have the majority of possession, Hearts could not add to their two-goal advantage. The introduction of Graham Weir for the ineffectual Denis Wyness and then Joe Hamill for the rapidly tiring Paul Hartley almost paid dividends nine minutes from time when the pair combined to provide Mark de Vries with yet another headed attempt. But again the Zeljo keeper Hasagic was up to the test.

HEARTS: MOILANEN MAYBURY KISNORBO PRESSLEY WEBSTER SEVERIN MACFARLANE HARTLEY (HAMILL) BOYAK (VALOIS) WYNESS (WEIR) DE VRIES. SUBS UNUSED: GORDON MCKENNA KIRK (A) MCCANN (N)

FK ŽELJEZNIČAR SARAJEVO: HASAGIC KAJTAZ ALIHODŽIĆ KARIC GREDIC (AVDIJA) MUHAREMOVIC SPAHIC JAHIL VUKSANOVIC (BISCEVIC) OBAD (RASCIC) AGIC. SUBS UNUSED: UROŠEVIĆ JOLDIC SMAILAGIC DŽEKO

If Craig Levein could be satisfied with the outcome, the same could not be said of Sabahudin Zujo, the Bosnian club's president. His immediate reaction was to sack the coach, Amar Osim, replacing him with his assistant, Kemal Alispahic. By the time Hearts arrived in Sarajevo on Tuesday 14 October, Alispahic's reign had also come to an abrupt end and Milomir Odovic had been handed the task of trying to overturn Hearts' healthy advantage.

Before the return leg, much had been made of the Željezničar fans, known as the Maniacs. A recent derby match against Sarajevo had been halted as riot police used tear gas to control the crowd violence. On Hearts' official party's arrival a police escort was provided for team and supporters alike, although this proved to be unnecessary as the locals looked to be more hospitable than hostile.

Despite only needing a draw to qualify, Craig Levein resisted the temptation to field a defensive line-up, with Graham Weir selected to partner Mark de Vries up front as they went in search of the all-important away goal that would almost certainly guarantee that Hearts became the first Scottish side to qualify for the second round of the UEFA Cup since Aberdeen seven years previously.

OLIMPIJSKI STADION – WEDNESDAY 15 OCTOBER 2003
FK ŽELJEZNIČAR SARAJEVO: 0
V
HEARTS: 0
REFEREE: A STREDAK (SLOVAKIA)

Immediately from the kick off Hearts fashioned the sort of opportunity that they could only have dreamt about. A clever through ball from Jean Louis Valois allowed Mark de Vries to run in one-on-one with Željezničar keeper Kenan Hasagic. Much to the disappointment of the 500 travelling support, it was the Bosnian international that won this particular duel.

It was a promising start by the visitors, but as the half worn on it was the home side that began to get the upper hand. Despite their dominance, Sarajevo did not trouble Tepi Moilanen unduly. Hearts, though, were reduced to some desperate defending, with Andy Webster and Jean Louis Valois finding their way in quick succession into the referee's book. By the half-time whistle the stalemate had not been broken, with Hearts looking comfortable holding on to their two-goal advantage.

After five minutes of the second period, Sarajevo centre Sanel Jahic put the lead under threat when he broke free on the right. Fortunately for Hearts his shot was just too high and Tepi Moilanen's goal survived. Eight minutes later it was Hearts' turn to fashion an opportunity that could have put the tie beyond doubt. Andy Webster unleashed a fierce shot from 18 yards, which Hasagic did well to stop. As the ball rebounded to Jean

Steven Pressley, Craig Levein and Alan Maybury celebrate after the 0-0 draw against FK Željeznicar in Sarajevo October 2003 © Davy Allan

Louis Valois, the Frenchman fired the ball towards the goal but once again Hasagic managed to get a hand to it to turn it wide.

With 15 minutes left it was Hasagic to the rescue again when a cross from Mark de Vries looked certain to find Graham Weir unmarked at the back post. But the keeper somehow managed to get his fingertips to the ball and the chance was gone.

It was to be Weir's last part in the action. Craig Levein began to introduce substitutes. Denis Wyness came on and was followed by Paul Hartley, who replaced Phil Stamp. Finally, with only a few minutes to go, Mark de Vries made way for Kevin McKenna as Hearts ran down the clock. There was still enough time left, though, for Tepi Moilanen to become the third Hearts player to be booked, ironically for time-wasting as the Gorgie men cruised into the second round.

FK ŽELJEZNIČAR SARAJEVO: HASAGIC BISCEVIC KAJTAZ MULALIC ALIHODŽIĆ KARIC GREDIC (JOLDIC) MUHAREMOVIĆ JAHIC VUKSANOVIĆ (AVDIJA) OBAD (DŽEKO). SUBS UNUSED: ADILOVIĆ SPAHIC RAŠČIĆ HADZIC
HEARTS: MOILANEN MAYBURY PRESSLEY WEBSTER KISNORBO STAMP (HARTLEY) MACFARLANE SEVERIN VALOIS DE VRIES (MCKENNA) WEIR (WYNESS). SUBS UNUSED: GORDON MCCANN KIRK (A) SIMMONS

When the draw for the second round was made in UEFA headquarters in Nyon Switzerland two days later, Hearts were paired with Bordeaux, with the first leg to be played in France. So began the scramble by supporters to make travel arrangements and it was not long before the Tynecastle ticket office announced that all of the 3,100 tickets that had been allocated were sold, thus ensuring the biggest away support since Munich over 14 years earlier.

In the lead-up to the game 20-year-old Craig Gordon had replaced Tepi Moilanen in goal after the big Finn had been beaten five times at Parkhead. Hearts had subsequently won the three following games, although Bordeaux would prove a stiffer test for Craig rather than Partick Thistle, Falkirk and Livingston, whom they had beaten 4-1, 2-1 and 3-1 respectively. Craig Levein also recognised this and altered his team to reflect the threat that the French side would pose. The normal 4-4-2 formation was replaced with an unfamiliar 3-6-1 line-up, with Mark de Vries being handed the lone striker's role. It was particularly harsh on Andy Kirk, who had notched five goals in the three games. The Ulsterman had to settle for a place on the bench on this occasion.

STADE CHABAN DELMAS – THURSDAY 6 NOVEMBER 2003
FC GIRONDINS DE BORDEAUX: 0
V
HEARTS: 1 (DE VRIES 78)
REFEREE: K JAKOBSSON (ICELAND)

By kick off time most of the large Hearts support had found their places in the impressive stadium, having wound their way in a giant conga from the Connemara Bar in the Cours d'Albret in town. Their encouragement for the team was relentless, despite the fact that neither side gave them much to shout about on the park for the first 20 minutes.

The noise from the stands increased considerably when it appeared that Robbie Neilson had been brought down in the box by Bruno Basto. The Icelandic referee thought otherwise, but awarded Hearts a free kick just outside the box near the bye line. From what appeared an impossible angle, Jean Lois Valois attempted to curl the ball into the far corner of the net, but his effort was just wide.

It was a rare attack from Hearts as the midfield and defence continued to work hard to contain the French side. When Bordeaux did break through they found that Craig Gordon was in excellent form. No better example was when in the 27th minute a shot from David Jemmali took a slight deflection, but the Scotland Under-21 keeper managed to pull off a tremendous stop.

With half-time looming it was Hearts that came closest to breaking the deadlock, albeit courtesy of Bordeaux midfield man Pascal Feindouno.

Hearts prepare to defend a corner against Bordeaux during the 1-0 victory in the UEFA Cup November 2003 © Davy Allan

When Hearts were awarded a free kick midway inside the French half, Jean Louis Valois played the ball out wide to Robbie Nielson, who crossed the ball to the far post where Feindouno attempted to cushion a header back to his keeper. However, his direction was out and Ulrich Rame was forced to pull off a magnificent fingertip save with Denis Wyness only inches away from connecting with the rebound.

Bordeaux were quick to show their intentions after the break when the ever dangerous Frank Jurietti shot just over after only a few minutes. His partner and, later, Rangers flop, Jean Claude Darcheville, was also proving to be a handful and with 50 minutes gone it appeared that Kevin McKenna took this a little to literally. The big Canadian appeared to use his arm to control the ball in the box with Darcheville in close attendance, but the offence was missed by the officials and Hearts survived.

Darcheville provided another scare on the hour mark when his shot rebounded off the post, then needed to be cleared off the line by Andy Webster. Craig Gordon got down well to clutch the ball after Paulo Costa fired the clearance back in.

With 20 minutes to go Hearts were forced into making a change after Robbie Neilson was caught late by the Moroccan international Marouane Chamakh, with Austin McCann taking his place. But it was another substitute, Paul Hartley, who had come on for Jean Louis Valois, who set up the move that led to Hearts going in front in the 78th minute. His free kick into the box was headed goalward by Kevin McKenna, but for the second time in the game Ulrich Rame managed to make a fantastic fingertip save. This time, though, he could only turn the ball onto the inside of the post and as the ball came back off the upright there was Mark de Vries to force the ball home.

Hearts immediately brought on Scott Severin for the tiring Phil Stamp as they attempted to see out the dying minutes and remained resolute until the very last minute, when Jean Claude Darcheville created an opportunity for himself eight yards out. Once again Craig Gordon pulled off another splendid save low to his right to ensure Hearts gained one of their best away results in Europe.

FC GIRONDINS DE BORDEAUX: RAMÉ ALICARTE BASTO JEMMALI JURIETTI (DE SOUZA) POCHETTINO E DA COSTA P DA COSTA (RIERA) FEINDOUNO CHAMAKH DARCHEVILLE. SUBS UNUSED: ROUX CANEIRA PLANUS DE OLIVERIRA SAHNOUN HEARTS: GORDON MCKENNA PRESSLEY WEBSTER NEILSON (MCCANN) MAYBURY STAMP (SEVERIN) WYNESS VALOIS (HARTLEY) KISNORBO DE VRIES. SUBS UNUSED: MOILANEN MACFARLANE KIRK WEIR

By the time Michel Pavon brought his side to Edinburgh three weeks later, Hearts had chalked up two impressive victories in the SPL. Firstly, Aberdeen were beaten 1-0 at Pittodrie, then Hibs were dispatched 2-0 at Tynecastle the following Sunday, leaving them third in the table behind the Old Firm.

The victory against Hibs came at a cost, with captain Steven Pressley sustaining a thigh injury that forced him off the park midway through the first half.

There were also injury doubts about Phil Stamp and Scott Severin, but it was not the fact that three key players could be missing from the stating line-up but the fact that Hearts held a one-goal lead that bothered Craig Levein. 'To be honest, I was expecting to be something like 1-0 down coming into this game,' he said, before admitting, 'Never did I ever imagine that the dilemma after the first leg would be whether to defend a lead or go for the kill.'

For Michel Pavon there was no such indecision. 'Do we believe we can go through? Of course, why else would we be here?' he stated.

Before the game, Frank Jackson, president of the Welsh, Irish, Scottish and English Sporting and Cultural Society (and landlord of the Connemara Bar) presented gifts to the Hearts directors on behalf of the Police Municipale for the outstanding behaviour of the support in Bordeaux. Off the field at least, Hearts had won – but could the players follow the fans' lead? Despite the game being broadcast live on BBC, nearly 18,000 were inside Tynecastle believing they could.

Phil Stamp had won his fitness battle and was included in the starting 11 but Scott Severin was only included on the bench, while Alan Maybury took over the role of captain from Steven Pressley.

TYNECASTLE STADIUM – THURSDAY 27 NOVEMBER 2003
HEARTS: 0
V
FC GIRONDINS DE BORDEAUX: 2 (RIERA 8; FEINDOUNO 66)
REFEREE: G GILEWSKI (POLAND)

The French side were quick to show their intent and squared the tie after only eight minutes. A careless pass in midfield by Jean-Louis Valois was picked by Jean-Claude Darcheville, who found Albert Riera 25 yards out. His swerving shot went high into the top corner, with Craig Gordon helpless.

Hearts struggled to keep Bordeaux at bay before they had a lucky escape 15 minutes later when a thunderous volley by Darcheville crashed back off the crossbar. On the half hour mark Hearts' cause was hampered when Paul Hartley had to be stretchered off after a collision with Albert Riera in midfield. Scott Severin took his place but could do nothing to stop a marauding run by Pascal Feinduno which resulted in Craig Gordon doing well to push the ball onto the upright before being scrambled clear.

There had been little seen of Hearts as an attacking force, but with five minutes to go before half-time Mark de Vries thought he had won a penalty when his shot appeared to come off the hand of Frank Jurietti. The Polish referee didn't agree and waved play on, much to the disgust of the big Dutchman. A minute later he was further incensed when Phil Stamp latched onto his pass and slammed the ball in the net, only for Mark de Vries to be pulled up by the assistant referee for offside.

There was still enough time left in the half for Hearts to have a second penalty claim when Robbie Neilson was sent tumbling in the box by Eduardo Cota. It looked a clear-cut award, but again Grezegorz Gilenski wasn't interested and the sides went in all square on aggregate.

In order to try and turn the tide, Craig Levein brought on Stephen Simmons in place of Neil MacFarlane. The change nearly made the difference. With an hour played he tried an over-head kick which was going well wide but fell at the feet of Mark de Vries, whose effort was blocked on the line and cleared.

With Hearts pushing forward, the French side were finding gaps in the home defence and six minutes later punished them with ruthless efficiency. The impressive Marouane Chamakh burst down the left, leaving Kevin

McKenna trailing. At the bye line he cut the ball back perfectly into the path of Pascal Feindouno, who made no mistake from just inside the 18 yard box.

To their credit, Hearts hit back almost immediately when Jean-Louis Valois fashioned a chance for Phil Stamp, only to see the Englishman blast the ball over the bar from inside six yards. They continued to battle away in search of the two goals required and with 20 minutes left, Ulrich Rame had to produce a wonder-save to prevent Stephen Simmons pulling one back.

A couple of minutes later Andy Kirk replaced Jean-Louis Valois and he came close with a diving header from a Robbie Neilson cross. But the visitors stood firm and eventually ran out worthy winners.

HEARTS: GORDON NEILSON MAYBURY WEBSTER MCKENNA STAMP MACFARLANE (SIMMONS) KISNORBO VALOIS (KIRK A) DE VRIES HARTLEY (SEVERIN). SUBS UNUSED: MOILANEN MCCANN (A) WYNESS SLOAN
FC GIRONDINS DE BORDEAUX: RAME CANEIRA ALICARTE, POCHETTINO JURIETTI COSTA DARCHEVILLE (CELADES) RIERA (DA COSTA) FEINDOUNO PLANUS CHAMAKH (SAHNOUN). SUBS UNUSED: ROUX, DEIVID, BASTO, MIRANDA

Hearts' European adventure was over for another season, but not before they had achieved one of their best results ever with the win in Bordeaux, a result that is still remembered fondly by many a Jambo. But it is the rather forgettable game against Željezničar that remains indelibly impressed in the memory of Hearts memorabilia collector and editor of the Hearts history magazine, *Eighteen 74*, Gary Cowan:

> Every so often in Sarajevo you stumble across a curiosity representing hope from despair: a patch of concrete pavement with a myriad of small irregularly shaped craters filled with red resin. The way the holes fan out in a rough semicircle looks like the petals of a flower. These are Sarajevo's roses. Created by the scars cut in the concrete by some of the thousands of mortar shells which fell on the city in the Bosnian war, where the bombs claimed a fatality, the holes in the concrete were filled with blood-red resin to create a permanent floral tribute out of the very destruction which caused death. Beauty from death and destruction. Flowers from blood.
>
> That the inhabitants of Sarajevo have chosen a way of commemorating the victims of the war by making something attractive out of the very rubble of war is typical of their attitude to it. They don't want to sweep it under the rug and forget about it. They want to move forward from it but they don't want to pretend it never happened. In the souvenir shops, for instance, you can buy empty mortar casings engraved into various designs and patterns. At the War Memorial near the city centre, an eternal flame burns bright.

Everywhere you looked in Sarajevo in October 2003 when my wife Amy and I went there for the match against Željezničar, the ravages of the war were still evident. That was barely surprising because the siege of the city had been lifted for only some seven years before Hearts' (and our) visit. Surrounded on all sides by the forces of the Yugoslav People's Army and then the army of Republika Srpska, the city was besieged for almost four years between April 1992 and February 1996, before the settlement thrashed out in the Dayton Accord finally released the city from its deadly embrace.

The figures are staggering and just writing them down doesn't begin to tell the story. Nearly 10,000 civilians were killed or went missing in the city. Some 1,500 of them were children. 56,000 civilians were wounded, 15,000 of them were children. On 5 February 1994 shells fired into the Markale marketplace, which was crowded with shoppers trying to buy up the few goods that remained, killed 68 civilians and wounded over 200. The following year, the same market was shelled again, massacring a further 37 civilians. We wandered through it on our visit, silent and thoughtful. It is estimated that during the four years of the siege, there was an average of 329 shell impacts in the city every single day. On one day, 22 July 1993, 3,777 shells fell on Sarajevo.

To say that Sarajevo was bombed back to the dark ages is no cliché. In their opening statement in the prosecution of Radovan Karadzic, the Bosnian Serb leader who faced one charge relating to the siege amongst many others, prosecutors said that 'The siege of Sarajevo, as it came to be popularly known, was an episode of such notoriety in the conflict in the former Yugoslavia that one must go back to World War II to find a parallel in European history. Not since then had a professional army conducted a campaign of unrelenting violence against the inhabitants of a European city so as to reduce them to a state of medieval deprivation in which they were in constant fear of death. In the period covered... there was nowhere safe for a Sarajevan, not at home, at school, in a hospital from deliberate attack.' If you want a moving but unchallenging read which brings home the reality of the siege, try *Zlata's Diary* by Zlata Filipovic.

During our trip we paid a visit to Željezničar's stadium; the game against Hearts was being played at the Olympic Stadium. Zeljo's home ground is in the Grbavica area of Sarajevo, one of the many areas of 'front line' in the fighting. Seven years on, there was not a single building around the area of the stadium which was not affected. Concrete buildings had huge chunks missing, shell holes in every wall and bullet holes pockmarking every surface. Little repair work had taken place. Metal signposts around the ground itself had shafts of sunlight pouring through the numerous bullet holes. When you create a new nation which immediately finds itself in a bloody, brutal and wearing civil war, it is little wonder that only some seven years later, Sarajevo was still a mess; a cross between a building site and war zone.

And yet... there was hope in Sarajevo. What would be your reaction if your city had been shelled over 300 times every day for four years, if you had lived without water, electricity and gas for over three years, if your loved ones – your children – had been killed or wounded, if, as the prosecutors said, you lived in constant fear of being killed at any moment in your own home, in your school, in a cemetery at a funeral, at a football match? There must have been a temptation for Sarajevo to give up; to imagine that life could never go on as before and to just stop trying.

But seven years later, Sarajevo was a fascinating vibrant city with sophisticated bars, upmarket shops, interesting and varied architecture and people who appeared delighted to see a relatively happy band of Hearts supporters.

We flew via Vienna. An hour's transfer time was always going to be tight and when our flight from London touched down in Vienna half an hour late, there was a real risk that we'd be spending 24 hours in the Austrian capital. Instead, we were whisked through to the waiting Sarajevo flight, which took off almost before we had fastened our seat belts. When we touched down, it soon became clear that whilst we had been whisked through Vienna airport, our luggage had not been quite so fortunate and was still languishing there.

As we sat in a taxi travelling into the city, farms and smallholdings gave way to suburbs and slightly larger houses and the first signs of the scars of the war became clear. Buildings with shell holes became more common and as we arrived at our hotel, one of the iconic sights of the aftermath of the siege of Sarajevo; the bombed out parliament building, a huge multi-storey block entirely destroyed by Serbian tanks, sitting like a huge monument to futility in the very centre of the city. It was here that demonstrations were first held against Serb aggression. In April 1992, as a crowd of between 50,000 and 100,000 peace demonstrators marched close to this building, snipers shot and killed two young women, Suada Dilberovic and Olga Sucic, the first casualties of the siege.

Opposite the parliament building was our hotel, another Sarajevo icon, the Holiday Inn. Constructed for the 1984 Winter Olympics – think Torville and Dean's *Bolero* – the building is an odd-looking one. A strange yellow colour, it looks a little like someone has placed a huge cubic block of cheddar cheese eight storeys high in the middle of the city. It was actually very comfortable and was almost certainly the most luxurious hotel in Sarajevo at the time. The choice of a large section of the travelling support, it was also the base for the Hearts squad who could be seen at various times traipsing across the lobby, which also doubled as the bar and lounge, to and from the dining room, glancing enviously at the beer glasses on our tables. Occasionally our paths would cross and Mark de Vries was very friendly, stopping to chat on several occasions. But it was Steven Pressley who impressed me with his attitude when, completely unbidden, he made a detour towards us. The ultimate club captain, he wanted nothing more than to thank us for making the long trip to Sarajevo and to check that we were being well looked after in the hotel. There is a (to my mind misguided) element of our support that seemingly is prepared to forget the years of wonderful service both on and off the pitch that Pressley gave to our club.

The Holiday Inn overlooked the wreck of the parliament building. Did I mention before that the shots fired at the demonstrators marching on the parliament building came from the upper floors of the Holiday Inn itself? Was it possible that we were sleeping in the very room which witnessed the catalyst of the siege of Sarajevo? It was enough to send a shiver down the spine, as was any trip across the main dual carriageway which separated those two buildings. Dubbed 'sniper's alley', anyone who ventured on to that roadway quite literally risked their life as they ran the gauntlet of Serb snipers whose sights were trained on the wide open spaces of the roadway. When we visited, the worst that might happen would be to be run over by a tram or car, but it was still difficult to cross that road on foot as we did several times without looking around nervously and perhaps even ducking one's head involuntarily.

The luggage eventually turned up and Davy Brunton and I ventured out into Sarajevo for a beer. For some reason which I can't now recall, Amy and the remaining London Hearts members intrepid enough to make the trip were not flying out until a day or so later so Dave and I had some time to familiarise ourselves with the city before the hordes arrived. Naturally, we went to a bar. I'd love to be able to report that everything we did in Sarajevo was culturally significant, that every waking moment was spent improving ourselves through our study of art, architecture, history and the cultures and traditions of others. However, as any Hearts fan who has ever travelled on a European trip following the team abroad will tell you, that is far from realistic. Dave and I hit the first of many bars over the course of that night and they were not to be the last.

I'm not sure I can recall which bars we went to on that first night which may be a product of a lapse of memory over the intervening years but may also have something to do with the amount of the local brew consumed. I do recall many of the bars quite well as Sarajevo seemed to have a wide variety of them. We definitely went to one near the main drag into town with wood panelled walls, a huge range of optics and a television showing football results from all over Europe. Someone cheered as the Danish second division results came through. I also recall one which was approached down an alley – it appeared to have been created out of bits of corrugated iron and sheets of plastic with a bar propped up at the end and some bar stools in front. I have vague memories of Calum Anderson holding court in here but might be wrong. Near the war memorial, there was a neon nightmare of a bar, all stainless steel fittings and uncomfortable chairs. A look back in there later in the week showed that the owner had at least had the good sense to put a Hearts scarf prominently behind the bar, attracting custom he might not otherwise have had. I also recall a dim basement bar approached through an innocuous looking entrance door but which turned out to be a nightclub where, above the dull thump of the bass, we chatted to some Hearts fans who had in turn been talking to Husref Musemic, former Hearts legend (anyone who scores a winner against Hibs automatically being granted such status by law) and then manager of Sarajevo's other team, FC Sarajevo. Given that rumours still abounded that Musemic had been killed in the Bosnian conflict, it was good to have confirmation in so far as it was still needed that Husref was alive and well and living in Sarajevo making a decent living out of football.

Dave and I headed back out to the airport to welcome the other members of London Hearts including Amy. Holding up a sign which said 'London Hearts' (quite possibly in Swedish) in case they didn't recognise us was, I am certain, Dave's idea as, despite having been away from home for more than 48 hours, I was reasonably confident that Amy would still recognise me. Naturally, as Dave and I had been in Sarajevo for comfortably a day and a half longer than the others, we were experts in every aspect of the city's infrastructure, layout, history and cultural references. Oh, and we knew where the bar was in the hotel.

We went for a wander. There's an interesting area near the centre of Sarajevo. A series of long main roads houses shops, bars and restaurants. One day, as it started to rain, we dived into a clothes shop to see if they sold umbrellas and were very pleasantly surprised to find an upmarket, rather chic boutique which wouldn't have looked out of place in London. However, it was still something of a surprise; without wanting to repeat the obvious, this was only seven short years after the end of a hideous siege where basic utilities were cut off, let alone designer clothes. A little way down the same road, there were more surprises as the tall stone buildings gave way almost instantaneously to the old Turkish or Muslim quarter. Huge buildings housing elegant shops or bars gave way to small single storey buildings selling souvenirs or Islamic art or rough and ready cafés selling huge kebabs and steaming cups of Turkish coffee.

This sudden change of scenery was bizarre (as opposed to bazaar) and was a little like some sort of strange movie effect; not really going back in time so much as being instantly and abruptly transported to a different country, a different culture. Opposite was the tall and wonderfully ornate Emperor's mosque, the serene grounds of which we walked through on our last day in the city. It was a lovely area to wander around in just taking in the sights and smells. I don't know whether it was because it was a commercial area, whether it was a tourist area or whether it was just that the buildings were smaller but the area looked a lot more intact than the rest of Sarajevo; there didn't seem to be the same obvious damage that you saw everywhere else. Yet, walk right through and beyond that area and down towards the river and you very soon come across the National Library, destroyed by Serb shelling from the hills which surround the city and still lying in ruins when we were there.

Just before you get to the Library, there's a stone on the ground marking the other great event in Sarajevo's history. Long before they were a guitar-based band from Glasgow, Franz Ferdinand was the name of the Archduke of the Austro-Hungarian Empire. Parading down the streets of Sarajevo in his open-top car in 1914, Franz was assassinated together with his wife by Gavrilo Princip, a 19-year-old Serb Irredentist. That led to Austro-Hungary declaring war on Serbia and to cut a very long story short, the assassination was seen as the catalyst for the outbreak of World War 1. It isn't hard to make the connection between the futility of a war which was fought largely on the green fields of France and Belgium and which cost the lives of six Hearts players as well as countless thousands of other young men and the futility of another much later war in which Sarajevo was literally right in the firing line rather than merely being a bit-part player. As you look around you in this area of the city, you can see why the Serbs found it relatively easy to keep the city under siege for such a long time, the hills around each side surrounding it like the sides of a bowl and providing an easy vantage point for the shelling and sniper fire.

On our third day in Sarajevo, we wandered down to Grbavica, to Željezničar's 12,700 capacity stadium. Approaching the ground, two things struck us. The first, which I have already mentioned, was the sheer devastation of the housing and infrastructure in that area. It was an area which saw a lot of fighting and the scars were there for all to see. Indeed, Grbavica's wooden stands had been burned down during the war and one side of the ground was home to small temporary seated areas. The second was that the stadium itself looked strange. In these days of corporate football, you lose track of the number of times you hear about proposed 'retail opportunities' in new stadiums but notwithstanding that this stadium wasn't new, it appeared to have been a step ahead of the game. Approaching the stadium on foot, if you hadn't glanced above ground floor level, you might not even know there was a stadium there as the two storeys immediately behind the end stand comprised dozens of small shops and outlets including, if memory serves, a Daewoo garage and a hardware store. Cars were parked immediately in front of the shops and only the stand looming above the shops and the floodlights looming further above the stand gave a clue that you were in the right place for a football match. Even then, you had to walk down the side of the stadium before you could gain access to the ground. As we approached, we were greeted by Mirza, a Bosnian Tartan Army member who had met Scottish soldiers during the conflict and had fallen further for the charms of the travelling Scots football fans after they had visited Sarajevo in 1999 and who had gone on to follow his adopted country rather than that of his birth. Under the username 'MacMirza', he had already made a valuable contribution to the travelling Hearts support by answering numerous questions about accommodation, match tickets, travel arrangements and the strength and cost of local beer on the Hearts Internet message board, 'Kickback', and it was good to meet him in person rather than as a name on a screen.

We did a guided tour of the stadium including – and you wouldn't get this sort of hospitality at a Scottish ground if you had turned up uninvited out of the blue – the changing rooms and directors' lounge where we were treated to coffee and cakes by a lady wearing a white coat like a doctor's coat but who, one assumed, was part of the catering rather than the medical staff at Željezničar. Before she left the room, Mirza quizzed her on the team photos which adorned the walls of the room and it became apparent that, having been at the club for several decades, she was something of an expert in the club's history, rattling off the names of the great teams and stories about them at some length. One wall of the lounge was a huge, glass-fronted cabinet full of trophies, pennants and gifts from the club's many forays into European and local competition. There was a bronze statue of a ram, a gift from Derby County in 1972, and a pennant from Kilmarnock who had played in Sarajevo in 1998. A trophy carved from an old bullet-casing served as a reminder of the recent past. A request for a replica shirt had the staff scrambling around, not in a club shop but in the team's own kit cupboard.

Željezničar was formed by railway workers in Sarajevo and everything about the club is true to its roots in the railway industry. The club's crest features wings, a symbol of the railways and the club's colours are blue and white, also long associated with the railways. A railway line used to run right behind the ground and train drivers would make a point of making sure their trains let off a loud whistle if a match was in progress. However, it was something of a surprise to cast a glance across the terraces at the ground and to see, at the far end of the stadium, planted firmly and squarely in the middle of the terraces, an old steam locomotive, probably 40 feet long and beautifully restored with black livery and bright red wheels. How it got there, I never quite established but it looked rather magnificent sitting in the middle of a football stadium. If that had been in Britain, it would have been removed long ago on health and safety grounds. Such a thought would no doubt have been laughable in Bosnia.

What's that? I haven't mentioned the match? Well, those of you who have travelled abroad to watch Hearts in Europe will know that the experience is rarely about the match itself. Sarajevo was a case in point. Leading by a reasonably comfortable 2-0 from the first leg, a 0-0 draw in freezing conditions in the Olympic Stadium was sufficient to see Hearts through to the next round. I can barely tell you what happened during the game; it was so cold that several brass monkeys were seen nervously crossing their legs. All I can recall is that despite everyone hopping from foot to foot to try to get any sort of feeling back in their toes, Neil Mackay, fuelled by the day's partying in the Fiss Bar, insisted on supporting the team topless throughout much of the 90 minutes. I also recall some very European-style flares being lit by the 'Maniacs', the Željezničar 'ultras' but in all honesty, in a crowd of 15,000 in the vast bowl of the stadium, it looked less than menacing. Hearts clung on gamely for a draw and at the end, the players, led by Pressley, jogged over to the 300 or so travelling fans to show their appreciation and, possibly spotting Neil, fling some jerseys into the crowd.

These days, the Tartan Army generates mixed emotions among Scottish football fans. There are very many Hearts supporters in the Tartan Army and they follow their country with enthusiasm and pride. There are others – I would venture to guess a small minority – who see the kilts and Glengarry's and the 'never mind the result, we're only here to party' mindset as something of an embarrassment to the nation, up there with shortbread tins and bagpipes for tourists. Whatever your view (and I align myself with the majority), one thing for which you cannot criticise the Tartan Army is its belief in fundraising for local charities whenever they play abroad. Many thousands of pounds have been raised for local children's charities in parts of Europe where help is desperately needed and it's probably fair to say that many of the local population's perceptions of football fans has been altered by the generosity of the Scots.

The Hearts support in Sarajevo followed in the generous footsteps of their compatriots in their support of the Christine Witcutt Centre during the trip. A busload of Hearts supporters drove from Edinburgh to Sarajevo and brought with them a veritable mountain of donated clothes and toys for the kids from the centre. We had caught a lift from the hotel from Craig Levein and Peter Houston who were making a trip to the centre to meet some of the staff and kids and watch the bus arriving and making their donations.

Christine and Alan Witcutt were volunteers with the Edinburgh Direct Aid charity. Formerly a teacher in Wishaw, Christine and her husband along with other EDA members volunteered to deliver food and medical aid to the people of Sarajevo during the siege. In July 1993, whilst travelling along 'sniper's alley' in a truck forming part of the third EDA convoy to reach Sarajevo, a sniper shot and killed Christine Witcutt.

The Christine Witcutt Centre was opened in 2001 in her memory as a day care centre for disabled children. It offers teaching in a wide variety of areas and over the course of a couple of hours, we were shown music equipment and other specialist educational materials which the children badly needed and the children themselves put on a show for the visitors, performing short songs and dances and reciting poems for the assembled visitors.

It is difficult to put the effect of a visit like that into words, and something of a cliché to say that it was humbling. But I felt humbled for three reasons. First for the obvious reason, that these children of Sarajevo, physically or mentally disabled in some way, had clearly worked hard to put on a show for a group of visitors from across Europe who they had never met and whose common bond was football. Second, I felt humbled to be a part of that group; we hadn't travelled in on the bus but had brought our own donations with us and added our small offering to the colossal mountain of donations which had arrived from Edinburgh. Football fans so often get a bad press but this group of visitors – including guys who, on another day, might have been cursing the loss of valuable drinking time – were generous with their gifts, their time and their obvious affection for the children. It was genuinely uplifting to be a Hearts fan that day. Finally, I felt humbled watching the faces of the kids as maroon scarves were wrapped round their necks and they smiled the wide-eyed smiles of the innocent. Although no one else in our party knew it yet, Amy and I had found out only a few weeks earlier that we were expecting our first baby, the next generation of Hearts fans. It was therefore a poignant experience that taught us that even kids who had very little, who had experienced war first-hand and who would have struggled against difficult odds in any country, let alone in Bosnia after the war, could experience joy and, fittingly for Sarajevo, hope from despair.

CHAPTER 17

2004–05 UEFA Cup

ONCE AGAIN A third-place finish behind the Old Firm gave Hearts entry into the first round of the UEFA Cup, allowing them to avoid the qualifying rounds where one of Scotland's other representatives, Dunfermline, had fallen to Icelandic giants Fimleikafelag Hafnarfjaroar. If Hearts could avoid similar humiliation, an aggregate win would then see them progress to the lucrative group stage which had been introduced for the first time.

After the draw was made on 27 August in the Grimaldi Forum in Monte Carlo, the team in their way turned out to be SC Braga of Portugal who were competing in Europe for the first time in their history. Forever in the shadow of Benfica, Porto and Sporting Lisbon, Braga qualified for the competition by finishing fifth in the Portuguese Primeira Liga after manager Jesualdo Ferreira's first full season in charge. They were only two games into the new season and had opened with two draws, the latest being against champions, Porto.

Hearts, on the other hand, had made a steady if unspectacular start and after five games were lying fifth in the league. Their latest result had been a 0-0 draw against Rangers, a game witnessed by Braga's Rui Águas. Although identifying Mark de Vries and Graham Weir as the men to watch, he was more intrigued by the fact that Hearts had taken the controversial decision to switch the game to Murrayfield. 'The atmosphere was superb, much better than we are used to. I don't understand why the match can't be played there,' he said.

It was a contentious decision, as a claim by club CEO Chris Robinson that the ground no longer met UEFA standards had been hotly contested by others. However, whether to maximise the income from the game or as a trial to assess the feasibility of Robinson's plan to sell Tynecastle and move location, the game went ahead at the home of Scottish rugby.

On the day before the game, one of the players identified by Braga as posing a threat to their chances, Graham Weir, was ruled out of Craig Levein's plans when he was sent home suffering from mumps. He joined a fairly lengthy injury list, with Ramon Pereira, Steve Simmons and Kevin

McKenna all unavailable for selection. Mark de Vries, the other player to impress the Portuguese, was struggling with a hamstring injury and looked unsure to play the full 90 minutes if risked.

MURRAYFIELD STADIUM – THURSDAY 16 SEPTEMBER 2004
HEARTS: 3 (WEBSTER 52; HARTLEY 62; KISNORBO 90)
V
SPORTING CLUBE DE BRAGA: 1 (ALMEIDA 65)
REFEREE: A GENOV (BULGARIA)

Despite calls from fan groups to boycott the game in protest at the decision to approve the sale of Tynecastle taken at an EGM earlier in the week, almost 19,000 turned up at Murrayfield to watch the tie. It was certainly more that could have been accommodated in Gorgie, but in the 67,000 capacity arena they looked a little lost. However, everyone inside the home of Scottish rugby joined in creating tremendous backing for the team and at times some venomous disapproval of Chris Robinson and his plans for Tynecastle.

For the game Craig Levein sprang a couple of surprises by using Phil Stamp as Mark de Vries's striking partner and handing Jamie McAllister his first starting place of the season. The move looked to be a profitable one when in the first few minutes McAllister went close to opening the scoring after his left-foot volley drifted inches wide following a knock-down from de Vries.

With 36 minutes played, Phil Stamp and de Vries combined well only for José Nuñes to fell the big Dutchman inches outside the box. Stamp took the kick but the opportunity was wasted when he slammed the ball into the defensive wall. Two minutes later, though, he did test Paulo Santos in the Braga goal when a neat pass from de Vries allowed him through on goal. His lob was brilliantly palmed away one-handed by the keeper; although it fell to Jamie McAllister he could not keep his shot down as the ball landed on the top of the net.

It was true to say that Hearts had the better of the half but Braga were dangerous on the break. Craig Gordon had to be alert when a shot from Jaime Aquino took a deflection off Andy Webster, but the goalie was able to turn the ball round the post to keep the sides level at half-time.

Within six minutes of the restart Hearts grabbed the goal that their dominance deserved. Robbie Neilson made good progress down the right before putting over a decent cross that Mark de Vries nodded back across goal, where Andy Webster was on hand to head home a goal reminiscent of his strike the previous season against Željezničar.

Ten minutes later and things got even better for the Edinburgh side when another superb cross from Robbie Neilson was met perfectly by Paul Hartley, whose volley left Santos with no chance. Despite the thousands of empty seats Murrayfield was rocking but only two minutes later, Braga managed to silence the boisterous crowd.

They were awarded a free kick – taken by Wender – which Hearts' zonal marking system failed to deal with. Paulo Sérgio found room for a free header which he placed behind a despairing Craig Gordon.

The away goal was vital to Braga's aspirations and certainly hurt Hearts' chances of progressing to the group stages. For the next 25 minutes they battled gamely to restore their two-goal advantage and with 90 minutes on the clock substitute Denis Wyness looked to have done just that. His quick turn fooled the Portuguese defence, allowing him the time and space to fire off a shot which agonisingly spun inches wide of the left-hand post.

It looked as though the opportunity had gone but deep into stoppage time, Hearts forced a corner. From the subsequent kick, Patrick Kisnorbo managed to control the ball with his chest before volleying it into the net from eight yards. It was his first goal for the club and there was no doubt he had picked the perfect time to open his account.

HEARTS: GORDON NEILSON MAYBURY WEBSTER PRESSLEY HAMILL (MACFARLANE) KISNORBO HARTLEY STAMP (WYNESS) MCALLISTER DE VRIES. SUBS UNUSED: MOILANEN JANCZYK SLOAN BERRA STEWART
SPORTING CLUBE DE BRAGA: SANTOS, GOMES DIAS LOUREIRO ALMEIDA KENEDY (TOMAS) WENDER FERREIRA BAHA (JAIME) NUNES VANDINHO. SUBS UNUSED: GONCALVES BARROSO FERNANDES COSTA

Manager Levein knew the value of the goal. 'That third goal was vital for us, it has given us a great chance,'he said, going on to curb speculation on his own future with the words 'I've got two years left of my contract here and I'm happy at the club.'

There was little doubt that the win had added to his managerial CV. However, his next game in charge certainly did nothing for his credentials. He made six changes to the side that were then comprehensively beaten by Dunfermline who were rooted to the bottom of the SPL. In the crowd were representatives of Lithuanian banker Vladimir Romanov who had shown signs of taking a controlling interest in the Gorgie club. After the display against the Pars, they could hardly have taken back a favourable report to Kaunas.

Hearts' form improved marginally as they took care of Kilmarnock in the CIS Insurance Cup then against Inverness Caley in the SPL, although the biggest cheer on that day was reserved for the return to Tynecastle of Hearts legend John Robertson, now manager of the Highland club.

For the trip to Portugal, the manager's team selection was still being hampered by injuries to vital players, particularly the strikers. Graham Weir was recovering from his bout of mumps, while Ramon Pereira and Mark de Vries were both carrying knocks, with Levein stating that the Dutchman would have to make a 'Lazarus-type recovery' to play any part. As a back-up, Kevin McKenna was included in the travelling party, even although he had not started a game all season due to a knee injury.

Not on the plane was under-fire CEO Chris Robinson who, rumour had it, was staying behind in Edinburgh to sell his shares in the club to Vladimir Romanov. It was news that sparked scenes of wild celebration amongst the 1,500 supporters that had made the journey to north-west Portugal.

Stevie Frail meets Batman and a chicken before the game in Braga © Davy Allan

Perhaps buoyed by a 0-0 draw against Benfica in the Stadium of Light, Braga boss Jesualdo Ferreira was confident of his side's chances. 'I don't think we will qualify, I know we will,' he said prior to the game. It was a bold statement and one that riled both the Hearts manager and players. 'That is insulting to me and the players, and to be honest it's very annoying. We will see what happens this evening but we're not too happy about what has been said, that's for sure,' Levein said.

ESTÁDIO MUNICIPAL DE BRAGA – THURSDAY 30 SEPTEMBER 2004
SPORTING CLUBE DE BRAGA: 2 (TOMAS 12; AQUINO 75)
V
HEARTS: 2 (DE VRIES 27 & 48)
REFEREE: A STREDAK (SLOVAKIA)

Set in Mount Castro overlooking the town and built for Euro 2004, the stadium featured a rock face behind each goal. Another claim to fame was the 270 square metre TV style scoreboard, the biggest in Europe, and it was the home side that were the first to feature on the giant screen.

Having already come close through Jaime and Wender, Braga went ahead after 12 minutes when Tomas pounced on a mix-up between Robbie Neilson and Craig Gordon following a corner by Paulo Sérgio.

Having sprung a surprise by including Mark de Vries in the starting line-up, Craig Levein's gamble was justified 15 minutes later when another defensive error allowed the Dutchman to pull the sides level. Paulo Jorge was woefully short with a back header that allowed de Vries to nip in before rounding Paulo Santos and rolling the ball into an empty net.

The goal was the signal for the Portuguese to introduce some indiscipline into their play but the Slovakian referee was quick to react by showing a flurry of yellow cards to both sides. Mr Stredak, who had also been in charge when Hearts played in Sarajevo, further enraged the home side for turning down a penalty claim ten minutes before the end of the half, when Phil Stamp appeared to handle a volley from Wender in the box.

What had already been an excellent performance got even better three minutes into the second half when once again Mark de Vries got his name on the score sheet. Collecting the ball in midfield, he drifted past two or three challenges before stroking a left-foot shot from 20 yards. The ball took a deflection off Nem which left Santos wrong-footed, and Hearts were deservedly ahead.

Now needing four goals to go through, Braga seemed to realise that the task was beyond them as their attacks became less frequent and with less conviction. However, with 15 minutes left they did manage to snatch an equaliser. Robbie Neilson had been on hand to make a goal-line clearance from Cesinha, before a corner from the right seemed to hit Jaime on the shin. Robbie was on the line again, but an unkind bounce took it past the defender and into the net.

Minutes before the end, Tomás also had the ball in the net but his effort was rightly ruled out for offside as Hearts became the first Scottish club to reach the group stages of the competition.

SPORTING CLUBE DE BRAGA: SANTOS GOMES NEM LUIZ ALMEIDA TOMÁS JAIME KENEDY (CASTANHEIRA) WENDER (CESINHA) ABEL (BAHA) VANDINHO. SUBS UNUSED: GONCALVES BARROSO NUNES COSTA
HEARTS: GORDON NEILSON MAYBURY WEBSTER PRESSLEY MACFARLANE KISNORBO HARTLEY STAMP (PEREIRA) MCALLISTER DE VRIES (MCKENNA). SUBS UNUSED: MOILANEN WYNESS BERRA STEWART HAMILL

When the draw was made in Switzerland on Tuesday 5 October, Hearts were handed the stiffest of tasks in the five-team group stage. Included in Group A were three former winners of the tournament (in its various guises), Feyenoord, Schalke 04, the Hungarian side Ferencvaros with Swiss outfit Basel, completing the group.

First up was a trip to Holland, followed by a home game against the Germans, then a journey to Switzerland before rounding off the series of games against Ferencvaros in Edinburgh. Although three teams would qualify from the group, Hearts had been seeded fourth and reaching the knockout stage would be a difficult job considering the quality of opposition they would face.

On returning to the domestic scene, Hearts suffered a European 'hangover', only managing a draw against lowly Livingston before being soundly trounced 3-0 by Celtic at Parkhead. After the game the management team headed off throughout Europe to spy on their opponents. Stephen Frail went to Munich to watch Shalke take on Bayern while Peter Houston was sent to Hungary to report on Ferencvaros against Újpest Doza. Along with Gary Kirk, Craig Levein travelled to Kerkrade in the Netherlands to see Feyenoord play Roda.

Managed by Dutch legend Rudd Guillit, they had a comfortable 2-0 win with goals from 19-year-old Salomon Kalou and Dutch international Dirk Kuijt, both of whom impressed the watching Tynecastle duo. Although the two strikers caught the manager's eye, he was quick to point out that the whole side was littered with quality players, which was the reason they sat at the top of the Erdivisie.

Once again Mark de Vries was an injury doubt, this time with a poisoned toe, but after receiving treatment for the infection at the Western General hospital, he was considered fit enough to be included in the travelling party. Although he made the journey to Holland on the Wednesday, it was obvious by the next day that he had no chance of making a dream return to Holland, so with an Edinburgh Derby on Sunday in mind, he decided to return to Edinburgh hours before the kick off.

FEIJENOORD STADION – THURSDAY 21 OCTOBER 2004
FEYENOORD: 3 (KUYT 22 & 83; GOOR 58)
V
HEARTS: 0
REFEREE: T POULSEN (DENMARK)

Craig Levein's priority was finding a way to stop the Dutch side from scoring and unsurprisingly his side had a defensive look, with striking duties handed to Kevin McKenna in the absence of de Vries. Also missing from the line-up was influential midfielder Phil Stamp, who had suffered from a stomach upset in the afternoon, his place being taken by Joe Hamill.

Hearts had taken their full allocation of 2,500 tickets for the game in De Kuip and the fans that had travelled from Edinburgh gave them a raucous reception when the sides made their entrance but they were quickly silenced – Salomon Kalou created a great chance for himself straight from the kick off, proving to be the threat that Craig Levein had predicted. On this occasion Craig Gordon was alert to the danger and confidently dealt with his shot, but Kalou was a constant menace. After six minutes he was harshly adjudged to be offside when his diving header found the net – a let-off for the visitors and the first of many controversial refereeing decisions from Mr Poulsen, the Danish referee.

Feyenoord again came close to opening the scoring on 20 minutes when Pascal Bosschaart got the better of Robbie Neilson before rounding Craig Gordon. He hit the ball goalward and turned away to celebrate his goal but he did not bargain for Andy Webster, who chased back to clear the ball off the line.

The clearance only delayed the opening goal for two minutes, and when a cross from Patrick Paauwe was met by Dirk Kuyt at the back post. His header beat Craig Gordon, but the keeper was clearly obstructed by Karim Saidi who also looked to be standing two yards offside. Unbelievably the goal was allowed to stand, perhaps in an effort to compensate for the one wrongly disallowed earlier.

It was an unbelievable decision, and worse was to follow after 36 minutes when Joe Hamill won the ball just outside the Feyenoord box, then squared it to Kevin McKenna who rifled an angled volley into the net. Instead of signalling a goal, the referee gave a free kick for an offside decision against Paul Hartley who, although nowhere near the ball, was adjudged to have been interfering with play.

Perhaps encouraged by the disallowed goal, Craig Levein made a tactical change a couple of minutes later by substituting Neil McFarlane with Graham Weir and switching to a more attack-minded 4-4-2 formation.

Two minutes after the start of the second half, Weir did well to make room for himself inside the Feyenoord goal area only to be brought down by a rash tackle from Karim Saidi, but once again the referee frustrated Hearts when he waved away any claim for a penalty.

Although working hard, Hearts were finding it difficult to match the home side whose slick passing moves continued to create chances for their hard-working forwards. It looked as if it was just a question of time before they added to their lead and the second goal duly arrived on the hour mark. Salomon Kalou chipped a ball through the heart of the defence for Bart Goor to run onto and clip the ball over the advancing Craig Gordon.

Being two down, Craig Levein then went for broke with 20 minutes left and introduced Denis Wyness in place of Jaimie McAllister, changing to a 4-3-3 formation. Despite the bold move, Feyenoord continued to dominate the game and Dirk Kuyt brought out a magnificent one-handed save from Craig Gordon after 75 minutes.

The Maroons continued to battle hard and with ten minutes left Joe Hamill went close to reducing the deficit with a long-range effort that went just wide. But it was the home side that got the next goal three minutes later when a cross from the Belgian international Bart Goor was headed home by Dirk Kuyt from six yards.

At the end of the game Craig Levein confronted the referee and his assistants about their controversial performance. Although there was no doubt that certain key decisions went against his side, there was equally no doubt that the better side had won the game.

FEYENOORD: BABOS SAIDI BOSSCHAART KUIJT ONO GOOR PAAUWE KALOU (BUFFEL) BASTO (MITILIGA) CASTELEN (LAZOVIĆ) ZUIVERLOON. SUBS UNUSED: LODEWIJKS GHALY LOOVENS GYAN
HEARTS: GORDON MAYBURY KISNORBO (STEWART) WEBSTER PRESSLEY MCKENNA HARTLEY MACFARLANE (WEIR (G)) NEILSON MCALLISTER (WYNESS) HAMILL. SUBS UNUSED: MOILANEN JANCZYK SLOAN BERRA

With Schalke and Basel drawing 1-1, the defeat left Hearts at the foot of the table and with the German side set to visit Edinburgh in two weeks' time. Another defeat would put a huge dent in their ambitions to be one of the three qualifiers for the knockout stages.

Their SPL form improved when a comfortable derby win against Hibs was followed by a 1-1 draw at Tannadice. With a new owner in charge there was fresh optimism at the club ahead of the next UEFA cup clash, but things were thrown into disarray a week before the game when Craig Levein announced that he was leaving the club to take up the manager's post at Leicester City. Rumours of his departure had been circulating for a few days but it was still a shock for most. His assistant, Peter Houston, was put in temporary charge for the home game against Dundee, which was won 3-0, but with it being generally accepted that he too would head to the West Midlands, the search for a new manager began.

There was one clear favourite: Hearts legend John Robertson, who was currently in charge at Inverness Caledonian Thistle. The race was on to get the former hero in place before Schalke came to town and on the day before the game, chairman George Foulkes was happy to announce that they had got their man.

Their opponents had also recently had a change of manager: after a few games of the new season, with the club sitting second bottom of the Bundesliga, general manager Rudi Assauer had sacked former German international Jupp Heynckes and brought in Ralf Rangnick.

Rangnick was no stranger to Hearts as he had been the manager of the Stuttgart side that had scraped through to the next round four years earlier, after the one of the most dramatic European games ever witnessed at Tynecastle. However, the following year he was sacked after a run of poor results and he moved to second division side Hannover '96 where, in his first season in charge, he led them back into the Bundesliga after a 13-year absence. Rangnick then managed to establish the side in the top flight but after a loss of form he was relieved of his post in March 2004. Briefly touted for the post of assistant manager to the international side, he was brought to Schalke in September. His success was instant and the club won all five league games they had played under his stewardship.

However, he had to be grateful in part to his predecessor for being able to bring his side to Edinburgh, as it was under Jupp Heynckes that Schalke had qualified for the UEFA Cup after being one of *three* winners of the Intertoto Cup, a competition in which Hearts' city rivals Hibernian had failed to progress past the second round after being beaten by Lithuanian giants FK Vetra. The Germans' achievement allowed them passage into the first round where, now under Rangnick, they had comprehensively beaten the Latvian side Liepajas Matalures 9-1 on aggregate.

Schalke were former winners of the tournament, having beaten Inter Milan on penalties back in 1997. Rangnick obviously considered that the current side could repeat the success. After a training session at Murrayfield he stated, 'If we play the way we have in the last two games we can beat any team in Europe.' Like many, he remembered the game at Tynecastle well. 'It was a close match played in a great atmosphere,' he said, but it was the presence of one player that he remembered in particular. 'Hearts played a guy that normally didn't play in the team in attack. He was a huge guy, the tallest footballer I have seen in my life. We nicknamed him "Jaws" from the James Bond movie'.

'Jaws' was of course Kevin James who was no longer at the club, but the player struggled to contain him that night was the Brazilian International Marcelo Bordon who was now in the Schalke ranks. If Hearts could get someone to cause Bordon as much discomfort as James did that night, then surely they would have a terrific chance of getting the win the needed.

Although this was billed as John Robertson's first game in charge, he rightly decided not to interfere with John McGlynn's preparation for the game as the youth coach had taken over the reins following the departure of Peter Houston. McGlynn was also given the responsibility for team selection and in a remarkable parallel to the game in 2000, he had to contend with an injury doubt about his main striker. Mark de Vries was still not fully recovered from the poisoned toe problem that had kept him out for a few weeks, so perhaps with the Stuttgart game in mind, McGlynn decided that Kevin McKenna would make the perfect partner for the enigmatic Ramon Pereira up front.

MURRAYFIELD STADIUM – THURSDAY 4 NOVEMBER 2004
HEARTS: 0
V
FC GELSENKIRCHEN SCHALKE 04: 1 (LINCOLN 73)
REFEREE: N IVANOV (RUSSIA)

With former manager Craig Levein and his assistant Peter Houston among over 27,000 spectators watching from the stands, John Robertson took his place in the dugout to rapturous applause. There was no doubt that his presence had added to the attendance, there being over 9,000 more inside the home of Scottish rugby than had been at the Braga game. The match was also being broadcast live on German TV which, along with income from advertising, meant that the tie would be the most lucrative in the club's history, grossing an estimated £1 million.

Even this sizable amount would not be enough to pay the annual salary of Schalke's star man, Ailton who, rumour had it, was being paid £1.8 million a season. Bought from Werder Bremen, 'Tony' had angered the Schalke support by saying that he much preferred life in the more cosmopolitan Bremen than Gelsenkirchen. They soon forgave him when he started scoring the goals that saw the club rise to second place in the league.

As early as the third minute he showed the type of talent this money bought when he tested Craig Gordon with an audacious chip from almost 25 yards. His aim was a shade out on this occasion and the ball went inches over the bar, but it was an indication of the threat that the German side posed.

Hearts struggled to get a foothold in the game and Patrick Kisnorbo let his frustrations boil over after 19 minutes when he was booked for dissent after passing comment to an assistant referee. It was a senseless booking and one that would contribute significantly to the outcome of the game.

Hearts created their first real chance a minute later when Jamie McAllister gathered a clearance on the edge of the box. Frank Rost in the Schalke goal could only parry his shot as it fell into the path of Paul Hartley, but the midfielder was unable to control it properly and was blocked out at the expense of a corner.

Towards the end of the first period, two incidents in quick succession

Kevin McKenna challenges Christian Pander in the UEFA Cup match against Schalke 04 at Murrayfield in November 2004 © Getty Images

brought the strangely subdued crowd to life. Firstly, Hamit Alintop took a rather theatrical tumble after a challenge from Robbie Neilson. The right back was not the only man in the stadium surprised to see the Russian referee flash the yellow card for what appeared to be a harmless tackle.

Within a minute Mr Ivanov further incensed the home support after Ramon Pereira fell in the box under pressure from Marcelo Bordon. With Pereira looking for a penalty, Ivanov took no action, although the incident bore similarities to the clash that had seen Neilson punished seconds earlier. There is no doubt it would have been a soft award but it was the sense of injustice that had angered the fans.

Barely two minutes into the second half, Hearts had another claim for a penalty when Patrick Kisnorbo burst into the box, only to be impeded by Niels Oude-Kamphuis. Once again the referee ignored any pleas and waved play on. After the ball went out, he called over Kisnorbo and for the second time in the game showed him the yellow card. The Australian did seem to make the most of the contact that was made but to be cautioned for 'diving' was harsh in the extreme.

Down to ten men, Hearts battled hard to stay in the game as the visitors started to use their numerical advantage to good effect. Both Ebbe Sand and Oude-Kamphuis hit the woodwork in a two-minute spell.

Hearts' management team's reaction was to gamble on the fitness of Mark de Vries and sent him on to replace Kevin McKenna with 25 minutes to go. It was a bold move but nine minutes later it was Schalke that made the breakthrough. The Brazilian Lincoln dispossessed Paul Hartley in midfield then took a couple of strides forward before unleashing an unstoppable strike from 30 yards.

It was a hammer blow to Hearts' hopes. Even the introduction of an extra forward in the shape of Graham Weir could not produce the equaliser, and the German side played out the remainder of time with ease.

HEARTS: GORDON NEILSON MAYBURY WEBSTER PRESSLEY MCALLISTER KISNORBO HARTLEY HAMILL (WEIR G) MCKENNA (DE VRIES) PEREIRA (MACFARLANE). SUBS UNUSED: MOILANEN WYNESS BERRA STEWART
FC GELSENKIRCHEN SCHALKE 04: ROST POULSEN BORDON ALTINTOP (KOBIASHVILI) AILTON LINCOLN SAND (HANKE) ASAMOAH (VARELA) WALDOCH OUDE-KAMPHUIS PANDER. SUBS UNUSED: HEIMEROTH KLÄSENER RODRIGUEZ VERMANT

In the group's other game Ferencvaros and Feyenoord drew 1-1, a result that left Hearts rooted to the bottom of the table. After two games they were the only team that had yet to gain a point.

The Schalke manager still thought that Hearts had a chance of qualifying. 'If they win their next two games they will be in the reckoning,' Rangnick said, also suggesting that the result might have been different if Hearts had not taken the game to Murrayfield: 'It would have been tougher for us if the game had been played at Tynecastle. My memory of that was it was worse for the away team.'

The truth was that the result might have been different if Hearts had not suffered from yet another woeful display of refereeing.

In the three weeks until the next game, away to Basel, John Robertson's side had mixed results with a win, draw and a defeat against Aberdeen, Kilmarnock and Motherwell respectively. The latter game, billed as 'the legend's return', was the new manager's first game in charge at Tynecastle. The disappointing 1-0 defeat angered Robertson, not because of a poor performance by his team but by the referee, and the fact that he had also seen a man sent off. All very reminiscent of the game against Schalke.

With a win essential to kickstart the European campaign, it was a tough test ahead. Basel had an impeccable record at home in European competitions. Recently, teams such as Liverpool, Valencia, Juventus and Celtic had all failed to win in St Jacob Park. Managed by former Tottenham Hotspur boss Christian Gross, the Swiss side appeared in the group stages of the UEFA Cup via the 'parachute' system employed by UEFA for teams beaten in the qualifying stages of the Champions League. They had been unfortunate in being paired against Inter Milan and were beaten 5-2 on aggregate after having held the Italians to a 1-1 draw in Basel. Recently, results had gone against them and at the weekend before the tie they had exited the Swiss Cup at the hands of FC Thun.

Despite Basel's dip in form it was obvious that Hearts had a tough task in hand, but John Robertson took a positive approach to the game. Without the suspended Paul Hartley and Patrick Kisnorbo, he selected Denis Wyness, Mark de Vries and Ramon Pereira to start the game.

ST JACOB PARK – THURSDAY 25 NOVEMBER 2004
FC BASEL: 1 (CARIGNANO 76)
V
HEARTS: 2 (WYNESS 31; NEILSON 89)
REFEREE: K JAKOBSSON (ICELAND)

The 2,000 Hearts fans who had made the journey to Switzerland were congregated in one corner of the stadium, their flags and banners showing that they had travelled from all parts of the UK and beyond to see if their favourites could get the necessary victory. At the opposite end, the home support displayed a banner that read 'Brave Enough To Break Hearts' – but it was not a case of being brave enough, it was a question of whether they were good enough.

It looked as though they might be when they almost opened the scoring as early as the second minute. Australian Scott Chipperfield played in a free kick from the right touchline and Benjamin Huggel rose in between Steven Pressley and Robbie Neilson, but his header went inches wide. It was an early warning which was heeded and the defence then dealt comfortably with any attack that came their way.

There was a scare after 16 minutes when Craig Gordon could only parry a long-range effort from the Argentinean Matais Delgado. The ball bounced out to Julio Rossi but with no defenders near him, he directed his diving header into the ground, giving the Hearts goalie the opportunity to gather the ball as it bounced into his arms.

Hearts looked content to hit the home side on the break but all too often the final pass would go astray. Then, with 25 minutes gone, a stroke of good fortune provided them with a golden opportunity. An attempted clearance from Sterjovski rebounded off the referee to Michael Stewart, who quickly played it inside to Denis Wyness. In space on the edge of the box, he could only drag his left-foot shot wide of the goal with Pascal

Zuberbühler rooted to the spot.

Six minutes later he made amends for the miss after Ramon Pereira cut in from the left along the edge of the box before playing the ball to Joe Hamill, who touched it on to Wyness. He took one touch with his right foot before hitting a low shot into the bottom of the net with his left. Ramon Pereira had continued his run and strayed into an offside position, even going as far as to trying to connect with the ball. Despite turning to celebrate the goal, he had failed to get a touch, something the assistant referee had also spotted as he allowed the goal to stand. That was the signal for half a dozen over-exuberant supporters to run onto the park from the Hearts enclosure, but order was quickly restored with a heavy security presence now surrounding the travelling fans.

The decision to let the goal stand was certainly contentious but was probably the first refereeing decision that had gone Hearts' way in the three games so far. Two minutes later they got another break when Icelandic referee Kristinn Jakobsson waved away a strong penalty claim when Alan Maybury clashed with Mile Sterjovski in the box. Mr Jakobsson had been in charge the previous year in Bordeaux, so perhaps this was to be Hearts' night.

At the start of the second half the home side went on the attack straight from the kick off and succeeded in winning a free kick on the edge of the box. Scott Chipperfield took the kick but he failed to test Craig Gordon as the wall did its job. Chipperfield did call on Gordon to show what he could do after 56 minutes, after a Mile Sterjovski cross from just inside the box on the right went to the back post where the Australian reacted quicker than Joe Hamill. His diving header from inside the six yard box looked to be a goal all the way until the Scottish international dived to his right to pull of a top class save.

Basel's frustration at their failure to make a breakthrough began to grow and it was no more clearly illustrated when Christian Giménez became the first name to be entered into the referee's book following an outrageous foul on Steven Pressley after 65 minutes – although whether the Mr Jakobsson used his actual name or the rather odd 'JIMMY' he displayed on the back of his number 13 shirt is not known.

Their failure to score was also becoming a source of frustratation for the home crowd and their irritation increased eight minutes later when once again Basel went close. For once, Craig Gordon was beaten when Chipperfield's corner was met by substitute César Carignano but Alan Maybury was on the line to head clear. Marco Zwyssig looked ready to pounce but Gordon made a flying dive to punch the ball clear. Carignano had better luck three minutes later when he latched onto a through ball from Matias Delgado and managed to shrug off the attention of Alan Maybury and Andy Webster to finish off from eight yards out.

The mood of the Swiss crowd changed instantly as their team went in search of a winner, but as had been the case throughout the game Basel found it difficult to break down the well-organised Hearts defence. With only two minutes left on the clock, Graham Weir latched on to a long clearance from defence then bundled it out to Joe Hamill on the left. Hamill played it to

Steven Pressley, Robbie Neilson and Craig Gordon are amongst the players who celebrate with manager John Robertson at the end of the 2-1 win over Basel
© Davy Allan

the back post where Phil Stamp, who had come on for Ramón Pereira, was waiting. His downward header took a deflection off his marker and dropped in the path of the inrushing Robbie Neilson, whose first-time shot went under the body of Pascal Zuberbuhler. It was Robbie's first goal after eight years at the club but it could not have come at a better time.

Basel were stunned and threw everything at Hearts in an effort to get the equaliser. At one stage their keeper ran the length of the park after his side won a corner. Ironically, he was then penalised for using his hands to control the ball. In the remaining seconds Hearts should have added a third goal when Graham Weir was left clear with only Zuberbuhler to beat, but his weak effort was palmed away by the goalkeeper as the final seconds ticked down.

After four minutes of added time had been played, the referee finally ended the game to give Hearts one of their best results in their long history of playing in Europe. The team were naturally delighted, as was the new manager, who ensured that the players went to applaud the travelling support who had also played their part in the important victory.

FC BASEL: ZUBERBUHLER ZWYSSIG HUGGEL STERJOVSKI (DEGEN D) CHIPPERFIELD GIMÉNEZ KLEBER DELGADO (BARBERIS) DEGEN (P) SMILJANIC ROSSI (CARIGNANO). SUBS UNUSED: QUENNOZ MANDL
HEARTS: GORDON NEILSON MAYBURY WEBSTER PRESSLEY MCALLISTER STEWART (MACFARLANE)

HAMILL WYNESS DE VRIES (WEIR G) PEREIRA (STAMP). SUBS UNUSED: MOILANEN BERRA SLOAN
JANCZYK

On the same evening as Hearts were winning in Switzerland, Schalke had a comfortable 2-0 win at home against Ferencvaros. These results lifted the Germans into top spot in the group, with Hearts in third place. However, as they did not have a fixture in Matchday Four, the placings were sure to change going into the final round of games in mid-December.

In the clash of the top two sides Feyenoord came out on top, 2-1 against Schalke; meanwhile, in a game taken in by Hearts' Donald Park and John McGlynn, Basel defeated Hearts' next opponents, Ferencvaros, by the same scoreline in Budapest. With only one game left, Hearts had dropped out of the qualifying places into fourth place. Schalke and Feyenoord were already assured of qualification, so the home tie against the Hungarians was a 'must win' if they were to stand any chance of going through to the lucrative knockout stages. Even then, they would have to rely on the previously unbeaten Feyenoord avoiding defeat in Basel.

Ferencvaros were another team whose route to this stage had come via the 'parachute' method from the Champions League. Eliminated by Sparta Prague, they were then entered into the first round of the UEFA Cup where they beat Millwall 4-2 on aggregate.

Like Hearts, they had just undergone a period of financial restructure when in 2003 they became the first Hungarian club to become a 'PLC' with shares being traded on the Budapest Stock Exchange. Also like Hearts, they had a new manager in charge – Romanian-born Hungarian Csaba László. With only one point his club was bottom of the group and he, like John Robertson, was looking for Feyenoord to get a win in Basel if they were to stand any chance of progressing.

MURRAYFIELD STADIUM – THURSDAY 16 DECEMBER 2004
HEARTS: 0
V
FERENCVÁROSI TC: 1 (RÓSA 30)
REFEREE: L PANIASHVILI (GEORGIA)

It may have been that Ferencvaros needed a favour from the Dutch side but they also needed to get a win in Edinburgh, a fact that seemed to elude them for the opening period of the game. They posed little threat and Hearts controlled the game from the first blast of the referee's whistle.

Paul Hartley was dominant in the midfield area and was unfortunate not to put the home side ahead when Lajos Szücs had trouble dealing with his angled drive after ten minutes. Hartley beat the Hungarian keeper three minutes later when he charged down a clearance from Gábor Gyepes before slamming the ball into the net. He barely had time to celebrate before the Georgian referee awarded a free kick against him for alleged deliberate use of his hand to control the ball. It was a harsh decision, considering that he was no more than two feet away from Gyepes when the defender slammed the ball against him.

As Hearts continued to press forward in search of the vital opening goal, Csaba László's men were content to defend in depth, often breaking up the play by reacting dramatically when being pressurised. It was a tactic that began to frustrate both the home team and the crowd as Levan Paniashvili, the Georgian referee, continued to award fouls for the most innocuous of challenges.

On the half hour mark Hearts were caught out by the classic sucker punch when the Hungarians broke out of defence in a move that saw Péter Lipcsei thread a ball through the middle of their back four. Dénes Rósa looked offside as he ran onto the pass, but he was allowed to advance on Craig Gordon by the officials. The Scottish international blocked Rósa's first effort and did even better to dive to his right to save the rebound, but with his defenders still watching on, Gordon could do nothing to prevent the Hungarian from finding the net with his third attempt.

Ferencvaros retreated back into their defensive shell but almost came unstuck three minutes later when Mark de Vries made a surging run, then unleashed a powerful drive from 25 yards. Gábor Gyepes instinctively stuck out his leg and was relieved to see the ball glance off the post, with his goalkeeper Lajos Szücs helpless.

The remainder of the half was played out in the same acrimonious manner. Mr Paniashvili eventually began to take some action with the names of Lipcsei and Zavadszky entering his book after a melee involving half a dozen players from each side. With things threatening to boil over, Andy Webster became the third player to be shown the yellow card as the referee brought the proceedings to a close.

The break did little to take the heat out of the game. Dániel Tőzsér continued the hostilities and was promptly booked for his troubles. It was almost his last action in the game – Csaba Lázló introduced Hungarian international Szabolcs Huszti in his place. Huszti had made a name for himself when he scored two goals against Scotland in a friendly international a few weeks earlier, but despite his proven goal threat the visitors continued with their defensive strategy. With half an hour to play, news started to filter through that Basel had taken the lead against Feyenoord and much of the urgency seemed to be lost from both sides' play. Csaba Lázló continued to remain animated on the touchline which eventually saw his antics brought to the referee's attention by the fourth official. After a short lecture, the Hungarian was sent to the stand to watch the remainder of the game beside the other club officials.

Hearts remained positive, with John Robertson bringing on Ramon Pereira, quickly followed by Denis Wyness in a move that saw them chase the equaliser with four forwards on the pitch. But as they pressed forward, Ferencvaros were quick to exploit the gaps at the back and Craig Gordon was the hero of the hour with a fine stop from a drive from Leandro, which he quickly followed up with a save from a Thomas Sowunmi header.

Those opportunities were the closest either side came to scoring before the referee brought the proceedings to a close. There was still time, though, for a remarkable incident when the coaches of both sides clashed, with John Robertson appearing to take a kick at his opposite number and the pair having to be separated by Lothian and Borders officers.

In the press conference afterwards Robbo explained, 'He called my side cheats and stood on my foot. I got him off my foot.' Lázló, unsurprisingly, saw it differently: 'He said I am crazy. I said he is crazy. He came to me and gave my leg a kick. This is not nice.' When told this, the Hearts manager responded by saying, 'If I had kicked him he wouldn't be standing.' The final word went to the Hungarian manager when he said of Hearts, 'This is a good team. Maybe with a better coach, who knows...'

HEARTS: GORDON NEILSON MAYBURY WEBSTER PRESSLEY STEWART KISNORBO (WYNESS) HARTLEY MCALLISTER (PEREIRA) DE VRIES WEIR G (MCKENNA). SUBS UNUSED: MOILANEN HAMILL BERRA MACFARLANE
FERENCVÁROSI TC: SZÜCS VUKMIR GYEPES BALOG RÓSA LIPCSEI ZAVADSZKY LEANDRO TŐZSÉR (HUSZTI) BAJEVSKI (TAKÁCS) PENKSA (SOWUNMI). SUBS UNUSED: UDVÁRACZ, SZKUKALEK SOMORJAI BOGNÁR

The result saw both sides eliminated from the competition, with Feyenoord, Schalke and Basel all going through to the knockout stage. It was as far as they went, as all three were eliminated at the first hurdle in the 'Round of 32'.

For Hearts, it had been their first taste of playing in the new group format which brought about many unforgettable moments, none more so than the last-gasp winner in Switzerland scored by former club captain Robbie Neilson. Modestly, he does not make too much of it:

Although I've left the club, I still run into Hearts fans wherever I go and I still get asked about either 'that' tackle in the Cup Final or 'that' goal in Basel, but to be honest that was a case of being in the right place at the right time. It is among many great memories of European ties, from my very first appearance after replacing Colin Cameron in the game against Stuttgart in German, to my last in the Toyota Arena in Prague. Of all the European games I played in, the trip I recall most was when we got a chance to play in the Champions League a couple of seasons later when we travelled to Bosnia to play Široki Brijeg.

Most journeys abroad just involve a bit of training at the ground and then hanging about a hotel until game time. However, this time the lads decided to do a bit of sightseeing and it really was a culture shock compared to tranquil Edinburgh.

We were based about 25 kilometres from Široki, in Mostar, a place everyone had heard about – not just because Hearts had played there before, but because of the Bosnian war back in the early '90s.

We were amazed to see the street which marked the divide between east and west in the city and had obviously been the front line during the trouble. The buildings were derelict and what was still standing was full of holes from bullets and artillery shells.

Just round the corner was the famous Stari Most bridge that spans the Neretva river. I don't think it was that long since it had been rebuilt after being destroyed during the conflict. But the most remarkable thing about it was the locals who, for a few euros, would dive off into the water 80 foot below. I can think of easier way to make a living!

Once we arrived in Široki the residents were not just as friendly – one tried to swipe the hamper containing our strips for the game. He hadn't reckoned on Tom, our fitness coach, who was after him quicker than Neil McCann.

The game itself was unremarkable really as we played out a 0-0 draw to qualify to play AEK Athens. The thing that I still remember was the condition of the stadium. There had been a lot of talk that Tynecastle was not of a standard to host European ties but if that was the case I have no idea how the Pecara stadium met the requirements. There was no stand, just a wall behind one of the goals and behind that was a block of flats. At one point I looked up and could see into someone's living room – they were watching the game live on TV.

After the game we could not leave from Mostar airport, so the plane had been scheduled to leave from Dubrovnik. At the last minute that was rescheduled to Split, which meant a tiring, three-hour journey, just to get the flight home.

Add the fact that I heard the news that I had been called into a Scotland training squad by Walter Smith, and that trip will stay in my memory for some time to come.

CHAPTER 18

2006–07 Champions League

THE ARRIVAL OF Vladimir Romanov as Hearts' new supremo signalled the start of a managerial merry-go-round at Tynecastle. John Robertson's reign was brought to an end and Steven Pressley, John McGlynn, George Burley, Graham Rix and Valdas Ivanauskas all had spells in the hot seat, with varying degrees of success.

The 05–06 season saw the last three managers in charge, with Burley setting up the foundations before Lithuanian Ivanauskas watched as a Paul Hartley penalty after 52 minutes in the second-last game of the season (against Aberdeen) was good enough to see Hearts finish as runners-up in the SPL, thus gaining entry to the qualifying stages of the Champions League. Coupled with a Scottish Cup triumph ten days later, the season was the most successful for many a long year.

It meant that the following season Hearts had an earlier start than normal, with the Champions League qualifier first leg having to be played a few days before the SPL opening day. Hearts were drawn against the relatively unknown NK Široki Brijeg from Hertzegovia. More familiar to some was their manager Ivica Barbaric who had played in the Velež Mostar side that Hearts defeated in the UEFA Cup in 1988.

Hearts were not only firm favourites to go through to the third qualifying round, they also had history on their side, having a perfect two out of two record against sides from Bosnia having beaten not only Velež Mostar but also Željezničar Sarajevo a couple of seasons earlier.

MURRAYFIELD STADIUM – WEDNESDAY 26 JULY 2006
HEARTS: 0
V
NK ŠIROKI BRIJEG: 3 (ANIC OG 53; TALL 78; BEDNAR 85)
REFEREE: E BERNTSEN (NORWAY)

The decision to make the venue Murrayfield was vindicated: despite the game being shown live on TV, over 28,000 – Hearts' biggest European attendance since 1960 – turned up to watch them ease past the Bosnian minnows. Perhaps it was the change of venue, or the fact that it was a particularly warm July evening, but it took until the second half before they managed to take control of the game.

It might have been so different if Bruno Aguair had managed to do better than to knock a Neil McCann cross over the bar after only 20 seconds. After that early let-off, Široki started to cause problems and had a decent claim for a penalty waved away after the ball seemed to strike Neil McCann on the hand when he tried to clear from a corner.

Due to the empty spaces in the stands and the poor showing from the team, the Hearts support were becoming restless and slack finishing by Edgaras Jankauskas ten minutes before the interval did nothing to help the atmosphere.

The mood was not lightened when Bruno Aguair clumsily brought down the Brazilian, Celson, 25 yards out. It gave Wagner Lago the chance to blast a shot that went inches over the bar. The jeers were ringing out as the Norwegian ref blew for the end of an uninspiring half.

Hearts started the second period with a bit more urgency and a typical long throw from Robbie Neilson found Roman Bednář in the box. With his back to goal, he fired in a shot on the turn but the Široki defenders somehow managed to block and the danger was cleared.

A few minutes later another Robbie Neilson throw-in caused more panic and in an attempt to clear the danger Branimir Anic headed the ball past his own keeper.

The goal enlivened the home side, with Steven Pressley, Deividas Česnauskis and Bruno Aguair all coming close to grabbing the vital second goal. Neil McCann and Edgaras Jankauskas made way for Saulius Mikoliunas and Michal Pospisil respectively, and with 12 minutes to go it was Pospisil that started the move that saw Ibrahim Tall put Hearts two up. His first attempt was a complete mis-kick, but he recovered his composure to make no mistake from six yards out.

With five minutes left, Roman Bednář was quick to pounce on an attempted pass back by Ivica Landeka and beat Široki goalie Tomislav Bašić easily.

HEARTS: GORDON NEILSON PRESSLEY BERRA FYSSAS CESNAUSKIS TALL AGUIAR (BRELLIER 88) MCCANN (MIKOLIUNAS, 56) JANKAUSKAS (POSPISIL 56) BEDNÁŘ. SUBS UNUSED: BANKS MOLE NEILL DRIVER.
NK ŠIROKI BRIJEG: BAŠIĆ PANDŽA LANDEKA ŠILIĆ BUBALO (DOCI) ANIC WAGNER CARVALHO (PAPIC) GOMES CELSON KAROGLAN (KOVACIC). SUBS UNUSED: VASILJ LUKACEVIC STUDENOVIC DZIDIC.

The emphatic win put Hearts firmly in the driving seat to progress to the next qualifying round where they would face a stiffer task against AEK Athens.

The ground at Široki which met UEFA standards while Tynecastle didn't. Note the houses in the background where Robbie Neilson was able to watch the game on TV!
From author's collection.

But first there was a trip to south-eastern Europe to take care of.

The squad and around a hundred intrepid supporters arrived in sun-drenched Bosnia in the early afternoon and were then bussed to the hotel in Mostar which would be their base during their stay. The town of Široki Brijeg lay some 22 kilometres away high in the mountains, but lacked the facilities that Hearts required. This meant that the team had to leave Mostar in the early evening for a training session in the compact Pecara stadium. There they were surprised to see that the ground only had three sides with the area behind one goal only being a brick wall. The whole set-up had some of the players questioning how the Pecara was UEFA compliant yet Tynecastle wasn't.

The following day the squad relaxed with a stroll round Mostar old town before heading back up the winding road for the game. There were two changes to the team from the first leg, with Julian Brellier getting the nod in front of Ibrahim Tall and Michal Pospišil taking over from Edgaras Jankauskas who had a hamstring injury.

Vladimir Romanov made an appearance at the game and brought with him 50 workers from his Bosnia-based aluminium company to boost the small number of travelling fans.

STADION PECARA – WEDNESDAY 2 AUGUST 2006
NK ŠIROKI BRIJEG: 0
V
HEARTS: 0
REFEREE: V KASSAI (HUNGARY)

Hearts made a confident start and the thousands back in Scotland watching the game live on the BBC benefited from an instant replay that showed if Hungarian referee Viktor Kassai was correct in disallowing a Hearts goal after eight minutes. It was technology that the away support did not have and they remained convinced that Široki keeper, Viktor Kassai, blundered by punching a Neil McCann corner into his own net – without any interference from Christophe Berra as the whistler had decided.

The home side also made some chances, the best coming after 15 minutes when a fiercely struck free kick from Mislav Karoglan was expertly dealt with by Craig Gordon.

Another chance came their way shortly before the break when Branimir Anic made good progress down the right-hand side before squaring the ball to Ronelle Gomes 15 yards out. Luckily for Hearts, the forward completely missed his kick but the ball fell to Josip Papic just outside the box. Perhaps surprised to get the opportunity, he blasted the ball wildly over the bar.

Široki began the second half the way they left off, and Craig Gordon had to be at his brilliant best again within five minutes of the restart. Wagner set up Celson a few yards out, but the Scotland keeper once again frustrated the Bosnians with a tremendous block.

As the game wore on it began to slip beyond the home side's grasp and their support, or Škripari as they are known, started to drift off into the night. The final straw for most came with 13 minutes left, when Craig Gordon pulled off yet another great save from a powerful drive from the rotund substitute, Hrvoje Erceg.

NK ŠIROKI BRIJEG: VASILJ ANIC ŠILIC WAGNER PAPIC (STUDENOVIC) PANDŽA IVICA LANDEKA GOMES KOVACIC (ERCEG) KAROGLAN CELSON (CARVALHO). SUBS UNUSED: BAŠIĆ DOCI DALIBOR KOZUL KVESIC.
HEARTS: GORDON NEILSON (TALL) FYSSAS PRESSLEY MCCANN (MIKOLIUNAS) AGUIAR POSPISIL BEDNAR CESNAUSKIS (BESLIJA) BERRA BRELLIER. SUBS UNUSED: BANKS MAKELA WALLACE MOLE.

In the third qualifying round Hearts were paired against AEK Athens, a side with a useful Champions League pedigree, having qualified for the group stages twice in the last decade. Their owner, Demis Nikolaidis, had been likened in the press to Vladimir Romanov inasmuch as he had taken over the Athens club when they were deep in debt. Nikolaidis then managed to get a court ruling to have the debt written off and now AEK were beginning to emerge from the shadows of rivals Olympiakos and Panathinaikos.

Although the Greek season did not start until the end of the month, AEK had just beaten a strong Benfica side 3-1 in a friendly at the weekend and a familiar face in new AEK coach Lorenzo Serra Ferrer's side that turned up for a workout at Murrayfield on Tuesday evening was former Rangers flop Emerson. He may have wished he had stayed back in Greece when their allotted time on the Murrayfield surface came to an end and Ferrer refused to take his team inside. When a second, firmer request was also ignored, Scottish ingenuity kicked in: the pitch sprinklers were turned on, soaking the bewildered Greeks.

Hearts didn't have any such problems at their training session and were also coming off a morale-boosting victory with a Roman Bednář double being good enough to see off champions Celtic at Tynecastle. The win had come at a cost, as Ibrahim Tall sustained ankle ligament damage and was ruled out for four weeks. On the day of the game both Julien Brellier and Deividas Censauskas were diagnosed as having a respiratory virus so manager Valdas gave a debut to new signing Christos Karipidis, deploying him in an unfamiliar midfield role. Fellow Greek Takis Fyssas also lined up against his countrymen.

MURRAYFIELD STADIUM – WEDNESDAY 9 AUGUST 2006
HEARTS: 1 (MIKOLIUNAS 61)
V
AEK ATHENS: 2 (KAPETANOS 89; BERRA OG 90)
REFEREE: N VOLLQUARTZ (DENMARK)

If Hearts needed any indication of the Greeks' intentions, it came as soon as the first minute when Robbie Neilson was forced to clear a net-bound shot from Julio César behind for a corner. A minute later and it was Takis Fyssas' turn to clear the danger, and from the resultant corner César swung in a dangerous ball that was met by Traianos Dellas and rattled the crossbar before being swept clear.

Craig Gordon's goal continued to be under siege and both the Brazilian César and Nikos Liberopoulos came close as Hearts struggled to try and find a way into the game.

With 11 minutes gone and against the run of play, Saulius Mikoliunas almost gave the home side a shock lead when in the first attack, he cut inside from the left and let fly towards goal. The ball struck Bruno Grillo on the thigh and spun away from keeper Stefano Sorrentino – but, agonisingly, onto the post before being cleared. AEK continued to pile on the pressure and Steven Pressley did just enough with a last-gasp tackle on Julio César to ensure that the Athens danger man did not give his side the lead. If the Hearts captain had been the hero at that moment, he quickly turned to sinner three minutes before the break when he badly miscued a clearance that fell straight to César, whose dipping effort forced Craig Gordon into a fantastic, fingertip save.

Although Hearts had been second best throughout the first period, they still managed to go in at half-time all square and, incredibly, went ahead after 15 minutes of the second 45. An incisive move between substitute Edgaras Jankauskas and Roman Bednář saw the Czech fire in a shot that hit the left-hand upright. Saulius Mikoliunas was first to react and stroked home a low drive from five yards.

The joy amongst the 32,500 crowd had barely died down when Hearts managed to shoot themselves in the foot. After Neil McCann was penalised for a tackle in midfield, Bruno Aguiar foolishly threw the ball away, earning himself a booking. As he had already received a caution in the first half for a foul on Liberopoulos, it meant that he had to leave the park.

Despite being a man short, Hearts continued to defend well as AEK went all out for the equaliser. Every man was a hero, none more so than Craig Gordon when with only four minutes left he defied Julio César once again with yet another stunning save. But disaster was to strike in the last minute of the 90. Robbie Neilson lost possession to Stavros Tziortziopoulos, who whipped in a cross into the middle of the Hearts box. Christophe Berra looked to have Panteus Kapetanos covered but somehow the lone forward managed to produce a miracle header that looped into the top corner of the net.

It was probably no more than the visitors deserved, but it was still hard to take as victory had beckoned. But even a hard-fought draw was taken away deep into time added on, when Nikolas Lymperopoulos seemed to run out of ideas and hit a speculative shot 25 yards out. Instinctively, Christophe Berra stuck out a leg in an attempt to block the ball but it took a wicked deflection past Craig Gordon. Hearts had lost in the cruellest manner.

HEARTS: GORDON NEILSON FYSSAS BERRA PRESSLEY MCCANN (N) MIKOLIUNAS AGUIAR KARIPIDIS (JANKAUSKAS) BEDNAR (WALLACE) POSPIŠIL (ELLIOT C). SUBS UNUSED: BANKS BESLIJA MAKELA MOLE
AEK ATHENS: SORRENTINO PAUTASSO (TZIORTZIOPOULOS) DELLAS CIRILLO GEORGEAS LAGOS (LAKIS) EMERSON IVIĆ JULIO CÉSAR LYMPEROPOULOS KAPETANOS. SUBS UNUSED: CHIOTIS PAPASTATHOPOULOS MORAS SOARES TÖZSÉR

After the match Valdas Ivanauskas insisted that Nicolai Vollquartz, the Danish referee, was the cause of Hearts' downfall, saying, 'I am very angry about the referee. He made mistakes, and the mistakes cost us the match. The sending off cost us the match.' Not surprisingly, his opposite number, thought differently. 'We feel that we dominated the match from the first minute to the last. We always thought that things would work out well as we have worked hard and these efforts paid off,' Lorenzo Serra Ferrer said.

Perhaps the shots count of 32-8 in his side's favour backs up his statement.

Following a disappointing 2-0 defeat to Rangers, Hearts had major injury worries for the second leg in Athens. Of particular concern were the forwards, with regular starters Roman Bednar and Michal Pospíšil both doubtful and the alternative being the slothful Edgaras Jankauskas and Calum Elliot, of whom the talk was that he was set to be farmed out on loan. Also, Paul Hartley was not considered fully fit after being out through injury.

By the time the squad left Turnhouse, Valdas Ivanauskas had decided that Roman Bednář was out, but with an estimated £6 million at stake for qualifying for the group stages, it was worth gambling on Paul Hartley.

OACA SPYRO LOUIS – WEDNESDAY 23 AUGUST 2006
AEK ATHENS: 3 (CÉSAR 79 & 86; LIBEROPOULOS 82)
V
HEARTS: 0
REFEREE: Y BASKAKOV (RUSSIA)

In an attempt to gain the psychological upper hand, before kick off the Greeks showed reruns of previous wins in Europe on giant screens behind each goal. The move backfired spectacularly as each goal was greeted by cheers from the 400-strong Hearts support. The Athenians had chosen games against Hibs and Rangers, hardly a move to upset the travelling masses.

What did silence the crowd temporarily was the news that Jamie Mole would lead the attack, a surprise move as he had not started a competitive game so far. But it was Mole that had a fabulous opportunity to grab the goal that would pull Hearts back into the tie.

After containing the home side comfortably for the first 15 minutes, Hearts broke out of defence with a move involving Paul Hartley and Neil McCann. The ball was moved to Jamie Mole, who was left with only stand-in keeper Dionisis Chiotis to beat, but his effort was weak and Nikos Georgeas had plenty of time to get back and clear easily.

It was a bad miss but the real turning point of the game came ten minutes later, when Julien Brellier became involved in the biggest jewellery scandal since Bobby Moore walked into a Bogotá jewellers shop in 1970.

After having received treatment for a head knock, Julien received a yellow card after the referee spotted that he was wearing a diamond earring. A strange decision, since the ref had checked the players in the dressing room before the start and several Greek players could easily be spotted wearing rings and gold necklaces.

Having incurred the wrath of the Russian referee, the last thing the Frenchman wanted to do was to come to his attention again but that is exactly what he did five minutes later. Jumping into a challenge with Traianos Dellas, he was adjudged to have struck the Greek with his elbow. It looked a fairly innocent clash, but Mr Baskakov thought otherwise and brandished a second yellow card. Brellier was gone, taking with him Hearts' chances of progressing to the next round.

From that moment AEK raised their game and within seven minutes Panagiotis Lagos had spurned two great chances to put them ahead. Hearts survived and went in at half-time all square, but still with the uphill task of having to grab the two goals that would put them through with only ten men.

If that seemed a tough ask, it became even harder. With 62 minutes gone, they were reduced to nine men when Neil McCann was shown a straight red card after a tackle on Serbian midfielder Vladimir Ivić.

Now it was obvious that there was only going to be one winner as the home side controlled the play and continued to create chances. To Hearts' credit, they defended stoutly and it took a dubious penalty decision to give AEK the breakthrough finally after 77 minutes. Winger Vasilis Lakis cut into the box but his progress was checked on the bye line by Deividas Cesnauskis. Craig Gordon gathered the ball but was as shocked as

Neil McCann is shown the red card after a foul on Vladimir Ivić in Athens © Davy Allan

everyone else in the stadium when he saw the referee point to the spot. The big keeper was sent the wrong way as the Brazilian Julio César expertly slotted home.

The flares set off by the crowd were still burning when, four minutes later, Nikos Georgeas sent in a cross from the left and Nikos Liberopoulos beat Takis Fyssas and Christoph Berra to head past Craig Gordon.

It was game, set and match to the Greeks with five minutes left when Edgaras Jankauskas was caught in possession by Julio César, who strode into the box before finishing neatly from 12 yards. With only a minute to go, manager Ivanauskas turned 'Greek Tragedy' into 'French Farce' when he brought on recent signing Mauricio Pinella in place of Jamie Mole. The Chilean forward did not have the opportunity to touch the ball before the referee brought the contest to a close. However, given Pinella's subsequent Hearts career, that minute was a rare opportunity to see him in action.

AEK ATHENS: CHIOTIS PAUTASSO (TÖZSÉR) CIRILLO DELLAS GEORGEAS EMERSON IVIĆ LAGOS (LAKIS) CÉSAR LIBEROPOULOS (KAMPANTAIS) KAPETANOS. SUBS UNUSED: ARABATZIS MORAS KIRIAKIDIS TZIORTZIOPOULOS
HEARTS: GORDON NEILSON PRESSLEY BERRA FYSSAS BRELLIER MIKOLIOUNAS MCCANN CESNAUSKIS (WALLACE) HARTLEY (JANKAUSKAS) MOLE (PINILLA). SUBS UNUSED: BANKS BESLIJA KARIPIDIS ELLIOT

AEK went through to play in Group H, finishing third behind eventual winners AC Milan who beat Liverpool in the final played in AEK's home ground in Athens. Finishing third, they then 'parachuted' into the 'Round of 32' in the UEFA cup but were beaten 4-0 on aggregate by Paris Saint-Germain.

Elimination from the Champions League did not mean the end to Hearts' European adventures for the season, as they now qualified for a place in the first round of the UEFA Cup. When the draw was made on 25 August in the Grimaldi Forum in Monaco, they found out that to make it to the lucrative group stages they would have to overcome Sparta Prague, a team with a fine European pedigree.

After a poor start to the season, Sparta had just replaced Stanislav Griga with former player Michal Bilek as manager when the teams were paired together. At Tynecastle there was also speculation that Valdas Ivanauskas's position was in jeopardy after the club had not only being dumped out of the Champions League but had suffered defeats at the hands of Falkirk, Rangers and St Mirren. Rumour was that Mr Romanov was running out of patience with his fellow Lithuanian and his mood was not helped by what he saw as biased refereeing, not only in the game against AEK but also at home in Scotland.

Prior to the game against Sparta, he chose to use the club's web site to vent his anger against Russian ref Yuri Baskakov and the 'football mafia in Scotland', a move that, unsurprisingly, brought comments from both the SFA and UEFA that they would 'investigate'. Perhaps the Hearts owner's outburst had been brought on by the fact that Italian referee Paulo Bertini had been appointed as the man in charge for the game at Murrayfield.

Bertini had recently been implicated in a bribes scandal that had rocked Italian football, involving Juventus, AC Milan, Lazio and Fiorentina. Calls for him to be handed a five-year ban were eventually ignored and he was cleared, but there was no doubt it was a controversial appointment.

Sparta arrived in Edinburgh on the Wednesday morning following a 2-0 win against Tescoma Zlin in the Gambrinus Liga, in Bilek's first game in charge. His squad included Tomáš Jun, a player Hearts had turned down the chance to sign from Besiktas back in January. Bilek's opposite number however, had seen his side slip to a 1-0 defeat against St Mirren at Tynecastle, plus had a number of injury doubts, and could now have been grateful for the services of the big Czech striker. As it was he decided to give record signing Mirsad Bešlija his first start of the season and the enigmatic Mauricio Pinella was also included in the starting line-up.

MURRAYFIELD STADIUM – THURSDAY 14 SEPTEMBER 2006
HEARTS: 0
V
AC SPARTA PRAHA 2 (KOLÁR 34; MATUSOVIC 71)
REFEREE: P BERTINI (ITALY)

Rain had been falling constantly since midday, which made the Murrayfield pitch extremely heavy. Puddles of water were clearly visible on the pitch as the teams emerged from the tunnel. Fireworks filled the air to greet them and the resultant plumes of smoke led the referee to delay the start for a few minutes.

The first real opening fell to the visitors after ten minutes when Ludovic Sylvestre worked a one-two with Libor Došek before shooting inches wide. Although Sparta dominated the play they found it difficult to create any real openings, with Hearts content to contain the Czechs in the opening exchanges.

With half an hour gone, Craig Gordon was called into action for the first time when he brought off a fine save from the hardworking Sylvestre. The forward's angled drive looked to be goal-bound until Craig managed to tip the ball over the bar for a corner. But it was a warning of what was to come – a few minutes later, Sparta took the lead.

Hearts' defence failed to clear the ball properly and it fell to Daniel Kolář on the edge of the box. The midfielder wasted no time in hammering it into the top corner of the net, with Craig Gordon helpless. Hearts continued to struggle and it was the Czechs who had the opportunity to increase their lead moments before half-time when Jiří Homola got on the end of a corner from Jan Simak, but he contrived to head over from only a yard out.

The rain had stopped for the start of the second period but the conditions did not help Hearts' passing game. Subsequently, it was the more direct route of a long throw-in from Robbie Neilson that nearly brought the equaliser. Under no real threat from a Hearts player, Michal Kadlec tried to clear the danger but made a bit a hash of it with the ball hitting the back of his head. The startled Jaromir Blažek was beaten, but luckily for him and sadly for Hearts, the ball spun just past the post.

Hearts increased the tempo of their game and a few minutes later Blažek was called into action to deal with a fierce shot from Jamie Mole. The keeper could only beat it out but Paul Hartley couldn't find the net with the rebound.

With just over an hour gone, Valdas Ivanauskas made a double switch with Pinilla and Beslija making way for Ibrahim Tall and Deividas Cesnauskas. It was a move that incensed Mauricio Pinilla who made his displeasure know as he stormed up the tunnel. Nor did it find favour with the 27,000 fans and was greeted with booing that echoed round the stands. Sparta also took the chance to make a substitution with Miroslav Matusovic replacing Jan Simak. The new man was only on the field for seconds when he had an opportunity to increase Sparta's lead, but missed the straightforward chance from only six yards.

With 20 minutes remaining and Hearts still chasing the game, they had Craig Gordon to thank for keeping the tie alive when he brought of an incredible triple save. First, he did well to block a shot from Libor Dosek and then was quick to react when Ludovic Sylvestre fired in the rebound. The ball fell to substitute Matusovic even closer to goal than his miss minutes earlier, but Craig somehow managed to push the ball behind for a corner.

The big forward made no mistake a minute later when he got the ball 25 yards out, but this time the Hearts goalie could do nothing as it flew into the net from long range. It was a killer blow to Hearts' hopes and signalled the start of the spectators filtering out into the dreich Edinburgh evening. When Signor Bertini blew his whistle for the final time, Hearts had been well beaten by a better side and on this occasion, the referee could not be blamed.

HEARTS: GORDON NEILSON WALLACE BERRA PRESSLEY BESLIJA (TALL) MOLE AGUAIR HARTLEY
BEDNAR PINILLA (CESNAUSKIS). SUBS UNUSED: BANKS FYSSAS PARK (M) MAKELA KARIPIDIS
AC SPARTA PRAHA: BLAŽEK REPKA POPŠECH HOMOLA KADLEC KISEL SIVOK, LUDOVIC
(LUSTRINELLI) KOLÁR (HAŠEK) ŠÍMAK (MATUSOVIC) DOŠEK. SUBS UNUSED: GRIGAR DROBNY
ZABAVNÍK, JUN

In the two weeks between the first and second legs, Hearts' results picked up considerably, with three wins away from home. Motherwell and Aberdeen were beaten in the league and Alloa had been seen off in the League Cup, with Hearts scoring eight goals in the process against the loss of only one. The improvement was such that Vladimir Romanov was happy to assure the media that whatever the result in Prague, Vladas Ivanauskas would remain as the manager.

The club's owner also took the opportunity to pronounce that he was satisfied with UEFA's choice of referee, Germany's Peter Sippel, whom he believed would be strong in his handling of the game and punish the 'crude, physical attacks' he thought the Sparta players used in the first leg.

Not surprisingly, Prague manager Michal Bílek defended his players' actions, responding that it had been 'a hard game but fair'. Like Hearts, Sparta had also put together a good run of results that included a 6-0 win against lower league opposition in the Czech cup and more recently a convincing 3-0 win over Ceska Budesovice in the league. Given the form of both sides, it looked as though it would be a closer contest than that at Murrayfield, with Hearts having to make a little piece of history as no Scottish club in the 51 years of European competition had gone through after losing the first leg at home.

LETENSKY STADION – THURSDAY 28 SEPTEMBER 2006
AC SPARTA PRAHA: 0
V
HEARTS: 0
REFEREE: P SIPPEL (GERMANY)

Voted one of Scotland's best-dressed men a few days earlier, Steven Pressley notched up another milestone as he led the team out into the Toyota Arena, equalling the mark set by Henry Smith for European appearances. In the side Jamie Mole had been preferred to Roman Bednář, denying the Czech the opportunity to make his appearance on home soil as Hearts went in search for the goals that would keep them in the competition.

It was the home side, though, that started the game brighter and they nearly went ahead in the sixth minute, but a combination of Paul Hartley and Craig Gordon kept the sides level. From a corner, Zdeněk Pospěch fired in a powerful header that Hartley managed to clear off the line. Then seconds later Craig Gordon did well to tip a shot from Daniel Kolář onto the crossbar and again Hartley was on hand to clear the danger.

The game then settled down, with neither side creating any clear-cut chances, the only incident of note coming after 25 minutes when Steven Pressley had to leave the pitch to receive attention for a head wound that he received in a clash with Libor Došek. He had just returned with his head swathed in bandages when a corner from Daniel Kolář caused confusion in the Hearts defence. Perhaps it was because they were still organising with the reintroduction of the captain, but somehow Tomáš Sivok was left totally unmarked. Fortunately, he placed his header wide with Craig Gordon looking beaten.

Deividas Cesnauskas had Hearts' first real chance of note but it had taken 39 minutes to arrive. A telling pass from Robbie Neilson found the little Lithuanian, but he blasted the ball over when he was in a good position 15 yards out. He was wasteful again right on the stroke of half-time when a clearance from a free kick from Paul Hartley fell to him, but this time, although he kept the ball down, his effort was wide of the target.

Despite the fact that the game was being broadcast live by the BBC, over 3,000 had made the journey from Scotland and they thought they were about to witness Hearts score the goal they needed to get into the game only three minutes after the break. A header from Paul Hartley found Mauricio Pinella, who played the ball into the path of Jamie Mole. With only the keeper to beat, his effort was tame and Jaromir Blažek had little trouble clearing the danger.

Minutes later and Pinella created another chance, this time for Saulius Mikoliunas, but again it was squandered as he failed to get the ball on target.

It was to prove to be the last real opportunity that Hearts created and all that was left was for their manager to make a couple of baffling substitutions. Firstly, after 66 minutes he replaced Robbie Neilson with Ibrahim Tall, the 'like for like' change doing nothing to alter the chances of breaking the deadlock. Then, with only seven minutes left, he withdrew Chilean striker Pinella for midfield player Bruno Aguair. It was a move that angered the travelling support, who showed their disapproval by loudly booing the decision as Hearts' European aspirations ended for another season.

AC SPARTA PRAHA: BLAŽEK POPŠECH REPKA HOMOLA KADLEC KISEL LUDOVIC, SIVOK KOLÁR

(JUN) SIMAK (MATUSOVIC) DOŠEK (LUSTRINELLI). SUBS UNUSED: GRIGAR HAŠEK DROBNY
ZABAVNÍK
HEARTS: GORDON NEILSON (TALL) WALLACE BERRA PRESSLEY BRELLIER MIKOLIOUNAS MOLE
(BEDNÁR) CESNAUSKIS HARTLEY PINILLA (AGUIAR). SUBS UNUSED: BANKS BESLIJA LITHGOW
MAKELA

Sparta Prague went on to finish fourth in Group F, failing to qualify for the knockout stage of the competition which was eventually won by Sevilla in the final at Hampden.

Many have lingering memories of Hearts' first foray into Europe's premier tournament, none more so than Scottish International Christophe Berra who has a variety of reasons to remember the trip to Bosnia:

The games in 2006 were obviously a bit special for me as it was when I got to make my debut in Europe for Hearts. I had been involved back in 2004 when Craig Levein included me in all six UEFA Cup games, but I never got a start as Andy Webster, Steven Pressley and Patrick Kisnorbo were the men in charge. I was only 19 then, and just happy to have the chance to be involved.

By the time we qualified for Europe again, Andy Webster had moved on and I had established myself in the team and not only were we in Europe but we were in the Champions League. Well, the qualifiers at least.

Like most folk I had never heard of Široki Brijeg and like most folk thought we had a good chance to make the next round. As it was, we did, quite easily, but I knew when we drew AEK Athens things would be a bit tougher. And out of all the European games I have played, this is the one that sticks in my memory the most – and not for the right reasons.

Although the game was our home leg, Athens flew at us right from the start. I remember thinking this isn't supposed to happen. Most teams would usually sit off a bit, but not AEK, and we were under pressure from the word go. To be honest, we didn't expect them to be so good and we were more than happy to go in at half-time all square.

I was delighted when we nicked a goal after about an hour but then Bruno [Aguair] was sent off, leaving us a man short and with a bit of defending to do. We were doing all right until a few minutes before the end when a ball came in from wide on the right. I was marking a big guy in the middle of the box and thought I had done everything right defensively, but although the ball was a bit behind him he managed to somehow get his head to it and it looped over Craig [Gordon] for the equaliser.

I felt bad but it wasn't as bad as I felt minutes later. It had to be about the last kick of the game and one of their forwards tried a speculative shot from outside the box. It was a natural reaction to stick a leg out, hoping to block it, but it took a deflection and ended up sending Craig the wrong way and into the net.

I know it was just one of those things, but to say I was devastated is an understatement. I was fighting back the tears and I spent ages in the shower after the game. Even leaving the ground, I could hardly speak to anyone.

We were well beaten in Athens, although I don't believe the scoreline reflects the game and the same could apply to the games against Sparta in the UEFA cup. We were always in with a chance in both matches and were never outplayed. In fact, I would even say we were the better team in Prague. However, we were out of Europe and these games have been my only ones so far, but I hope to have a chance again sometime to make up for the bad luck I suffered against AEK.

CHAPTER 19

2009–10 Europa League

IT TOOK A FURTHER three years before a third place finish in the SPL was good enough to see Hearts qualify for European competition once again. In the intervening years Valdas Ivanauskas had vacated the manager's chair in somewhat mysterious circumstances, his place being taken by Eduard Malofeyev. Malofeyev's tenure lasted only 23 days in which Hearts lost all six games they played, thus giving him the distinction of being, statistically, the worst manager in the club's history. It came as little surprise when he was replaced by Ukrainian Anatoly Korobochka. However, Korobochka's managerial style was unpopular with fans and players alike and after some indifferent results, he was given the title of 'Director of Football' and his assistant, Stevie Frail, moved into the hot seat. Frail was *in situ* from January 2008 until the end of the season when he was replaced by Csaba László, known to Hearts fans as the manager that felt the force of John Robertson's right foot at the end of Hearts' UEFA Cup tie against Ferencvaros a few years earlier. In his first season in charge, László managed to give the club some stability and was rewarded with a place in Europe.

The 09–10 season was the first occasion that the Europa League was introduced, although it was simply another rebranding of the UEFA Cup. No matter the title of the competition, once again the draw was unkind: Hearts were paired with Croatian giants Dinamo Zagreb.

In recent years Zagreb had been more used to qualifying for the Champions League, and further back had built an impressive European record, with the highlight coming in 1967 when they defeated Leeds United to win the Inter-Cities Fairs Cup. In Hearts' favour, though, was the fact that the first leg was to be played in Croatia and any decent result there would give them an excellent opportunity to win the tie at Tynecastle.

STADION MAKSIMIR – THURSDAY 20 AUGUST 2009
GNK DINAMO ZAGREB: 4 (MANDŽUKIĆ 5; PAPADOPOULOS 36; VRDOLJAK 56; BIŠĆAN 60)
V
HEARTS: 0
REFEREE: N IVANOV (RUSSIA)

A concert by U2 a few weeks earlier had left the playing surface in the Stadion Maksimir in ruins. A replacement surface was laid only 48 hours before the tie but the pitch was in far from perfect condition, with ruts and gaps everywhere. The Dinamo stadium announcer was obviously proud of the new addition to the ground, blasting out the likes of 'Fields of Gold' by Sting and 'The Green Green Grass of Home' by Tom Jones over the PA before the game. The thousand or so travelling fans were left wondering whether this was in tribute to the new turf or just in fact a couple of tunes from the latest Croatian Top Ten.

However, Hearts could not blame the state of the pitch for their inept performance. Dinamo grabbed the initiative from the start. Boosted by the return of Lee Wallace from injury and Marius Žaliūkas from suspension, Hearts lined up in a 4-5-1, formation hoping to limit the home side's opportunities while relying on Christian Nadé to perhaps grab a vital away goal. The plan was exposed as early as the second minute when a Pedro Morales free kick tested Marián Kello.

The Hearts keeper appeared to be badly at fault when Hearts inevitably fell behind five minutes later: he let a cross from Zagreb's Brazilian winger, Sammir, over his head to the back post where Mario Manduzkić had the easiest of tasks to nod the ball into the net.

Hearts struggled to keep up with the Croatians and the 30°C heat did little to help their cause. Neither David Obua nor Christian Nadé looked as though they were expending much energy as Hearts chased the game, with only 'Suso' Santana offering any attacking option but too often his efforts were easily snuffed out by the home defence.

Half an hour after opening the scoring, Dinamo doubled their lead through Greek international Dimitrios Papadopoulos. The scorer of the first goal, Manduzkić, was first to react when Marián Kello could only palm out a shot from Sammir. Although in a good position he slid the ball to Papadopoulos who tapped in from six yards.

Hearts were in disarray and both Eggert Jónsson and Marius Žaliūkas were seen exchanging words with Csaba László on the touchline before Christian Nadé made his first contribution to the game when he received a booking for a crude tackle on Ivica Vrdoljak. It was obvious changes needed to be made and at the start of the second half Ian Black came on for Ismaël Bouzid – the only surprise was that it took the Hearts manager a further few minutes before Christian Nadé left the action to be replaced by Gary Glen.

The changes provided instant dividends as 'Suso' Santana managed the visitors' first effort on target after 50 minutes. Unfortunately, it didn't

Marián Kello is beaten by a shot from Ivica Vrdoljak as Dinamo Zagreb go 3-0 ahead
© Davy Allan

trouble Tomislav Butina in the Zagreb goal as the game settled back into an all too familiar pattern and five minutes later Hearts were further behind. Ian Black lost possession to Pedro Morales who was allowed the time and space to move forward and supply Ivica Vrdoljak, who unleashed an unstoppable shot past Marián Kello from 25 yards.

Hearts had no sooner restarted the game when possession was lost again and Zagreb mounted yet another attack. The ball eventually went out for a corner which was taken by Morales. Former Liverpool defender Igor Bišćan was allowed to rise unchallenged and Hearts found themselves four behind after less than an hour.

Dinamo might have been expected to take their foot off the pedal with such a healthy advantage but Hearts had their goalkeeper to thank for keeping the score down only eight minutes later. He somehow managed to pull off a double save from firstly Milan Badelj and then the ever dangerous Popadopoulos before Eggert Jónsson finally cleared the ball from Badelj's second effort. In the closing minutes it was the post that came to Hearts' rescue as a Popadopoulos strike went close to consigning them to their worst ever defeat in Europe.

After the game Csaba László bemoaned the fact that that he had a bench of young, untried players. 'If you saw our bench, the oldest player was 19, I think,' he said. 'This is the biggest question for me. If you come to the Europa League and you play against a team like Dinamo Zagreb

Manager Csaba László and skipper Michael Stewart discuss what went wrong at the end of the game against Dinamo Zagreb © Davy Allan

who have scored over 20 goals in four games in the league, this is not an accident. With all these young players on the field, to feel, to explain and to have the duties is not easy. They tried and I am not angry about the team. I was realistic for the game.' To add insult to injury, he saw fit to emphasise the scale of the defeat: 'I said you must not lose very high, but this is different... we lost 4-0' – a fact of which the travelling support were only too well aware.

GNK DINAMO ZAGREB: BUTINA, ETTO (TOMEČAK) BIŠĆAN BARBARIĆ CARLOS SAMMIR (KRAMARIĆ) VRDOLJAK BADELJ MORALES (CALELLO) PAPADOPOULOS MANDZUKIC. SUBS UNUSED: LONČARIĆ GLAVINA SLEPIČKA SIVONJIC
HEARTS: KELLO JÓNSSON WALLACE(L) ŽALIUKAS BOUZID (BLACK(I)) SUSO (NOVIKOVAS) PALAZUELOS STEWART OBUA NADÉ (GLEN) CONCALVES. SUBS UNUSED: BALOGH THOMSON C STEWART (J) KUCHARSKI

In the days between the first and second legs Hearts had gone down 2-1 to Rangers at Tynecastle, leaving them at the foot of the SPL after two games. During the Rangers game both Calum Elliot and Eggert Jónsson had picked up injuries that ruled them out of the return tie. On a more positive note, Andy Driver had returned to training on the Tuesday before the game and had experienced no reaction to the foot injury that had kept him out of action for some time, and was considered fit enough to take a place on the bench.

Joining him among the substitutes was a famous name from Hearts' past in Gordon Smith, a product of the youth academy. Another academy graduate, Craig Thomson, was given a place in the starting line-up in place of the injured Jónsson and János Balogh replaced Marián Kello in goal.

TYNECASTLE STADIUM – THURSDAY 27 AUGUST 2009
HEARTS: 2 (STEWART 17; ŽALIUKAS 55)
V
GNK DINAMO ZAGREB: 0
REFEREE: K KIRCHER (GERMANY)

Despite the fact the game was being broadcast live by the BBC and that Hearts were four goals behind, a reasonable crowd of just under 12,000 turned up to witness the first European tie to be played at Tynecastle in over six years. Whether the game would actually go ahead was put in doubt when a power generator blew, leaving one set of floodlights at the Gorgie Road end out of action. After inspection, German referee Knut Kircher and the UEFA delegates in attendance decided it could go ahead with only three sets of lights in working order.

Dimitri Papadopoulos fashioned the first chance of the evening when he created room for himself on the right and fired in an angled drive that went behind, off the outside of the post. 'Suso' Santana soon showed that he could be as elusive as the Greek when a neat bit of footwork took him past two Croatian defenders after 11 minutes. Tomislav Butina in the Zagreb goal looked particularly nervous in dealing with Suso's cross and needed the help of Igor Bišćan to get the ball clear.

Five minutes later Gary Glen missed a great opportunity to grab a goal back when he did well to control a pass from David Obua before turning his marker. His shot was weak on this occasion and the Dinamo goal survived, but a matter of seconds later Hearts made the breakthrough. Butina collected a cross from Christian Nadé with ease and then elected to throw the ball out to Milan Badelj who was taken off guard and robbed by Michael Stewart 23 yards out. The club captain strode forward unchallenged for ten yards before stroking the ball into the net with his left foot. Stewart almost further reduced the deficit ten minutes later when he was on the end of a great move involving Craig Thomson, David Obua and Gary Glen. Unfortunately, his shot from Glen's knock-down was a shade to high and crashed against the crossbar.

Stewart, Glen and Obua were involved again towards the end of the half when another flowing move allowed Christian Nadé a clear sight of goal on the left. Typically, the Frenchman couldn't control the ball and let it run out for a goal kick, much to the annoyance of the home support and manager László.

The second half began with some of Lothian and Borders finest having to move into the section of the Roseburn Stand occupied by the small band of travelling supporters. A few seats had been set alight and stewards and police were still dealing with the matter when Marius Žaliūkas took a kick to the head and had to leave the pitch to get a cut on his mouth dealt with. He was soon back on the park and was responsible for further reducing Zagreb's lead on 55 minutes. A corner from Craig Thomson was only partially cleared by Sammir to the team captain standing at the edge of the box, and his hooked shot managed to make it through the crowded goalmouth and past the startled Butina.

There was no doubt Hearts were in the ascendancy. Now Gordon Smith and Andy Driver were introduced to help get another two goals that would extend the tie. Their cause was not helped when the German referee waved away a strong penalty claim when Suso was sent tumbling in the box after 68 minutes. Then with 12 minutes left Ismaël Bouzid did well to send in a powerful header from a Craig Thomson free kick, but Butina in the Dinamo goal did just enough to turn the ball away for a corner.

As time ran out, so did Hearts' chances. David Obua should have set up a storming finish but could only hook his shot over the bar when handily placed with seven minutes left.

It turned out to be the last chance and Hearts were out of Europe once again, although at least on this occasion they had done so after a magnificent performance that went a long way to restoring their reputation.

HEARTS: BALOGH THOMSON (C) CONCALVES ŽALIUKAS BOUZID SUSO PALAZUELOS (BLACK (I)) STEWART OBUA NADÉ (SMITH(G)) GLEN (DRIVER). SUBS UNUSED: KELLO KUCHARSKI THOMSON (J) NOVIKOVAS
GNK DINAMO ZAGREB: BUTINA LOVREN BARBARIĆ BIŠĆAN CARLOS MORALES (CALELLO) VRDOLJAK BADELJ SAMMIR (TOMEČAK) MANDŽUKIĆ PAPADOPOULOS (SLEPICKA). SUBS UNUSED: LONCARIC KRAMARIC GLAVINA SIVONJIC

As in so many other seasons, Hearts' eagerly awaited participation in Europe had come to an abrupt end against what was a competent rather than outstanding side which then failed to make it out of the group stages of the competition. It was perhaps one of the least remarkable campaigns, but for leading lights of the London Hearts Supporters Club Drew Goldie and Davy Allan, their trip to Zagreb epitomised just what following Hearts means, despite the result. Drew recalls:

One of the ways the world has changed, disappointingly in some respects, is that nowhere seems exotic as it did in former times: the media has shrunk the world to a global village. We're all so aware of place-names, of where they are, and even what they look like. Many years ago, sporting events from the other side of the world could have come from the dark side of the moon for all we knew, the television coverage being either non-existent or beamed through several low-grade satellites onto an old black-and-white telly, the commentary crackling through the wires.

I commented to a Manchester United fan of a certain vintage that these days European football has a very dull edge when the draw is made for the curiously named Champions League. No longer do you look forward to playing Górnik Zabrze, Slovan Bratislava or Vitória de Setúbal and marvel at the names, wonder where they come from. It's, 'Oh... Roma again.' For Manchester United and their ilk, playing away at Southend or Exeter must be about as exotic as it can ever be.

The UEFA Cup, however, is still a repository of possibility and wonder, even romance. Many teams such as Heart of Midlothian aren't regular attendees for the draw, so it's only every so often we're on the edge of our seats, wondering if it might possibly be something special. Some of us have memories of Hamburg, Prague, Vienna and Munich, but what you don't want, to be fair, is Stavanger and the like. So when the name Dinamo Zagreb came up, it was a dream come true, a name that we recalled from the mists of the 1960s, a team that has a European pedigree from the days of the Inter-Cities Fairs Cup, and a city which, in the post-Yugoslavia geographic turmoil, was now the capital of a new country.

There are advantages to living in London for a Hearts supporter (one is that you can choose not to go to games, which is more difficult when it's just up the road...). A major plus is that, when Hearts do get to Europe, we're nearer the destination and enjoy better transport links. But the best thing is the journeys to and from Edinburgh, which Davy Allan and I have been doing for 25 years, nearly always by train. Door-to-door, it takes the same time as flying, and as the London Hearts website will demonstrate, sitting on a train is not the worst way to pass five hours, especially when one of you has a wine collection. So it seemed entirely natural that we should decide to journey to Croatia by rail, especially when Davy's 'Extremely Significant Other' realised it would be a great place to go, and a few quiet days on a train across Mitteleuropa would be a tranquil and serene experience for her.

Heather was keen to make the arrangements to suit her needs, which by coincidence suited our needs too; and the three of us, the oddest of ménages à trois, made our way to St Pancras early one Tuesday morning and plonked ourselves in First Class on the Eurostar.

Was a glass of champagne imbibed? I can't remember, which invariably means there was. A stroll between Gares (Nord to l'Est) later, and we were on our way to Innsbruck, through the rolling beauty of the French countryside into and through the ski resorts of the Alps; a change at Zurich, where the clocks are big, and thence to Innsbruck by nightfall.

A wonderful place, Innsbruck, especially out of season when there's no snow and, more importantly, no skiers. It was quiet, relaxing and full of quiet, relaxing bierkellers, and we knew we'd have more time on the return journey to bask in the triumph of a Hearts victory. Or just to go the bierkellers if the unthinkable happened.

The thing very few people realise is how much of Europe is simply there, but not really recognised or populated. It's not easy to get to, as train schedules resemble those of Ivor the Engine rather than Trans-Europe Express. So some time was spent decanting ourselves onto the platform of various stations simply to catch a connection, with the constant worry when a train turned up of wondering if this was the one we should be getting on.

As we moved east, First Class lost something in translation. However, all proved well when more Hearts fans got on the train having flown to Llubljana, and even the obligatory 1960s border guards who got on to examine '*papieren*' etc seemed somewhat less cartoonish or scary than we might have feared.

Zagreb was wonderful, not unlike Edinburgh – in size, a hill in the middle, an Old Town, trams (oh, hold on), and quite cosmopolitan, with plenty of places to congregate; pizza was a speciality, though we wanted to see if there was a local delicacy (warning: unlikely to be delicate) to remember the trip by. Not always a good thing, granted, but having climbed the 1,000 steps up to the top of the hill, built into the rock was a rather dark restaurant which turned out to be Michelin-worthy, showing just how far we've come since the Wall came down.

On the outskirts of town there were some genuinely communist-era housing estates – some of which could rival one or two of our genuinely capitalist era housing estates – but as a venue for a football match, Zagreb couldn't be beat.

Unlike Hearts, who played like a team which hadn't been introduced to each other (which was true, of course: a pity that we couldn't have leased back Karipidis, Aguiar and Berra for that one tie...) though, to be fair, we were playing a team that had actually qualified for the Champions League and weren't too shabby. It was a poor 90 minutes, but in the context of five excellent days that's not a bad return. You know you've lost interest in a game when you realise that you watched some athletics championship there in 1973...

Davy and I decided to walk the Walk of Shame back to the town centre, rather than get stuffed onto the buses back (we turned down the numerous friendly offers from some locals of 'a fight') but the bars in central Zagreb were more than happy to let us drown our sorrows all night long.

Then, not to put too fine a point on it, there was Innsbruck to look forward to, its windy little alleys, plentiful portions of everything, a couple of very decent restaurants, views of the mountains from below and a trip up the cable-car to see as far as the eye could see (if you've never seen a ski-jump from above, you've not lived). Oh, and did I mention the bierkellers?

This was one journey we didn't want to finish, and as we moved further towards Paris and further away from Zurich (with a little nod to Basel not far away) we knew we'd done something wonderful (again). Add it to the list: Mostar, Tallinn, Basel. It's something that bigger teams won't get: it's still something special, and for Hearts fans especially.

CHAPTER 20

2011–12 Europa League

THE WIN AGAINST Zagreb turned out to be one of the few highlights of the first part to the 09–10 season as Csaba Lázló struggled to find the formula that had seen him crowned as 'SPL Manager of the Year'. After a succession of poor results, his time in Gorgie was finally brought to an end after a comprehensive 3-0 home defeat at the hands of Aberdeen on 27 January 2010.

Former manager Jim Jefferies, who had recently left the manager's post at Kilmarnock, was the instant favourite to fill the vacancy at Tynecastle and few were shocked to discover that he was the man that Vladimir Romanov turned to. For the remainder of the season the results were mixed and Hearts finished in a disappointing seventh place.

Jefferies began his restructuring of the side by raiding his former club for the bustling striker Kevin Kyle, with former fans favourite Rudi Skácel also signing for the club, although there was a doubt as to whether the Czech international had been the manager's choice.

The side played well and by mid-January they were being considered as genuine contenders to break the Old Firm's domination. However, defeat at the hands of both Celtic and Rangers within the space of a week more or less put paid to any thoughts of a title challenge.

Despite the defeats Hearts had opened up a 15 point gap on the fourth-placed side and with games running out it looked as though European football was once again assured. The loss of Kevin Kyle through injury sparked a dramatic loss of form as Dundee United emerged from the pack to challenge for third place. Eventually, with two games remaining, United went down 4-0 at home to Rangers, making certain that European football would return to Tynecastle once again.

Hearts entered the competition as a seeded team in the third qualifying round and were placed in Group Six when the draw was made in Geneva on Friday 15 July. If the draw had been eagerly anticipated, the result was something of an anti-climax when they were paired against either Paksi of Hungary or Tromsø from Norway. Little was know of either side, but having played out a 1-1 draw in Hungary the previous evening, the Norwegians looked favourite to qualify. Despite having home advantage and already being halfway through their season, Tromsø lost 3-0 in the return leg and rather unexpectedly it was Paksi that progressed to meet Hearts a week later.

Perennial underachievers, Paksi shocked not only their own 2,000 supporters but the whole of Hungary when under manager Karoly Kis they won the Ligakupa, beating Debrecen 4-2 over two legs. They followed up their first ever major success with a second-place finish behind Videoton in the Monicomp Liga which allowed them entry into European football for the first time in their history.

In the first qualifying round they easily beat UE Santa Coloma of Andorra before their surprise win against Tromsø. Both their home ties had to be played in the Sóstói stadium, home of Videoton, as their own ground Stadion PSE only had a capacity of 4,000 and did not meet UEFA standards. The game against Hearts would also take place in the Sóstói, located in Székesfehérvár, approximately 40 miles south-west of Budapest.

By the time Hearts arrived in Hungary Jim Jefferies had already accumulated an impressive amount of air miles building a dossier on Paksi. Following a journey to Norway to watch the second leg, he returned to Edinburgh to oversee a creditable 1-1 draw against Rangers at Ibrox on the opening day of the SPL season. Straight after that game he headed to Hungary to take in Paksi's 4-0 defeat against Videoton the following day. Jefferies had just enough time to repack his bag before returning to Edinburgh airport on Tuesday morning to board the team charter to Budapest.

Missing from the squad on the plane were recent signings Andy Webster and Mehdi Taouil, who had both picked up injuries at Ibrox; also, it transpired that David Obua's Ugandan passport had been allowed to expire which meant that he was sent to London for whirlwind visits to the Ugandan and Hungarian embassies to obtain the correct documentation. He could not travel to Budapest until the following day and then the visa he had been issued was considered to be incorrect. It took hours of negotiation to resolve the matter, and Obua arrived at the team hotel just before midnight the day before the game. Hardly the best preparation for a vital European tie.

SÓSTÓI STADION – THURSDAY 28 JULY 2011
PAKSI SPORTEGYESÜLET: 1 (SIPEKI 31)
V
HEARTS: 1 (HAMILL PEN 45)
REFEREE: M GESTRANIUS (FINLAND)

The rain that had fallen throughout the day in Székesfehérvár had stopped by the time the teams entered the almost deserted stadium. Despite tickets costing only the equivalent of £4.50, only 2,800 were inside, but the 300 that had made the trip from Edinburgh were determined to make themselves heard as Hearts began the game in an assured fashion. With David Obua in the side despite his travel difficulties, the team enjoyed the majority of possession although goal-scoring opportunities remained at a premium.

Completely against the run of play, it was the home side that went ahead after 31 minutes through István Sipeki. With Ian Black off the field receiving treatment for an injury, Paksi exploited their numerical advantage with a rare attack. A shot by László Bartha was blocked by Eggert Jónsson but the ball rebounded to Sipeki on the edge of the box. Instinctively he stuck out his right boot and the ball looped over Marián Kello into the net. Whether it was a stroke of luck or a stroke of genius was hard to tell, but it meant that Hearts were behind as the hosts started to push forward in greater numbers in an attempt to increase their advantage.

With the half almost over, Hearts were awarded a free kick out on the left-hand side of the park. Danny Grainger played the ball into the box but the opportunity looked to have gone when no one could make any contact. However, Mattias Gestranius, the Finnish referee, had spotted that Tibor Heffler had wrestled John Sutton to the ground and pointed to the spot. It looked a harsh award as Heffler was booked for his protests.

Jamie Hamill now stepped up confidently, crashing the ball high into the net to pull Hearts level. The goal was the club's first away goal in Europe for almost seven years since Robbie Neilson's strike in Basel had proved vital – and who could argue that this goal (ironically, by another right back) would not be as equally important.

Play was cautious in the second half, although the Hungarians did try to be slightly more adventurous in the opening period. Hearts remained resolute, restricting their opponents to very few opportunities. In turn, the visitors created a couple of chances but both Jamie Hamill and John Sutton could not find the required finish to grab a second away goal.

Marián Kello had to be alert in the 72nd minute when he pushed a header from Tamás Sifter around the post, following a corner from Gábor Vayer. Minutes later another set-piece from Vayer caused Kello a further anxious moment when his free kick sailed narrowly past the post, although the Slovakian keeper did look to have the effort well covered.

Time was beginning to run out and Hearts looked as though they were content to settle for the draw as Arvydas Novikovas and Ryan Stevenson

Jaime Hamill blasts the ball past Paksi goalkeeper Csernyanszki to pull Hearts level in
Hungary, July 2011 © Callum Marshall

were introduced to the action. Stevenson himself was then substituted in
stoppage time when he had to be stretchered from the pitch after injuring
his hand in a tackle. His replacement, Stephen Elliott, was hardly on the
park before the referee brought the proceedings to a close. With Hearts
having secured an away goal, they would surely be favourites to progress
to the next round in seven days time.

PAKSI SPORTEGYESÜLET: CSERNYÁNSZKI HEFFLER SIFTER FIOLA BÁLÓ BODE SIPEKI BARTHA
MAGASFÖLDI (MONTVAI) VAYER KISS. SUBS UNUSED: POKORNI NAGY GÉVAY MÉSZÁROS HREPKA
SZABÓ.
HEARTS: KELLO MCGOWAN JÓNSSON ŽALIUKAS GRAINGER MROWIEC BLACK (I) HAMILL (J) OBUA
TEMPLETON (NOVIKOVAS) SUTTON (STEVENSON (ELLIOTT S)). SUBS UNUSED: MACDONALD (J)
BARR SMITH (G) ROBINSON

As so often happens, Hearts suffered yet another 'European hangover'
and produced a lacklustre display in their next SPL game against Dundee
United. The 1-0 defeat at Tynecastle was a disappointment after the two
good results against Rangers and Paksi, but few could have anticipated
that it would lead to the removal of Jim Jefferies from his role as manager.
The axe fell on Jim and his assistant Billy Brown the following day when
Mr Romanov decided to once again ring the changes by bringing in Paulo
Sérgio as Hearts' tenth manager in six years.

Hailing from Portugal, Paulo Sérgio Bento Brito had been head coach
at several clubs in his home country, all with limited success. His contract
at his last club, Sporting Lisbon, had been terminated in February after a

series of poor results, including a 2-0 aggregate defeat to Rangers in the Europa League.

For his first game in charge, Sérgio was unable to call on Jim Jefferies for assistance as the former manager had turned down the role of Director of Football that had been offered, choosing to break his ties the club for a second time. He took along with him his assistant Billy Brown, but the club retained the services of Gary Locke who joined Sérgio's assistants António Cabral and Sérgio Cruz in the dugout before the game.

TYNECASTLE STADIUM – THURSDAY 4 AUGUST 2011
HEARTS: 4 (STEVENSON 33 & 45; DRIVER 50; SKÁCEL 71)
V
PAKSI SPORTEGYESÜLET: 1 (BODE 89)
REFEREE: R MALEK (POLAND)

As had happened the previous week in Hungary, rain fell persistently through the day but had stopped an hour or so before kick off, giving an almost perfect evening for football. However, both sides struggled to find any rhythm as they settled into the game.

The first incident of note came around the five-minute mark when László Éger announced his intentions with a heavy tackle on Stephen Elliot. The Irish international carried on after treatment but only lasted a few more minutes before John Sutton came on in his place.

Hearts continued to dominate but their play did not have the necessary cutting edge until the game sparked into life after half an hour. A Danny Grainger corner from the right was allowed to reach the far post where Ryan Stevenson had been left unmarked. His downward header bounced in front of Norbert Csernyánszki, who managed to get a hand to the ball but couldn't stop it crossing the line.

The goal lifted both the side and the crowd and the tempo went up a notch. Just before the interval, Paksi made a rare break from defence and a shot from István Sipeki almost brought an equaliser. Marián Kello was alert to the danger and his clearance upfield reached John Sutton who played the ball to Ryan Stevenson. Fom a tight angle six yards out he was able to make it 2-0 with a crisp strike that left the Paksi keeper red-faced once again.

Marius Žaliūkas took a knock just before the end of the first half and did not reappear for the second half. His place was taken by Jamie Hamill who took up a role in midfield, with Adrian Mrowiec dropping into the back four.

The second period was only five minutes old when Ryan Stevenson found John Sutton in the Paksi box. With his back to goal and surrounded by a couple of defenders, he cleverly played the ball into the path of Andy Driver who slammed it high into the net for goal number three.

With the tie all but over, Hearts allowed the visitors to stage a late rally and twice Daniel Böde was denied by Marián Kello. The keeper got his fingertips to a looping header, managing to push the ball onto the bar, then moments later he did even better when he came out best after being left one on one with Böde.

With 20 minutes to go, Hearts effectively snuffed out Paksi's mini-revival when Rudi Skácel was the first to react after Norbert Csernyánszki could only block a fierce shot from David Templeton. Skácel arrived just ahead of Ian Black and the Paksi defence to tap in from five yards, making it 4-0.

In the final minute Daniel Böde eventually got the goal that his overall play probably deserved when his diving header left Marián Kello rooted to his line. The goal, though, did little to take the shine of what had been an impressive display and the perfect start for Paulo Sérgio.

The new manager showed great humility in victory and was quick to praise the role his predecessor had played in the success: 'No one can change things in two days,' he said, adding, 'I want to dedicate this win to Mr Jefferies.'

HEARTS: KELLO MCGOWAN JÓNSSON ŽALIUKAS (HAMILL) GRAINGER MROWIEC DRIVER (SKÁCEL) BLACK STEVENSON TEMPLETON ELLIOTT (S) (SUTTON). SUBS UNUSED: MACDONALD BARR NOVIKOVAS ROBINSON.
PAKSI SPORTEGYESÜLET: CSERNYÁNSZKI SIFTER BÁLÓ KISS (MONTVAI) BÖDE HEFFLER (T) MAGASFÖLDI (CSEHI), FIOLA SIPEKI BARTHA ÉGER. SUBS UNUSED: POKORNI GÉVAY MÉSZÁROS HREPKA HEFFLER (N)

With the Hungarians dispatched, all eyes turned to the draw for the final qualifying round in Nyon the following day. As an unseeded team in Group Three, Hearts could have faced opposition from Russia, Israel, Greece or Spain, but it was the final option of England in the shape of Tottenham Hotspur that the Gorgie side were matched up against.

It was a draw that brought back many memories from the past. Former Hearts manager Joe Jordan was currently Harry Redknapp's assistant at White Hart Lane and Spurs had provided the opposition when Hearts celebrated their centenary in 1974. One of Hearts most famous sons, Dave Mackay, had gone on to great success with the London club and further back in history Hearts had defeated Tottenham 3-1 over two games in 1901 to become unofficial 'World Champions'. A similar result 110 years later would be a magnificent achievement, considering their pedigree.

In the build-up to the game, Hearts played with the usual 'Euro lethargy' and went down 1-0 at Motherwell, but recovered some form the following week with a confidence boosting 3-0 win over Aberdeen at Tynecastle, despite injuries to several key players.

Spurs had encountered problems themselves: days earlier, civil unrest in North London had led to their first Premiership game of the season, against Everton, being postponed with the whole of the Tottenham area being classed as a 'crime scene' by the Metropolitan Police. Their preparations were further hampered when, due to the Edinburgh Festival, they failed to find suitable accommodation in the city. They chose to base themselves 50 miles away in St Andrews, foregoing the opportunity to train at Tynecastle the previous evening.

TYNECASTLE STADIUM – THURSDAY 18 AUGUST 2011
HEARTS: 0
V
TOTTENHAM HOTSPUR: 5 (VAN DER VAART 4; DEFOE 12; LIVERMORE 27; BALE 63; LENNON 77)
REFEREE: P TAGLIAVENTO (ITALY)

Spurs' first introduction to Tynecastle was when they stepped out into an atmosphere that only special European nights seem to create and the capacity crowd needed little encouragement from stadium announcer Scott Wilson to '*Make some noise!*'.

With their slick, accurate passing it became apparent that the home side were up against team full of talented players with skills rarely seen at Tynecastle and it was no surprise that the visitors went ahead after only four minutes. Jermaine Defoe cut inside and attempted to play a one-two with Rafael Van der Vaart. Marius Žaliūkas managed to cut out the pass but then proceeded to hammer his clearance off the Dutchman. With the Hearts defence appealing in vain for a hand ball, Van der Vaart strode forward and smashed the ball into the net.

Tottenham continued to dominate and eight minutes later doubled their lead when Jermaine Defoe finished off a slick move involving Niko Kranjčar, Van der Vaart and Jake Livermore that sliced open the Hearts defence once again.

Hearts tried to match Spurs by attempting to play a similar passing game but more often than not it ended with the ball being played back to Marián Kello who in turn would hit a long ball up the park in the general direction of lone striker John Sutton. It was a tactic that did little to trouble the Tottenham back line and the visitors continued to control the game.

With just under half an hour gone, the game was over as a contest when Defoe, Van der Vaart and Livermore combined again to allow 21-year-old

Livermore to stroll through to make it 3-0.

It took a further ten minutes before Hearts managed to manufacture their first chance of the evening when Ryan Stevenson made a good run on the right before firing a vicious swerving shot that went narrowly past Heurelho Gomes' left-hand post. It was to be their only attempt on goal as the Italian referee Paolo Tagliavento brought the half to a close.

After the break the hosts did start to take the game to the visitors, staging something of a revival. Marius Žaliūkas saw his header from a corner cleared off the line and then a shot from Andy Driver struck Ryan Stevenson which otherwise might have tested Spurs' erratic Brazillian goalkeeper.

With the Tynecastle crowd revitalised and encouraging the side forward in search of the goal that might start an improbable comeback, they were stunned back into silence when Spurs added to their tally in the simplest manner in the 63rd minute.

Gareth Bale sprinted on to a simple ball played over the middle of the Hearts defence by Tom Huddlestone. His first touch took him round Marián Kello and he was left with the easiest of tasks to knock the ball into an empty net. It was a goal that the Welsh international richly deserved and he received a standing ovation from both sets of supporters when he was substituted a few minutes later.

To their credit, Hearts kept trying to move forward in search of a consolation goal but with 13 minutes left they were undone for a fifth time.

Rafael van der Vaart turns away after putting Spurs 1-0 in front at Tynecastle, August 2011
© Davy Allan

Aaron Lennon completes the rout as he puts Spurs 5-0 ahead at Tynecastle © Davy Allan

Spurs defended a corner with the ball breaking to Andros Townsend, who sent Jermaine Defoe scampering down the right. With the Hearts defence struggling to get back, Defoe played the ball across the goal to allow Aaron Lennon to complete the scoring. Once again the crowd were on their feet to applaud the move that had taken under ten seconds to complete. Having been outplayed throughout, Hearts could have no complaints about being on the end of their heaviest European defeat in their history. The only consolation for the 16,279 inside Tynecastle was that they had witnessed a display of football far above the standard normally on offer week in, week out, in the SPL.

HEARTS: KELLO HAMILL ŽALIUKAS WEBSTER GRAINGER TEMPLETON STEVENSON MROWIEC (OBUA) BLACK, DRIVER (ELLIOTT (S)) SUTTON (SKÁCEL). SUBS UNUSED: MACDONALD JÓNSSON MCGOWAN NOVIKOVAS
TOTTENHAM HOTSPUR: GOMES WALKER DAWSON KABOUL ASSOU-EKOTTO LENNON LIVERMORE KRANJČAR BALE (TOWNSEND) VAN DER VAART (HUDDLESTONE) DEFOE (PAVLYUCHENKO). SUBS UNUSED: FRIEDEL BASSONG CORLUKA CUDICINI

After this comprehensive defeat, Hearts managed to recover some respectability in the SPL with a 0-0 draw at Kilmarnock the following Sunday. In England a Spurs team showing only one change from the team that played at Tynecastle lost 3-0 against Manchester United.

In London the day before the game, Paulo Sérgio took the unusual step of announcing the team that would attempt to regain some pride at White Hart Lane. It was a surprising move and the line-up certainly raised some eyebrows. Out went Kello, Hamill, Stevenson, Sutton, Driver, Black and Mrowiec, with MacDonald, McGowan, Novikovas, Robinson, Jónsson,

Smith and Skácel taking their places. With the tie as good as won, Harry Redknapp also took the opportunity to ring the changes, with only two players that started the game at Tynecastle retaining their places in his side.

WHITE HART LANE – THURSDAY 25 AUGUST 2011
TOTTENHAM HOTSPUR: 0
V
HEARTS: 0
REFEREE: A KAKOS (GREECE)

Despite the fact that they trailed by five goals, Hearts' allocation of tickets for the game were snapped up and an estimated 4,500 fans made a friendly invasion of North London. The boisterous nature of the support went down well with the locals and was in stark contrast to the civil unrest that had taken place in the area a few weeks before. When the teams emerged from the tunnel, the first chorus of 'We're gonna win 6-0' went up and from that moment there was non-stop vocal support for the Gorgie side.

Sadly the entertainment on the park did not match that in the stands and it took nearly ten minutes before Roman Pavlyuchenko produced the first shot on target, a speculative 25-yarder that did little to test Jamie MacDonald in the Hearts goal.

A few minutes later, though, Hearts went close to opening the scoring after Ryan McGowan made good progress down the right before playing the ball in to Gordon Smith just inside the box. With his back to goal, the youngster turned his marker, Spurs captain Michael Dawson, before crashing a shot against the crossbar.

It was a let-off for the home side but they had a tremendous opportunity to take the lead after 29 minutes when Harry Kane raced onto a through ball from Tom Carroll. Jaimie MacDonald rushed off his line, but only succeeded in bringing down the 18-year-old to concede a penalty. The foul might have also resulted in the keeper being sent off but Mr Kakos, the Greek referee, decided that a yellow card was sufficient punishment. Kane elected to take the kick himself and struck a firm shot low to MacDonald's right, only to see the stopper produce a stunning save to keep the sides level. The penalty was to be the last clear-cut opportunity of the game, with both sides struggling to break the deadlock. In the end Hearts regained some of their pride with a creditable 0-0 draw, but the real winners on the night were the magnificent travelling support who had been a credit to the club throughout.

TOTTENHAM HOTSPUR: CUDICINI DAWSON (KABOUL) BASSONG TOWNSEND CARROLL LIVERMORE (NICHOLSON) HUDDLESTONE FREDERICKS (KRANJČAR) PAVLYUCHENKO KANE. SUBS UNUSED: FRIEDEL VAN DER VAART DEFOE ASSOU-EKOTTO

HEARTS: MACDONALD MCGOWAN WEBSTER ŽALIUKAS GRAINGER TEMPLETON JÓNSSON ROBINSON (TAOUIL) NOVIKOVAS SKÁCEL (MROWIEC) SMITH (SUSO). SUBS UNUSED: KELLO DRIVER OBUA STEVENSON

Despite going on to become creditable challengers for the title in the Premier League, Spurs could not progress any further in the competition when they failed to qualify from Group A, a group that saw Greek side PAOK Salonika and Russian outfit Rubin Kazan go into the last 32.

It is perhaps fitting that the real winners were the supporters who created such a special atmosphere at White Hart Lane, gaining rightful recognition from all, including Dave Hines of the Metropolitan Police, who had been sorely tested by the riots a few weeks before:

> I am a football intelligence officer based at New Scotland Yard and have policed many supporters in the central London area on European nights. I was in and around Liverpool Street on the day of the game and spoke to many Hearts supporters during the afternoon and early evening. I have to say that I didn't get one negative comment from any Hearts supporter on the day and I thoroughly enjoyed talking to many of the supporters who all just seemed to be enjoying the day and occasion. Hearts supporters really know how to enjoy themselves, don't they? It was a pleasure speaking to them and I look forward to the next time Hearts are drawn against a London club.

CHAPTER 21

2012–13 Europa League

AFTER SALVAGING SOME PRIDE with the creditable draw at White Hart Lane, Hearts performances in the SPL could be described as 'average' at best. They could not find solace in the League Cup either, being dumped out of the competition at the first hurdle by Ayr United at Somerset Park.

By January the Scottish Cup was Hearts' only chance of silverware for the season. When it took a goal from Gordon Smith six minutes from time to see off Achinleck Talbot at Tynecastle, the prospects of an appearance at Hampden four months later seemed remote. However, despite needing replays to get past both St Johnstone and St Mirren, they found themselves paired against holders Celtic in the semi-final on 15 April.

Local rivals Hibernian awaited the winners in the final, having beaten Aberdeen 2-1 the day before. With time running out and Hearts holding a 1-0 lead through the talsimatic Rudi Skácel, it looked as it would be the first all-Edinburgh final since 1896. However, Gary Cooper snatched an equaliser for Celtic from a suspiciously offside position with only three minutes to play and most of the crowd sat back, expecting extra time. Hearts were made of sterner stuff and in the first minute of stoppage time were awarded a penalty when a shot from Marius Žaliūkas firstly hit Joe Ledley then Victor Wanyama on the arm. Referee Euan Norris had no hesitation in making the award, much to the chagrin of Celtic manager Neil Lennon. Up stepped Craig Beattie, signed on a free transfer only a few weeks earlier, and crashed the ball straight down the middle, leaving Celtic keeper Fraser Forster with no chance. The goal sparked wild celebrations both on and off the pitch, as Hearts were once again in the Scottish Cup final.

As could be expected, the build-up to the first Hearts versus Hibs final since 1896 was intense, with Hearts looking to win their third cup in 14 years and their rivals trying to end the 110-year drought since the cup last rested at Easter Road. However, despite the anticipation, the final did not live up to the hype. Hearts dominated the Leith side from start to finish. Two goals from Rudi Skácel plus others from Darren Barr, Ryan

McGowan and Danny Grainger saw the Gorgie men cruise to a historic 5-1 victory.

The win saw Hearts' name being entered for the final qualifying round for the Europa League the following season, a win seeing them reach the lucrative group stage. Unseeded for the draw on 10 August in Lyon, Hearts could hardly have been handed a tougher task than being drawn against European giants Liverpool.

Although five-times European champions and three-times UEFA Cup winners, the Anfield side were going through a transitional phase with new manager Brendan Rodgers having recently taken over the helm from Liverpool legend Kenny Dalglish.

Hearts had also made significant changes since their famous victory three months earlier. Paulo Sérgio had refused the offer of a new contract and had been replaced by former youth coach John McGlynn. On the playing side, the club had lost several members of the cup-winning side – Rudi Skácel, Ian Black, Craig Beattie, 'Suso' Santana and Stephen Elliot had all left, to be replaced in the main by members of the previous season's highly successful Under-19 squad as attempts were made to reduce expenditure.

Although Brendan Rodgers chose to leave the likes of Steven Gerrard, Glen Johnson and Luis Suárez at home, it was still a multi-million pound squad that arrived in Edinburgh ahead of the eagerly awaited clash.

TYNECASTLE STADIUM – THURSDAY 23 AUGUST 2012
HEARTS: 0
V
LIVERPOOL: I (WEBSTER OG 77)
REFEREE: F MAYER (GERMANY)

As the teams lined up, the difference in quality was immediately obvious. The English side was fielding £20 million Jordan Henderson, £10 million striker Fabio Borini and £7 million Scottish international Charlie Adam, among others, and thoughts of the previous season's mauling by Spurs could not help but come to mind. However, with the backing of the sell-out crowd Hearts took the game to their opponents from the first whistle.

In the opening minutes the home side matched their more illustrious opponents and it was Arvydas Novikovas who was first to come close to opening the scoring when Pepe Reina did well to keep out his long-range shot after the Lithuanian had created space for himself on the right-hand side. A few minutes later John Sutton sent an effort just wide as Hearts continued to press. At the same stage of the game the previous year the home side were already two goals behind and effectively out of the tie, but this game was a different matter. Liverpool, however, always posed a

Hearts prepare to defend a corner against Liverpool at Tynecastle © Callum Marshall

threat and no more so that through 17-year-old Raheem Sterling, whose trickery down the left-hand side was the main source of any chances that came their way. When he intercepted a wayward pass from Mehdi Taouil with a minute of the half left, he was allowed to run in on goal with Fabio Borini in support. With only Jamie MacDonald to beat, he unselfishly squared the ball to the Italian, who crashed a powerful shot against the post when it seemed easier to score. It was almost the last action of the half and Hearts justifiably went in on level terms.

Sterling and Borini continue the second period the way they left off, but without threatening to breach the solid home defence. The home side continued to impress and efforts by Paterson and Novikovas helped raise the noise level inside the ground.

With time running out, Liverpool managed to make an unexpected breakthrough when Martin Kelly was allowed to race forward from his right back position and send in a low cross into the box. Initially missed by Danny Grainger, the ball looked to be heading towards Borini before Andy Webster got a touch before the forward. Unfortunately, he could do no more than nudge it beyond Jamie MacDonald to hand the visitors the advantage with 12 minutes of the game remaining.

Still Hearts came forward looking for the equaliser and both Andy

Driver and Callum Paterson created great chances for themselves before the end, but on each occasion Reina, in the Liverpool goal, thwarted them.

The game ended with the English side taking the slender advantage back to Anfield but no one in the crowd that had created such a tremendous atmosphere throughout would be willing to admit that the tie was over after such a pulsating display by the Gorgie men.

HEARTS: MACDONALD GRAINGER MCGOWAN BARR (ROBINSON) WEBSTER ŽALIUKAS PATERSON TEMPLETON (DRIVER) TAOUIL SUTTON NOVIKOVAS (CARRICK). SUBS UNUSED: ENKELMAN MCGOWAN (D) MCHATTIE
LIVERPOOL: REINA AGGER CARRAGHER KELLY ROBINSON (DOWNING) HENDERSON SPEARING (ALLEN) ADAM STERLING SHELVEY BORINI (MORGAN). SUBS UNUSED: JONES COATES FLANAGAN LUCAS

Both teams returned to league business the following Sunday, Hearts away to Aberdeen and Liverpool at home to EPL champions Manchester City, and both teams ended up with one point, the Edinburgh side playing out a 0-0 draw, while the Reds held City 2-2.

For that game, Brendan Rodgers took the opportunity to reintroduce the likes of Steven Gerrard, Martin Škrtel, Joe Allen and the controversial Uruguayan Luis Suárez into his side and the quartet retained their places for the second leg of the Europa League tie. John McGlynn did not have any such luxury and named exactly the same line-up that had performed so well at Tynecastle; it was a case of a team costing well over £200 million against one that had cost the sum total of £50,000.

ANFIELD – THURSDAY 30 AUGUST 2012
LIVERPOOL FC: 1 (SUÁREZ 87)
V
HEARTS: 1 (TEMPLETON 84)
REFEREE: V BEZBORODOV (RUSSIA)

The opening minutes started in the same fashion as it had left off at Tynecastle, with both sides evenly matched. Callum Paterson was the first to have a shot on goal when his dipping volley drifted just wide of the post. Slowly, though, Liverpool started to get a grip on the game and Hearts had to survive a narrow squeak after 14 minutes.

A cross from Stewart Downing on the left was nodded back across goal to Luis Suárez at the back post. With Jaime MacDonald scrambling, it needed Marius Žaliūkas to knock the ball off the line and away for a corner.

The home side had the majority of possession with Hearts looking to hit their opponents on the break, which they did to good effect ten minutes later. The ball was played in to John Sutton, whose clever lay-off on the

Andy Webster tussles with Liverpool's Luis Suárez during the 1-1 draw at Anfield
© SNS Group

edge of the box found Callum Paterson. The youngster was looking to turn and fire in a shot, but was brought down when Jamie Carragher barged into him from behind. It looked like a penalty but the Russian referee was not interested and waved play on, something he had done constantly when a Hearts player went down.

Liverpool continued to dominate and Steven Gerrard created a chance for himself on the half-hour mark when he burst through the Hearts defence, but Jaime MacDonald did well to rush from his line and block the Liverpool skipper's shot with his legs.

The Hearts keeper was beaten a few minutes later when Suárez squared the ball to Adam Morgan, who tapped it into an empty net. However, the ball had crossed the bye line in the build-up before reaching the young striker. The referee's assistant had spotted the infringement, and the score remained 0-0. The incident turned out to be the last chance of the half and

John McGlynn's men went into the dressing room still well in contention.

When the game recommenced, the Reds continued to pass the ball between them, but the Hearts defence were well organised and it took nearly 20 minutes before their goal came under any real threat. Suárez sprung the offside trap and ran unopposed in on goal. But again Jaime MacDonald was quick off his line and forced the little forward wide, which gave the defence time to get back and clear the danger. The Uruguayan scorned another chances seconds later when he had a clear sight of goal but could only send his shot wide of the far post.

With the clock ticking down, Hearts started to push forward in search of the goal they needed to send the game into extra time. Only eight minutes remained when substitute Raheem Sterling brought down David Templeton just outside the box. This time Mr Bezborodov could not ignore the offence and awarded the free kick. However, the defensive wall did its job as Danny Grainger's effort was deflected behind. Andy Driver's corner was headed clear by Jonjo Shelvey, only to fall at the feet of Templeton who took a couple of steps inside before sending a long-range effort goalward. Pepe Rainer looked to have it covered but let the ball slip from his grasp and over the line, much to the delight of the large Hearts support behind his goal.

Their joy was short-lived. Three minutes later Luis Suárez once again broke free. Marius Žaliūkas managed to push him wide to the right, but the forward blasted his shot from a tight angle which beat Jaime MacDonald low at the near post.

There were only a few minutes left on the clock for Hearts to grab the goal that would put them through. It was a task that was just beyond them, and they were denied their full opportunity when the referee blew the final whistle after only two of the scheduled three minutes of stoppage time had been played.

LIVERPOOL: REINA CARRAGHER KELLY ŠKRTEL GERRARD DOWNING HENDERSON (BORINI) ALLEN SHELVEY SUÁREZ MORGAN (STERLING). SUBS UNUSED: JONES JOHNSON COATES ENRIQUE AGGER
HEARTS: MACDONALD GRAINGER MCGOWAN BARR WEBSTER ŽALIUKAS PATERSON TEMPLETON TAOUIL SUTTON (DRIVER) NOVIKOVAS (CARRICK). SUBS UNUSED: HAMILTON (J) MCGOWAN (D) MCHATTIE HOLT (J) ROBINSON

It had been a fantastic, if ultimately unsuccessful effort by the team over the two legs, producing probably one of the best results in Hearts' European history when gaining the draw at Anfield. Again, a feature was the backing for the club, both home and away, with those that travelled to Liverpool out-singing the world renowned Kop for the full 90 minutes. The whole repertoire from the Hearts songbook was sung and none more loudly than what has become known amongst fans as the 'European Song', an anthem heard wherever Hearts travelled since 1984. John Fairbairn, the man who penned the ode to following the club in Europe, was in the stand that night. Here he explains the origins of the song and gives us a new 'Liverpool' verse:

Half the excitement in the days after qualifying for Europe until the draw is made is all about dreaming where you will end up following the team. So when we were paired with Liverpool it was something of a disappointment really, hardly the most glamorous location. I had been there before for the Scotland against Wales World Cup qualifier (was it really 35 years ago?) so it wasn't even as if it was somewhere new. What was new, though, struck me as I drove down the M6 – and it was the fact that although I had written 'We travelled far by bus and car and other times we went by railway', this was actually the first time I had gone to a European tie by car! In fact, there were a few things about the song that took a few years to come true.

Our wee club of Gas Board Employees and associates that travelled home and away enjoyed a golden spell of home-made ditties, usually made more popular by drunken renditions in The Auld Worthies public house that generously sponsored 'The Gorgie Gas'. Barely a Saturday went by without a new Top Ten Hit being released. When the 'Euro' vision came along something special was required. Initially, one verse and bespoked to our club (the initial lines were 'We've travelled far in Co Co's car... sing ya b*ss we're the Gorgie Gas) Although the Frank Sinatra version is the more popular beat, our 'Song for Europe' was probably inspired by the more up-tempo style of the Sid Vicious rendition. The song was requested so many times by the patrons of The Auld Worthies that the more generic version was born and the second verse added well before work on the Channel Tunnel was started – hence our offer to 'dig' it for them. Also, when we did go to Paris we went by train and hovercraft, but try getting something to rhyme with hovercraft!

The song caught on in various bars that we visited and there were some memorable renditions over the years. It eventually found its way onto the terracing, culminating in tears of pride and joy when it was heard at the 1998 Cup final being sung by the huge Hearts support that day. It has been certainly become a favourite, and to hear it being sung at Anfield... WOW! Thirty years previously, Liverpool were Champions of Europe, League Champions, League Cup Holders and Charity Shield Holders. Hearts had been dismissed from the Scottish Cup by Forfar at home and there were cries to turn Tynecastle into a car park. All these years later... THIS IS ANFIELD... WE ARE THE HEARTS...

The game itself was tremendous, one of the best yet. To come so close to causing an 'upset' was a great achievement. It's difficult to say 'We were robbed' (perhaps not, seeing as we were in Liverpool, after all), but over the piece I thought we were every bit as good… 'We have no cares of other players'.

And while I think about it, I will settle the argument that seems to crop up every now and again. When I wrote the song the fantastic World Cup tournament of 1982, held in Spain, was still fresh in the memory. The hat-trick against Brazil by Paulo ROSSI, the skills of Zibi BONIEK that took Poland to third place and the iconic goal celebration of Marco TARDELLI… unforgettable!

It's been great to hear the song being belted out by the Gorgie faithful for so long now, and on the way to Merseyside I thought I might bring it up to date with this verse (maybe it won't catch on just as much as the original but you can bet I will be giving it a blast the next time the boys are in Europe):

To see HMFC we'll float our boat across the Mersey
We'll let them know that Blood won't show when you wear a Maroon Jersey
Rodgers Reds will be in their beds while The Gorgie Boys are havin a party
And The Fab Four? Well three were scored by Hat-Trick Hartley.

To compete in Europe is a highlight not only for the club but also the supporters. From the 13 fans that travelled to the first ever European Cup game against Standard Liège to the thousands that descended upon Liverpool to watch their side take on the English giants, every Hearts fan has a memory of a special match.

Vladimir Romanov once announced that Hearts would win the Champions League within ten years of his taking over the club, and although we may never see this lofty ambition realised, there is no doubt that competing in Europe always ensures a very special evening of football.

Along the way so far, there have been games against famous sides such as Benfica and Inter Milan in the early years; then later, there were famous wins over the mighty Bayern Munich and Atlético Madrid at Tynecastle. Many still talk of the three ties against both Lausanne Sports and Real Zaragoza, and who will ever forget the remarkable comeback against Lokomotive Leipzig. All who were there well remember Robbie Neilson's winner against FC Basel and Mark de Vries' goal against Bordeaux when Hearts have been on their travels. Then there was the controversy of the game in Majorca, another game that has not been forgotten but probably for the wrong reasons.

Whatever the competition or opponent, it is clear that European nights create very special memories for those involved and supporters alike. Let's hope that future generations enjoy as many exceptional evenings as we have in the past.

Appendix 1

Results at a Glance

	HOME	AWAY	NEUTRAL	AGGREGATE
1958–59 EUROPEAN CUP				
ROYAL STANDARD DE LIÈGE	2-1	1-5		3-5
1960–61 EUROPEAN CUP				
BENFICA	1-2	0-3		1-5
1961–62 INTER-CITIES FAIRS CUP				
UNION SAINT-GILLOISE	2-0	3-1		5-1
INTERNAZIONALE MILANO	0-1	0-4		0-5
1963–64 INTER-CITIES FAIRS CUP				
LAUSANNE-SPORT	2-2	2-2	2-3	6-7*
1965–66 INTER-CITIES FAIRS CUP				
VÅLERENGA IF	1-0	3-1		4-1
REAL ZARAGOZA	3-3	2-2	0-1	5-6*
1976–77 CUP WINNERS CUP				
HAMBURGER SV	1-4	2-4		3-8
1984–85 UEFA CUP				
PARIS SAINT-GERMAIN	2-2	0-4		
1986–87 UEFA CUP				
FK DUKLA PRAHA	3-2	0-1		3-3**
1988–89 UEFA CUP				
ST PATRICKS ATHLETIC	2-0	2-0		4-0
FK AUSTRIA WIEN	0-0	1-0		1-0
VELEŽ MOSTAR	3-0	1-2		4-2
BAYERN MÜNCHEN	1-0	0-2		2-1
1990–91 UEFA CUP				
DNIPRO DNIPROPETROVSK	3-1	1-1		4-2
BOLOGNA	3-1	0-3		3-4
1992–93 UEFA CUP				
SLAVIA PRAHA	4-2	0-1		4-3
ROYAL STANDARD DE LIÈGE	0-1	0-1		0-2
1993–94 UEFA CUP				
ATLÉTICO MADRID	2-1	0-3		2-4
1996–97 CUP WINNERS CUP				
RED STAR BELGRADE	1-1	0-0		1-1**

	HOME	AWAY	NEUTRAL	AGGREGATE
1998–99 CUP WINNERS CUP				
FC LANTANA	5-0	1-0		6-0
REAL CLUB DEPORTIVO MALLORCA	0-1	1-1		1-2
2000–01 UEFA CUP				
IBV VESTMANNAEYJAR	3-0	2-0		5-0
VFB STUTTGART	3-2	0-1		3-3**
2003–04 UEFA CUP				
FK ŽELJEZNIČAR SARAJEVO	2-0	0-0		2-0
FC GIRONDINS DE BORDEAUX	0-1	1-0		1-1**
2004–05 UEFA CUP				
SC DE BRAGA	3-1	2-2		5-3
FEYENOORD	3	3-0		3-0
SHALKE 04	0-1			0-1
FC BASEL		2-1		2-1
FERENCVAROS	0-1			0-1
2006–07 CHAMPIONS LEAGUE				
NK ŠIROKI BRIJEG	3-0	0-0		3-0
AEK ATHENS	1-2	0-3		1-5
UEFA CUP				
SPARTA PRAHA	0-2	0-0		0-2
2009–10 EUROPA LEAGUE				
DINAMO ZAGREB	2-0	0-4		2-4
2011–12 EUROPA LEAGUE				
PAKSI SPORTEGYESÜLET	4-1	1-1		5-2
TOTTENHAM HOTSPUR	0-5	0-0		0-5
2012–13 EUROPA LEAGUE				
LIVERPOOL	0-1	1-1		2-1

* HEARTS ELIMINATED AFTER PLAY-OFF

** HEARTS LOSE ON AWAY GOALS RULE

Appendix 2

Appearances

	PLAYED	SUB	UNUSED SUB	TOTAL
A				
ADAM, STEPHANE	4	0	1	5
AGUIAR, BRUNO	3	1	0	4
AIRD, KENNY	3	0	0	3
ANDERSON, ALAN	5			5
B				
BAIRD, IAN	3	0	0	3
BALOGH, JÁNOS	1	0	1	2
BANKS, STEVE	0	0	6	6
BANNON, EAMONN	12	3	3	18
BARR, DARREN	2	0	2	4
BARRY, ROY	3			3
BAULD, WILLIE	5			5
BEDNAR, ROMAN	4	1	0	5
BERRA, CHRISTOPHE	6	0	6	12
BERRY, NEIL	13	0	2	15
BESLIJA, MISRAD	1	1	3	5
BLACK, IAN	3	2	0	5
BLACK, KENNY	12	0	0	12
BLACKWOOD, BOBBY	5			5
BONE, JIMMY	2	0	0	2
BOUZID, ISMAËL	2	0	0	2
BOWMAN, ANDY	3			3
BOWMAN, DAVIE	2	0	0	2
BOYAK, STEVEN	1	0	0	1
BRELLIER, JULIEN	2	1	0	3
BROWN, JIMMY	4	0	0	4
BRUCE, ANDY	0	0	2	2
BRUNO, PASQUALE	2	0	0	2
BURRELL, SANDY	0	0	4	4
BURNS, HUGH	0	0	1	1
BUSBY, DREW	4	0	0	4
C				
CAIRNS, MARK	0	0	1	1
CALDER, JIM	0	0	1	1
CALLACHAN, RALPH	2	0	0	2
CAMERON, COLIN	5	0	1	6
CANT, JIMMY	0	0	1	1
CARRICK, DALE	0	2	0	2
CESNAUSKIS, DEIVIDAS	4	1	0	5
CLARK, SANDY	2	0	0	2
CLUNIE, DAVE	4	0	0	4

COLQUHOUN, JOHN	17	1	0	18
CONCALVES, JOSÉ	2	0	0	2
COWIE, GEORGE	1	0	1	2
CRABBE, SCOTT	0	2	3	5
CRAWFORD, IAN	3			3
CRUICKSHANK, JIM	10	0	2	12
CUMMING, JOHN	16			16
D				
DAVIDSON NORRIE	3			3
DE VRIES, MARK	7	1	0	8
DOCHERTY, JOHN	3			3
DRIVER, ANDY	2	3	2	7
E				
ELLIOT, CALUM	0	1	1	2
ELLIOT, MAURICE	2			2
ELLIOTT, STEPHEN	1	2	0	3
ENKELMAN, PETER	0	0	1	1
F				
FASHANU, JUSTIN	2	0	0	2
FERGUSON, DANNY	8			8
FERGUSON, DEREK	3	2	1	6
FERGUSON, IAN	8	3	3	14
FLÖGEL, THOMAS	4	2	0	6
FORD, DONALD	2			2
FOSTER, WAYNE	8	3	1	12
FRAIL, STEVIE	1	0	1	2
FRASER, CAMMY	0	3	1	4
FULTON, STEVIE	4	0	1	5
FYSSAS, TAKIS	4	0	1	5
G				
GALLACHER, JOHN	4	0	0	4
GALLOWAY, MIKE	8	0	0	8
GAULD, STEWART	0	0	1	1
GAVIN, MARK	0	0	1	1
GIBSON, WILLIE	2	2	0	4
GLIDDEN, FREDDIE	2			2
GORDON, ALAN	1			1
GORDON, CRAIG	14	0	2	16
GOSS, JEREMY	1	0	0	1
GRAINGER, DANNY	6	0	0	6
H				
HAMILL, JAIMIE	2	1	0	3
HAMILL, JOE	4	1	2	7
HAMILTON, JACK	0	0	1	1
HAMILTON, JIM	4	0	0	4
HAMILTON, JOHNNY	13			13
HAMILTON, WILLIE	1			1
HARTLEY, PAUL	10	2	0	12
HIGGINS, BILLY	9			9

HOGARTH, MYLES	0	0	1	1
HOGG, GRAEME	4	0	2	6
HOLMES, DAVID	0	3	1	4
HOLT, DAVIE	9			9
HORN, ROBBIE	0	0	2	2

J

JACKSON, DARREN	2	0	1	3
JAMES, KEVIN	1	0	2	3
JANCZYK, NEIL	0	0	3	3
JANKAUSKAS, EDGARAS	1	0	0	1
JARDINE, IAN	2	2	3	7
JARDINE, SANDY	4	0	0	4
JEFFERIES, JIM	2	1	1	4
JOHNSTON, ALLAN	0	0	1	1
JOHNSTON, WILLIE	1	1	0	2
JÓNSSON, EGGERT	4	0	1	5
JUANJO	3	0	1	4

K

KARIPIDIS, HRISTOS	1	0	2	3
KAY, ROY	4	0	0	4
KELLO, MARIÁN	4	0	2	6
KERRIGAN, DON	5			5
KIDD, WALTER	10	1	2	13
KIRK, ANDY	0	0	3	3
KIRK, BOBBY	8			8
KIRKWOOD, DAVIE	3	1	0	4
KISNORBO, PARTICK	9	0	0	9
KUCHARSKI, DAWID	0	0	2	2

L

LEITCH, SCOTT	2	0	0	2
LEVEIN, CRAIG	14	0	0	14
LITHGOW, ALAN	0	0	1	1
LOCKE, GARY	8	1	0	9

M

MAKEL, LEE	5	1	1	7
MAKELA, JUHO	0	0	4	4
MARSHALL, GORDON	8			8
MAUCHLEN, ALLY	2	0	0	2
MAYBURY, ALAN	10	0	0	10
MIKOLIUNAS, SAULIUS	1	2	0	3
MILLAR, JOHN	1	0	1	2
MILLER, GEORGE	3			3
MILNE, ANDY	2			2
MOILANEN, TEPI	2	0	8	10
MOLE, JAMIE	3	0	3	6
MOORE, ALAN	1	1	2	4
MROWIEC, ADRIAN	3	1	0	4
MURIE, DAVID	0	0	4	4
MURPHY, JIM	0	0	1	1
MURRAY, GRANT	0	2	2	4

MURRAY, JIMMY	5			5
MURRAY, MALCOLM	O	O	3	3
MAC				
MACDONALD, ALEX	I	I	O	2
MACDONALD, JAIMIE	2	O	3	5
MACDONALD, RODDY	O	O	2	2
MACFARLANE, NEIL	5	3	2	10
MACKAY, DAVE	2			2
MACKAY, GARY	18	3	I	22
MC				
MCADAM, COLIN	O	O	I	I
MCALLISTER, JAMIE	6	O	O	6
MCCANN, AUSTIN	O	I	3	4
MCCANN, NEIL	9	O	O	9
MCCLOY, PETER	O	O	2	2
MCCREERY, DAVID	I	O	O	I
MCDERMOTT, MURRAY	O	I	4	5
MCGOWAN, DYLAN	O	O	2	2
MCGOWAN, RYAN	5	O	I	6
MCHATTIE, KEVIN	O	O	2	2
MCKENNA, KEVIN	4	3	I	8
MCKENZIE, RODDY	O	O	6	6
MCKINLAY, TOSH	12	O	O	12
MCKINNON, RAB	I	O	I	2
MCLAREN, ALAN	9	2	3	14
MCPHERSON, DAVE	14	I	O	15
MCMANUS, ALAN	O	I	I	2
MCSWEGAN, GARY	2	2	O	4
N				
NADE, CHRISTIAN	2	O	O	2
NAYSMITH, GARY	7	O	O	7
NEILL, JOHN	O	I	I	
NEILSON, ROBBIE	14	2	O	16
NIEMI, ANTTI	4	O	O	4
NOVIKOVAS, ARVYDAS	3	2	3	8
O				
OBUA, DAVID	3	I	I	5
O'CONNOR, DEREK	O	I	I	2
O'NEIL, KRIS	I	I	2	4
P				
PALAZUELOS, RUEBEN	2	O	O	2
PARK, DONALD	5	O	I	6
PARK, MATHEW	O	O	I	I
PATERSON, CALLUM	2	O	O	2
PEREIRA, RAMON	2	2	O	4
PETRIC, GORDAN	2	O	O	2
PINILLA, MAURICIO	2	I	O	3
POINTON, NEIL	2	O	O	2
POLLAND, WILLIE	9			9

POSPISIL, MICHAL	2	1	0	3
PRENTICE, BOBBY	4	0	0	4
PRESSLEY, STEVEN	22	0	1	23
Q				
QUITONGO, JOSÉ	0	2	0	2
R				
RITCHIE, PAUL	6	0	0	6
ROBERTSON, JOHN	11	4	2	17
ROBINSON, SCOTT	1	1	3	5
ROSS, BOBBY	1			1
ROUSSET, GILLES	6	0	2	8
S				
SALVATORI, STEFANO	3	0	1	4
SANDISON, JIMMY	2	1	6	9
SANTANA, SUSO	2	1	0	3
SEVERIN, SCOTT	5	2	1	8
SHAW, GRAHAM	3	1	0	4
SHEVLANE, CHRIS	4			4
SIMMONS, STEPHEN	0	1	1	2
SIMPSON, FITZROY	1	0	3	4
SKÁCEL, RUDI	1	2	0	3
SLOAN, ROBERT	0	0	4	4
SMITH, GORDON	2			2
SMITH, GORDON*	1	1	2	4
SMITH, HENRY	22	0	0	22
SNODIN, GLYNN	2	1	0	3
STAMP, PHIL	5	1	0	6
STENHOUSE, ROBIN	1			1
STEVENSON, RYAN	2	1	1	4
STEWART, JOHNNY	0	0	1	1
STEWART, MICHAEL	4	1	3	8
SUTTON, JOHN	4	1	0	5
T				
TALL, IBRAHIM	1	3	0	4
TAOUIL, MEDHI	2	1	0	3
TEMPLETON, DAVID	6	0	0	6
THOMAS, KEVIN	0	3	1	4
THOMSON, CRAIG	1	0	1	2
THOMSON, GEORGE	4	0	0	4
THOMSON, JASON	0	0	1	1
TOMASHEK, ROBERT	2	0	0	2
TRAYNOR, TOMMY	8			8
V				
VALOIS, JEAN LOUIS	3	1	0	4
VAN DE VEN,PETER	4	0	0	4
W				
WALKER, NICKY	0	0	10	10
WALLACE, LEE	3	2	1	6

WALLACE, WILLIE	11			11
WARDHAUGH, JIMMY	2			2
WATSON, ANDY	0	2	0	2
WEBSTER, ANDY	14	0	0	14
WEIR, DAVIE	6	0	0	6
WEIR, GRAHAM	2	4	1	7
WEIR, JIM	1	0	1	2
WESTWATER, IAN	0	0	2	2
WHITTAKER, BRIAN	10	0	0	10
WILSON, BRIAN	2	0	2	4
WILSON, TOMMY	0	1	2	3
WRIGHT, GEORGE	2	1	1	4
WYNESS, DENIS	3	4	3	10

Y
YOUNG, ALEX	2			2

Z
ŽALIUKAS, MARIUS	8	0	0	8

SMITH, GORDON* (2009 – PREESENT)

Appendix 3
Scorers

ROBERTSON, JOHN	7	MIKOLIOUNAS, SAULIUS	1
GALLOWAY, MIKE	5	NEILSON, ROBBIE	1
DE VRIES, MARK	4	O'NEIL, KRIS	1
FOSTER, WAYNE	4	PARK, DONALD	1
WALLACE, WILLIE	4	PETRIC, GORDAN	1
GIBSON, WILLIE	3	PRESSLEY, STEVEN	1
KERRIGAN, DON	3	SEVERIN, SCOTT	1
ANDERSON, ALAN	2	SKÁCEL, RUDI	1
BAULD , WILLIE	2	SNODIN, GLYNN	1
BUSBY, DREW	2	STENHOUSE, ROBIN	1
COLQUHOUN, JOHN	2	STEWART, MICHAEL	1
DAVIDSON, NORRIE	2	TALL, IBRAHIM	1
FERGUSON, DANNY	2	TEMPLETON , DAVID	1
FERGUSON, IAN	2	TOMASCHEK, ROBERT	1
HAMILTON, JIM	2	WYNESS, DENIS	1
MCPHERSON, DAVE	2	YOUNG, ALEX	1
STEVENSON, RYAN	2	ŽALIUKAS, MARIUS	1
TRAYNOR, TOMMY	2	ANIC (OG) NK ŠIROKI BERG	1
WEBSTER, ANDY	2	CLAES (OG) UNION SAINT-GILLOISE	1
BAIRD, IAN	1		
BANNON, EAMONN	1	TOTAL	98
BEDNAR, ROMAN	1		
BLACK, KENNY	1		
BLACKWOOD, BOBBY	1		
BROWN, JIMMY	1		
CAMERON, COLIN	1		
CLARK, SANDY	1		
CRAWFORD, IAN	1		
CUMMING, JOHN	1		
DRIVER, ANDREW	1		
FLÖGEL, THOMAS	1		
FULTON, STEVIE	1		
HAMILL, JAIMIE	1		
HAMILTON, JOHNNY	1		
HARTLEY, PAUL	1		
HOLMES, DEREK	1		
JACKSON, DARREN	1		
KAY, ROY	1		
KISNORBO, PATRICK	1		
LEVEIN, CRAIG	1		
MACKAY, GARY	1		
MAKEL, LEE	1		
MCCANN, NEIL	1		
MCSWEGAN, GARY	1		

Playing Record

ALL EUROPE	PLAYED	WON	LOST	DRAWN	FOR	AGAINST
HOME	37	20	12	5	67	44
AWAY	37	8	17	12	29	59
NEUTRAL	2	0	2	0	2	4
TOTAL	76	28	31	17	98	107

EUROPEAN CUP	PLAYED	WON	LOST	DRAWN	FOR	AGAINST
HOME	2	1	1	0	3	3
AWAY	2	0	2	0	1	8
TOTAL	4	1	3	0	4	11

CHAMPIONS LEAGUE	PLAYED	WON	LOST	DRAWN	FOR	AGAINST
HOME	2	1	1	0	4	2
AWAY	2	0	1	1	0	3
TOTAL	4	1	2	1	4	5

CUP WINNERS CUP	PLAYED	WON	LOST	DRAWN	FOR	AGAINST
HOME	4	2	2	0	11	6
AWAY	4	1	2	1	4	7
TOTAL	8	3	4	1	15	13

UEFA CUP	PLAYED	WON	LOST	DRAWN	FOR	AGAINST
HOME	20	12	5	3	35	20
AWAY	20	5	10	5	12	25
TOTAL	40	17	15	8	47	45

INTER-CITIES CUP	PLAYED	WON	LOST	DRAWN	FOR	AGAINST
HOME	5	2	1	2	8	6
AWAY	5	2	1	2	10	10
NEUTRAL	2	0	2	0	2	4
TOTAL	12	4	4	4	20	20

EUROPA LEAGUE	PLAYED	WON	LOST	DRAWN	FOR	AGAINST
HOME	4	2	2	0	6	7
AWAY	4	0	1	3	2	6
TOTAL	8	2	2	3	8	13

Appendix 5
Milestones

MOST GAMES
STEVEN PRESSLEY: 22 + 1 UNUSED SUB

YOUNGEST PLAYER
CALLUM PATERSON: 17 YEARS 10 MONTHS 10 DAYS, LIVERPOOL, 23/08/2012

OLDEST PLAYER
MURRAY MCDERMOTT: 38 YEARS 7 MONTHS 5 DAYS, ST PARTICKS ATHLETIC, 07/09/1988

FIRST PLAYER SENT OFF
PATRICK KISNORBO: 4/11/2004, SHALKE 04

TOP SCORER
JOHN ROBERTSON: 7

FASTEST GOAL
WAYNE FOSTER: 40 SECONDS, FK DUKLA PRAHA, 17/09/1986

FIRST NON-SCOT
GORDON MARSHALL (ENGLAND): ROYAL STANDARD LIÈGE, 03/09/1958

FIRST NON-UK
PETER VAN DE VEN (HOLLAND): SK SLAVIA PRAHA, 16/09/1992

RECORD WIN
5-0, FC LANTANA, 27/08/1998

RECORD DEFEAT
5-0, TOTTENHAM HOTSPUR, 18/08/2011

RECORD AGGREGATE WIN
6-0, FC LANTANA, 1998–99

RECORD AGGREGATE DEFEAT
5-0: SPORT LISBOA E BENFICA, 1960/61; INTERNAZIONALE MILANO, 1962–63;
TOTTENHAM HOTSPUR, 2011–12
8-3: HAMBURGER SV, 1976–77

Also published by Luath Press

Is the Baw Burst?

Iain Hyslop

ISBN 978 1 908373 22 9 PBK £9.99

Football has to wake up to reality and get its house in order. Brave decisions must be taken and followed through. Huge changes are needed. Financial problems, falling attendances, poor quality football, crumbling stadiums, terrible catering… is the picture really as bad as it's painted? Time to have a look. IAIN HYSLOP

1 football fan
1 football season
42 football grounds

Written by a football fan, for football fans, this is the unofficial review of the state of Scottish football.

Spotting sizable gaps in the review by former First Minister Henry McLeish, Iain Hyslop provides a detailed look at the beautiful game in Scotland. Every Scottish league ground is visited in a 44-game tour that samples the football, the stadiums, the finances and the pies!

Each chapter covers a game from the 2011 season and portrays the experience in a friendly, casual style that resonates with supporters from all over the country. Does Scottish football have a future or is the baw burst? This view from the not-so-cheap seats (Hyslop is adamant that football has to be more realistic with its pricing policy) ought to be required reading for everyone involved at the top end of the game. THE SCOTSMAN

Stramash: Tackling Scotland's Towns and Teams

Daniel Gray

ISBN 978 1906817 66 4 PBK £9.99

Fatigued by bloated big-time football and bored of samey big cities, Daniel Gray went in search of small town Scotland and its teams. Part travelogue, part history, and part mistakenly spilling ketchup on the face of a small child, Stramash takes an uplifting look at the country's nether regions.
Using the excuse of a match to visit places from Dumfries to Dingwall, *Stramash* accomplishes the feats of visiting Dumfries without mentioning Robert Burns, being positive about Cumbernauld and linking Elgin City to Lenin. It is ae fond look at Scotland as you've never seen it before.

There have been previous attempts by authors to explore the off-the-beaten paths of the Scottish football landscape, but Daniel Gray's volume is in another league. THE SCOTSMAN

A brilliant way to rediscover Scotland.
THE HERALD

Hands on Hearts
Alan Rae with Paul Kiddie

ISBN 978 1 908373 54 0 PBK £9.99

[Rae] was one of the most trustworthy, wonderful, lunatic, crazy, loveable, straight-jacketed men I have ever met in my life. JOHN ROBERTSON (Hearts striker 1981–98; manager 2004–05)

[Rae] was an absolutely fantastic physio who even though he worked in tiny little physio room at Tynecastle got people back from injury very quickly. A wonderful man with a very dry sense of humour who was brilliant company. SCOTT CRABBE (Hearts midfielder/striker 1986–92)

As Heart of Midlothian FC's physiotherapist, Alan Rae was a vital member of the Tynecastle backroom staff for more than two decades. He was one of the few constants during a tumultuous period in the club's rich history and his behind-the-scenes recollections will fascinate and entertain in equal measure.

From international superstars to mischievous boot-room boys, Rae shares his unique insight into the life of a great Scottish football institution. Hands on Hearts is a must-read for football fans everywhere – Jambos or otherwise – and for anyone who has ever wondered about the healing properties of the physio's magic sponge!

Hands on Hearts *is a rich source of anecdotes about the more unusual characters who were on the club's books during the Rae years.* THE SCOTSMAN

100 Favourite Scottish Football Poems
Edited by Alistair Findlay

ISBN 978 1906307 03 5 PBK £7.99

Poems to evoke the roar of the crowd. Poems to evoke the collective groans. Poems to capture the elation. Poems to capture the heartbreak. Poems by fans. Poems by critics. Poems about the highs and lows of Scottish football.

This collection captures the passion Scots feel about football, covering every aspect of the game, from World Cup heartbreak to one-on-ones with the goalie. Feel the thump of the tackle, the thrill of victory and the expectation of supporters.

Become immersed in the emotion and personality of the game as these poems reflect human experience in its sheer diversity of feeling and being.

The collection brings together popular culture with literature, fan with critic, and brings together subject matters as unlikely as the header and philosophy.

[this book] brings home the dramatic and emotional potential that's latent in the beautiful game. THE LIST

Singin I'm No a Billy He's a Tim
Des Dillon

ISBN 978 1 908373 05 2 PBK £6.99

What happens when you lock up a Celtic fan?
What happens when you lock up a Celtic fan
with a Rangers fan?
What happens when you lock up a Celtic fan
with a Rangers fan on the day of the Old Firm
match?

Des Dillon watches the sparks fly as Billy
and Tim clash in a rage of sectarianism and
deep-seated hatred. When children have been
steeped in bigotry since birth, is it possible for
them to change their views?

Join Billy and Tim on their journey of
discovery. Are you singing their tune?

Explosive. EVENING NEWS

*Scotland will never be free of the shackles of
sectarianism unless we teach our youngsters
that bigotry is wrong.* JACK MCCONNELL, MSP,
FORMER FIRST MINISTER

*His raucous sense of humour and keen
understanding of the west-coast sectarian
mindset make his sisters-under-the-skin
message seem a matter of urgency and not just
a liberal platitude.* THE GUARDIAN

*The sheer vitality of the theatrical writing –
the seamless combination of verbal wit and
raw kinetic energy, and the pure dynamic
strength of the play's structure – makes [Singin
I'm No a Billy He's a Tim] feel like one of the
shortest and most gripping two-hour shows in
current Scottish theatre.* THE SCOTSMAN

Over the Top with the Tartan Army
Andrew McArthur

ISBN 978 0 946487 45 5 PBK £7.99

Thankfully the days of the draft and
character-building National Service are no
more. In their place, Scotland has witnessed
the growth of a new and curious military
phenomenon. Grown men bedecked in tartan,
yomping across most of the globe, hell-bent
on benevolence and ritualistic bevvying. Often
chanting a profane mantra about a popular
football pundit.

In what noble cause do they serve? Why,
football, of course – at least, in theory.
Following the ailing fortunes of Scotland isn't
easy. But the famous Tartan Army has broken
the pain barrier on numerous occasions,
emerging as cultural ambassadors for
Scotland. Their total dedication to debauchery
has spawned stories and legends that could
have evaporated in a drunken haze but for
the memory of one hardy footsoldier: Andrew
McArthur.

Taking us on an erratic world tour, McArthur
gives a frighteningly funny insider's eye
view of active service with the Tartan Army.
Covering campaigns and skirmishes from
Euro '92 up to the qualifying drama for
France '98 in places such as Moscow, the
Faroes, Balarus, Sweden, Monte Carlo,
Estonia, Latvia, New York and Finland.

*I commend this book to all football
supporters... You are left once more feeling
slightly proud that these stupid creatures are
your own countrymen.*
SCOTLAND ON SUNDAY

We Are Hibernian: The Fans' Story
Andy MacVannan
ISBN 978 1906817 99 2 HBK £14.99

We are Hibernian explores the sights, sounds and memories of fans who have taken the 'journey' to watch the team that they love. Supporters from all walks of life bare their souls with humour, emotion and sincerity.

This book celebrates the story behind that unforgettable moment when Hibernian entered the childhood of its fans' lives and why, despite their different backgrounds, these loyal fans still support a sometimes unsupportable cause together.

Is it what happens on the field of play or the binding of tradition, memories and experience that makes Hibs fans follow their team through thick and thin? Featuring interviews with many different fans, this book takes you on a journey to discover why football is more than just a game and why Hibernian is woven into the DNA of each and every one of its supporters.

Everyone walked out that ground like they had just seen the second coming.
Irvine Welsh, writer

My family were Irish immigrants. My father had renounced his Catholicism but had retained a blind faith in Hibs.
Lord Martin O'Neill, politician

In the early 1950s Alan, Dougie and I caught the tail end of the legendary Hibs team when they were still the best team in the world.
Bruce Findlay, music business manager

Hibernian: From Joe Baker to Turnbull's Tornadoes
Tom Wright
ISBN 978 1908873 09 1 HBK £20

In Hibernian: From Joe Baker to Turnbull's Tornadoes, club historian Tom Wright marks a new dawn for the game and the end of an era for Hibs.

Hibernian begins in the turbulent 1960s, when relegation was avoided at Easter Road on the final day of the 1963 season.

The appointment of the legendary manager Jock Stein in 1964 saw an immediate improvement in the relegation haunted side. The Hibs side of the mid-'60s featured an all-Scottish international forward line, and the return of player Eddie Turnbull in 1971 saw the emergence of possibly Hibs' greatest-ever side – the magical Turnbull's Tornadoes.

Packed full of detail and interesting information, Hibernian is a must not only for Hibs supporters, but also for the general football fan who is interested in this defining period in the history of our game.

Luath Press Limited

committed to publishing well written books worth reading

LUATH PRESS takes its name from Robert Burns, whose little collie
Luath (*Gael.*, swift or nimble) tripped up Jean Armour at a wedding
and gave him the chance to speak to the woman who was to be his wife
and the abiding love of his life. Burns called one of the 'Twa Dogs'
Luath after Cuchullin's hunting dog in Ossian's *Fingal*.
Luath Press was established in 1981 in the heart of
Burns country, and is now based a few steps up
the road from Burns' first lodgings on
Edinburgh's Royal Mile. Luath offers you
distinctive writing with a hint of
unexpected pleasures.
Most bookshops in the UK, the US, Canada,
Australia, New Zealand and parts of Europe,
either carry our books in stock or can order them
for you. To order direct from us, please send a £sterling
cheque, postal order, international money order or your
credit card details (number, address of cardholder and
expiry date) to us at the address below. Please add post
and packing as follows: UK – £1.00 per delivery address;
overseas surface mail – £2.50 per delivery address; overseas airmail –
£3.50 for the first book to each delivery address, plus £1.00 for each
additional book by airmail to the same address. If your order is a gift,
we will happily enclose your card or message at no extra charge.

Luath Press Limited
543/2 Castlehill
The Royal Mile
Edinburgh EH1 2ND
Scotland
Telephone +44 (0)131 225 4326 (24 hours)
email sales@luath.co.uk